BIBLICAL GEOGRAPHY AND HISTORY

LECTOR HOUSE PUBLIC DOMAIN WORKS

BIBLICAL GEOGRAPHY AND HISTORY

CHARLES FOSTER KENT

ISBN: 978-93-93794-86-4

Published: 1926

LECTOR HOUSE LLP
E-MAIL: lectorpublishing@gmail.com

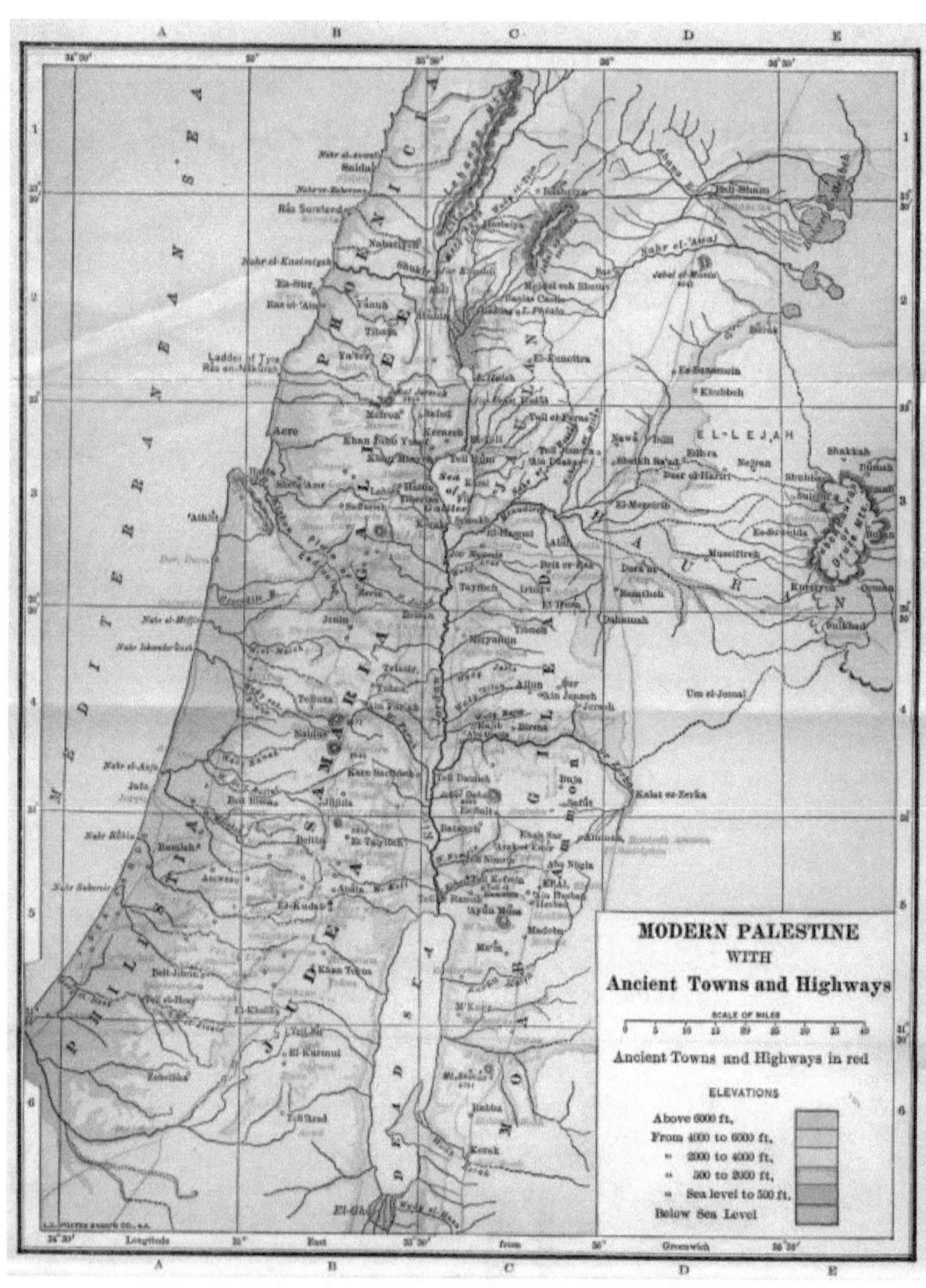

Modern Palestine, With Ancient Towns and Highways

BIBLICAL GEOGRAPHY AND HISTORY

BY

CHARLES FOSTER KENT, PH.D.

WOOLSEY PROFESSOR OF BIBLICAL LITERATURE IN YALE UNIVERSITY

1926

PREFACE

Geography has within the past few years won a new place among the sciences. It is no longer regarded as simply a description of the earth's surface, but as the foundation of all historical study. Only in the light of their physical setting can the great characters, movements, and events of human history be rightly understood and appreciated. Moreover, geography is now defined as a description not only of the earth and of its influence upon man's development, but also of the solar, atmospheric, and geological forces which throughout millions of years have given the earth its present form. Hence, in its deeper meaning, geography is a description of the divine character and purpose expressing itself through natural forces, in the physical contour of the earth, in the animate world, and, above all, in the life and activities of man. Biblical geography, therefore, is the first and in many ways the most important chapter in that divine revelation which was perfected through the Hebrew race and recorded in the Bible. Thus interpreted it has a profound religious meaning, for through the plains and mountains, the rivers and seas, the climate and flora of the biblical world the Almighty spoke to men as plainly and unmistakably as he did through the voices of his inspired seers and sages.

No other commentary upon the literature of the Bible is so practical and luminous as biblical geography. Throughout their long history the Hebrews were keenly attentive to the voice of the Eternal speaking to them through nature. Their writings abound in references and figures taken from the picturesque scenes and peculiar life of Palestine. The grim encircling desert, the strange water-courses, losing themselves at times in their rocky beds, fertile Carmel and snow-clad Hermon, the resounding sea and the storm-lashed waters of Galilee are but a few of the many physical characteristics of Palestine that have left their indelible marks upon the Jewish and Christian Scriptures. The same is true of Israel's unique faith and institutions. Biblical geography, therefore, is not a study by itself, but the natural introduction to all other biblical studies.

In his *Historical Geography of the Holy Land* and in the two volumes on *Jerusalem*, Principal George Adam Smith, of Aberdeen, has given a brilliant and luminous sketch of the geographical divisions and cities of Palestine, tracing their history from the earliest times to the present. Every writer on Palestine owes him a great debt. The keenness and accuracy of his observations, are confirmed at every point by the traveller. At the present time, the need of a more compact manual, to present first the physical geography of the biblical lands and then to trace in broad outlines the history of Israel and of early Christianity in close conjunction with their geographical background, has long been recognized. In the present work unimportant details have been omitted that the vital facts may stand out clearly and in their true significance. The aim has been to furnish the information that every Bible teacher should possess in order to do the most effective work, and the geographical data with which every student of the Bible should be familiar, in order intelligently to interpret and fully appreciate the ancient Scriptures.

This volume embodies the results of many delightful months spent in the lands of the eastern Mediterranean, and especially in Palestine, during the years 1892 and 1910. Owing to improved conditions in the Turkish Empire it is now possible, with the proper camp equipment, to travel safely through the remotest places east of the Jordan and to visit Petra, that most fascinating of Eastern cities. By securing his equipment at Beirut the traveller may cross northern Galilee and then, with comfort, go southward in the early spring through ancient Bashan, Gilead, Moab, and Edom. Thence, with great economy of time and effort, he may return through central Palestine, making frequent détours to points of interest. In this way he will find the quaint, fascinating old Palestine that has escaped the invasions of the railroads and western tourists, and he will bear away exact and vivid impressions of the land as it really was and still is.

The difficulties and expense of Palestine travel, however, render such a journey impossible for the majority of Bible students. Fortunately, the marvellous development of that most valuable aid to modern education, the stereoscope and the stereograph, make it possible for every one at a comparatively small expense to visit Palestine and to gain under expert guidance in many ways a clearer and more exact knowledge of the background of biblical history and literature than he would through months of travel. Through the courtesy of my publishers and the co-operation of the well-known firm of Underwood & Underwood, of New York and London, I have been able to realize an ideal that I have long cherished, and to place at the disposal of the readers of this volume one hundred and forty stereographs (or, if preferred for class and lecture use, stereopticon slides) that illustrate the most important events of biblical geography and history. They have been selected from over five hundred views taken especially for this purpose, and enable the student to gain, as he alone can through the stereoscope, the distinct state of consciousness of being in scores of historic places rarely visited even by the most venturesome travellers. Numbers referring to these stereographs (or stereopticon slides) have been inserted in the body of the text. In Appendix II the titles corresponding to each number are given.

The large debt that I owe to the valiant army of pioneers and explorers who have penetrated every part of the biblical world and given us the results of their observations and study is suggested by the selected bibliography in Appendix I. I am under especial obligations to the officers of the Palestine Exploration Fund, who kindly placed their library and maps in London at my service and have also permitted me to use in reduced form their Photo-Relief Map of Palestine.

C. F. K.

YALE UNIVERSITY,
January, 1911.

CONTENTS

PART I
PHYSICAL GEOGRAPHY

I

THE GENERAL CHARACTERISTICS OF THE BIBLICAL WORLD

II

THE GENERAL CHARACTERISTICS OF PALESTINE

III

THE COAST PLAINS

IV

THE PLATEAU OF GALILEE AND THE PLAIN OF ESDRAELON

V

THE HILLS OF SAMARIA AND JUDAH

VI

THE JORDAN AND DEAD SEA VALLEY

VII

THE EAST-JORDAN LAND

VIII

THE TWO CAPITALS: JERUSALEM AND SAMARIA

IX

THE GREAT HIGHWAYS OF THE BIBLICAL WORLD

PART II
HISTORICAL GEOGRAPHY

X

EARLY PALESTINE

XI

PALESTINE UNDER THE RULE OF EGYPT

XII

THE NOMADIC AND EGYPTIAN PERIOD OF HEBREW HISTORY

XIII

THE HEBREWS IN THE WILDERNESS AND EAST OF THE JORDAN

XIV

THE SETTLEMENT IN CANAAN

XV

THE FORCES THAT LED TO THE ESTABLISH-MENT OF THE HEBREW KINGDOM

XVI

THE SCENES OF DAVID'S EXPLOITS

XVII

PALESTINE UNDER THE RULE OF DAVID AND SOLOMON

XVIII

THE NORTHERN KINGDOM

XIX

THE SOUTHERN KINGDOM

XX

THE BABYLONIAN AND PERSIAN PERIODS

XXI

THE SCENES OF THE MACCABEAN STRUGGLE

XXII

THE MACCABEAN AND HERODIAN AGE

APPENDIX

APPENDIX I

APPENDIX II

LIST OF MAPS

PART I
PHYSICAL GEOGRAPHY

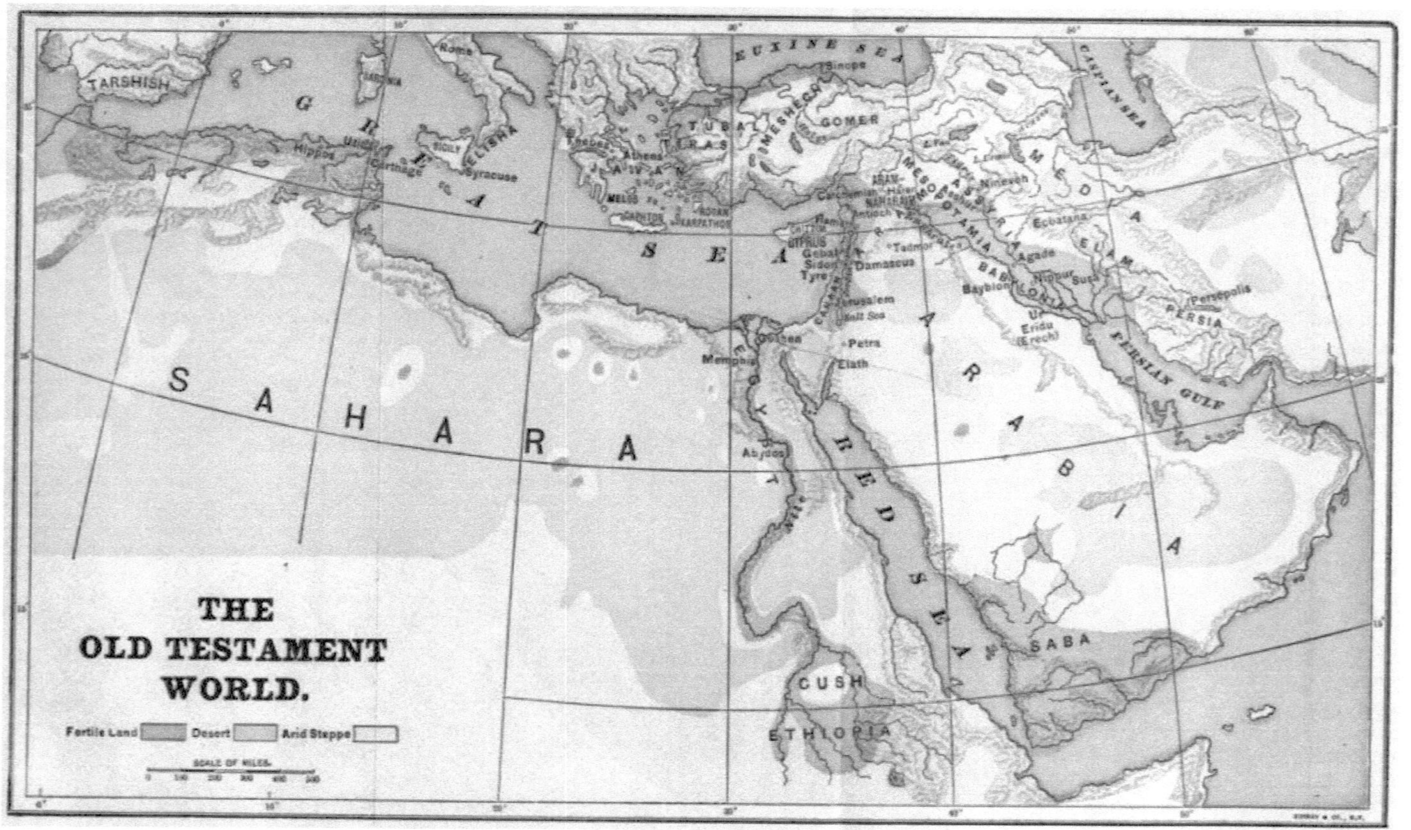

The Old Testament World

I

THE GENERAL CHARACTERISTICS OF THE BIBLICAL WORLD

Extent of the Biblical World.—Conditions Favorable to Early Civilizations.—Egypt's Climate and Resources.—Its Isolation and Limitations.—Conditions in the Tigris-Euphrates Valley.—Forces Developing Its Civilization.—Civilization of Arabia.—Physical Characteristics of Syria and Palestine.—Their Central Position and Lack of Unity.—Asia Minor.—Mycenæ.—Greece.—Italy.—Situation of Rome.—Reason Why Rome Went Forth to Conquer.—Résumé.

Extent of the Biblical World. In its widest bounds, the biblical world included practically all the important centres of early human civilization. Its western outpost was the Phœnician city of Tarshish in southern Spain (about 5° west longitude) and its eastern outpost did not extend beyond the Caspian Sea and Persian Gulf (about 55° east longitude). Its southern horizon was bounded by the land of Ethiopia (about 5° south latitude) and its northern by the Black Sea (about 45° north altitude). Thus the Old and New Testament world extended fully sixty degrees from east to west, but at the most not more than fifty degrees from north to south. With the exception of Arabia, all of these lands gather about the Mediterranean, for although the waters of the Tigris and the Euphrates ultimately find their way into the Indian Ocean, the people living in these fertile valleys ever looked toward the Mediterranean and for the most part found their field for conquest and commerce in the west rather than in the east and south.

Conditions Favorable to Early Civilizations. The greater part of this ancient world consisted of wastes of water, of burning sands or of dry, rocky, pasture lands. Less than one-fifth was arable soil, and yet the tillable strips along the river valleys on the eastern and northern Mediterranean were extremely fertile. Here in four of five favored centres were supplied in varying measure the conditions requisite for a strong primitive civilization: (1) a warm, but not enervating climate; (2) a fertile and easily cultivated territory which enabled the inhabitants to store up a surplus of the things necessary for life; (3) a geographical unity that made possible a homogeneous and closely knit political and social organization; (4) a pressure from without which spurred the people on to constant activity and effort; (5) an opportunity for expansion and for intercommunication with other strong nations. The result was that the lands about the eastern Mediterranean were the scenes of the world's earliest culture and history. From these centres emanated the great civic, political, intellectual, artistic, moral, and religious ideas and ideals that still strongly influence the life and faith of the nations that rule the world. The character of each of these early civilizations was in turn largely shaped by the natural environment amidst which it arose.

Egypt's Climate and Resources. The land of the Nile was peculiarly favorable for the development of an exceedingly early civilization. Lying near the equator and between extended areas of hot, dry desert, it possessed an almost perfect climate. While warm, it was never excessively hot, thanks to the fresh north winds which blew from the sea. The desert kept the atmosphere dry and cloudless through at least eleven months in the year. The narrow strip of alluvial soil which constituted the real land of Egypt was practically inexhaustible. The Nile, which rose during the hot summer months, furnished abundant water for irrigation. At the same tune the necessity for constant activity in order to develop the full resources of the land was a valuable incentive to industry. Finally, the uniformity of the Nile valley furnished an excellent basis for a unified social and political organization.

Its Isolation and Limitations. At first Egypt's isolation favored, but in the end fatally impeded the development of its civilization. On every side it was shut in, not only by miles of rocky desert on the east and west, but also on the north and south by almost impassable barriers. In the south the fertile territory narrows to a mere ribbon, with no natural highways by land, while several great cataracts cut off approach by water. On the north the Nile broadens out into a great impassable marsh with only two narrow gateways. One of these is the main western arm of the Nile, which reaches the Mediterranean near Alexandria; the other is the Wady Tumilat, which runs from the Isthmus of Suez through the biblical land of Goshen to the Nile valley. In early centuries these few narrow and uninviting avenues of approach on the north and south were easily guarded. The result was that the Egyptians, at a very early date, attained a high stage of culture, but they lacked that stimulus from without which is essential to the highest development. Once or twice, as in the days of the Hyksos and Ethiopian invasions, foreigners pressed into the land, and as a result the centuries immediately following were the most glorious in Egypt's history. In general, however, the civilization of the Nile valley was deficient in depth and idealism. It was grossly material; it developed too easily and the people were too contented. Even on the artistic side the brilliant promise of the earlier centuries failed of fruition. Moreover, the protecting natural barriers proved constricting, so that there was little opportunity for expansion. Hence Egypt's civilization was always provincial and by 500 B.C. had ceased to develop. From this time on the people of the Nile tamely submitted to the succession of foreign conquerors who have ever since ruled over this garden land of the eastern world.

Conditions in the Tigris-Euphrates Valley. Physical conditions in the Tigris-Euphrates valley were in many ways similar to those along the Nile. A warm but invigorating climate, fertile, alluvial soil, deposited by the great rivers and renewed each year by the floods, and the protection of the desert on the west favored the development of a virile civilization, as early if not earlier than that of Egypt. Starting from the same northern mountains, the two great rivers find their way to the Persian Gulf by widely different courses. The Tigris flows southeast in a comparatively direct course of eleven hundred miles. Its name, "The Arrow," suggests the rapidity of its descent. The Euphrates, on the contrary, makes a long detour westward toward the Mediterranean and then turns to the southeast, where for the greater part of the last half of its one thousand eight hundred miles it flows through the desert. The lands lying between the lower waters of these great rivers were by nature fitted to become the home of the earliest civilization. At a very early period these level plains attracted the nomadic tribes from the neighboring desert. Here they found soil that was exceedingly fertile, but covered to a great extent by the overflow of the great rivers. To be made productive it had to be drained in the flood and irrigated in the dry season by an extensive system of canals and reservoirs. Hence this region furnished powerful incentives to develop an energetic, enterprising civilization. The absence of natural barriers in the level plains of Babylonia and the uniformity of its physical contour meant that in time all the Tigris-Euphrates valley would inevitably be brought under one rule.

Forces Developing Its Civilization. Unlike Egypt, Babylonia was constantly subject to those thrusts from without which were essential to a great civilization. From the Arabian desert came nomadic invaders and from the mountains to the east and north and probably from northern Syria powerful, warlike peoples who either spurred the river dwellers on to strenuous activity in order to repel the hostile attacks or else as conquerors infused new blood and energy into the older races. On the other hand, the absence of constraining barriers gave ample opportunity for natural growth and expansion. The great rivers were the highways of commerce and conquest. The necessity of defence also suggested the advantages of conquest. The result was that at a very early period the armies of Babylonia had penetrated the mountains to the east and north and had carried their victorious rule as far as the shore of the Mediterranean on the west. Traders followed the armies, bearing the products of Babylonian art and in turn enriching the home-land with those of other nations. It was thus that Babylonia in time became not only the mistress of the ancient world, but also one of the chief centres from which emanated political, legal, artistic, and religious ideas and institutions that influenced all the peoples living about the eastern Mediterranean.

Civilization of Arabia. Very different was the site of the third Semitic civilization. The eastern shores of the Red Sea are rocky and barren. No important streams or harbors are found along this cheerless coast. The eastern slope of the range of mountains that runs parallel to the Red Sea is, however, one of the garden lands of the East. The clouds, chilled by the mountains, deposit their rains here, while mountain streams make it possible by irrigation to transform this part of Arabia into a rich agricultural land. Here from an early period was found a high type of civilization. Climate, soil, and the spur of foreign invasion fostered its development. Its products were famous throughout the ancient world. But it was in the highest degree isolated from the stream of the world's progress. Its one means of communication with outside nations was by the caravans which crossed the deserts. Hence a certain halo of mystery always surrounded this distant civilization. Like that of Egypt, it lacked opportunity for expansion and communication and so failed to rise above a certain level or to make any deep or significant impression upon the other Semitic nations.

Physical Characteristics of Syria and Palestine. In marked contrast with Arabia was the strip of hill and mountain country lying on the eastern coast of the Mediterranean, known in later tunes as Syria and Palestine. The dominant feature in this part of the Semitic world was the southern spurs of the Taurus mountains, which here run parallel with the coast in two ranges known as the Lebanons and the Anti-Lebanons. A warm, equable climate and fertile soil, especially in the broad valleys between the mountains, furnish the first necessities for a strong civilization. Frequent rain during the whiter and many perennial springs and brooks supply throughout most of this region the water needed for a prosperous, agricultural population. The desert on the east and the mountains in the north were the homes of active, migrating peoples whose ever-recurring attacks gave the inhabitants of Syria and Palestine a constant stimulus.

Its Central Position and Lack of Unity. This region was also the isthmus lying between the sea and the desert that connected Asia with Africa, and the ancient empires of Egypt and Babylonia. The great caravan routes led across it from Arabia on the south and Babylonia on the east to Asia Minor and thence by sea to the ports of the northern Mediterranean. One fatal defect, however, prevented it from becoming the permanent home of one strong, conquering people: it lacked physical unity. Its two rivers, the Orontes and the Jordan, were comparatively unimportant and flowed in opposite directions. Mountain ranges running from north to south and in the north one running from east to west divided the territory into eight or ten distinct areas. Wide variations in climate, flora, and fauna separated these different zones, making a uniform civilization practically impossible. No region, except the fertile valley between the Lebanons and Anti-Lebanons, possessed sufficient natural advantages to rule the whole territory immediately east of the Mediterranean. As a result Syria and Palestine were only at rare and comparatively brief periods completely dominated by native conquerors. The physical characteristics of this territory also suggested from the first a mixed civilization, combining those of the desert, of Babylonia, of Egypt, and of the other lands lying along the Mediterranean. The infusion of foreign elements largely explains the remarkable culture and religious life that flourished within the narrow bounds of Syria and Palestine. This land was at the same time the strategic point that commanded the rest of the ancient world and was destined to send forth influences that were to extend to the uttermost parts of the earth.

Asia Minor. Asia Minor, like Syria, is lacking in physical unity. Its centre is a high, barren plateau. This is encircled on the south, west, and east by fertile coast plains. These coast plains, however, are broken up into independent areas by lofty mountains. From the central plateau came the invaders, who spurred on the coast dwellers to put forth their strongest efforts. Communication by sea and along the great highways that run across the land from east to west brought to these maritime city states the culture of the East and the West. Under these conditions there naturally sprang up an exotic civilization, not unified, but gathered about different civic centres; not independent, but a brilliant fusion of native elements with Semitic and Hellenic culture.

Mycenæ. To the northwest, along the Dardanelles, the coastal plain broadens out into one of the most fertile regions in the ancient world. Frequent rains and perennial mountain streams water the gently rolling fields. Here, in a comparatively small area, were supplied in rich measure the five conditions essential to a strong, early civilization. Here was the seat of that ancient Mycenæan state, whose art and institutions for a brief period rivalled, and in many ways surpassed, those of Babylon and Egypt.

Greece. Of all the ancient centres of civilization Greece was in many ways the most unpromising. Its soil was for the greater part stony and unproductive. Less than one-third could be profitably tilled. The plains were not large and the mountain ranges dominated the land, dividing it into small, distinct areas. There were no navigable rivers and few perennial streams available for irrigation. Moreover, the streams brought down silt into the valleys, transforming them into malarious marshes. As a result, Greece is to-day and probably always has been the most malarial country in Europe. Its limited area gave no opportunity for a great and extensive civilization. Its great assets were a regular climate, a purifying north wind, and the protection of its insular position, which insured its security in its earlier days. While the land of Greece was insular it was also central and in close touch with the civilizations of Asia Minor and the eastern Mediterranean, for the islands of the Ægean Sea were like stepping-stones connecting Greece with the ancient East. The sea was also a great highway which led to the most distant lands. Finally, Greece was in a position to feel the invigorating shock of foreign invasion from the north and east. Its division into small areas meant the development of petty city states, with constant rivalry of arms as well as of wit and art. This keen rivalry and the intense civic loyalty that it kindled were the chief forces in the development of the civilization of ancient Hellas. Its physical character favored the rapid rise of a noble culture, but one which would fall with equal rapidity because of the lack of an opportunity for local expansion. It meant inevitably a scattered people and a widely dispersed civilization. The result was that even in the period of its decline Greek culture permeated and ruled the entire civilized world.

Italy. Further to the west Italy juts out into the heart of the Mediterranean. On the north the lofty Alps protect it from cold winds and snows. On almost every side it is encircled by the warm waters of the Mediterranean and its tributary bays. Throughout most of this narrow peninsula run the high Apennines. On the east they are so close to the coast that the descent to the sea is steep, the rivers insignificant, and the harbors few. On the western side, however, the slope is much more gradual and the coastal plains are exceedingly fertile. They are traversed by rivers fed by the melting snows. The result is that this western coast, with its many good harbors, and its abounding fertility, furnished from earliest times a favorable home for strong and active peoples. Here grew, mingled in great profusion, the fruits and grains of both the temperate and tropical climes. At many points, with the aid of irrigation, the soil yields four or more crops a year. Throughout most of this garden land the climate is semi-tropical without being enervating. The brilliant sunshine is tempered by the cool breezes from the sea and mountains. It is pre-eminently a land of contrasts. On one side is the blue sea, on the other the snow-capped mountains. On this western slope the temperature varies from that of the chill snows and storms on the mountains to the warm, humid air of the river basins. From the beautiful clear lakes on the heights the descent is sudden to the malarial marshes in the lowlands.

Situation of Rome. This western slope is cut midway from north to south by the Tiber, next to the Po the largest river in Italy. To the east the Apennines rise to their greatest height, insuring a heavy annual rainfall. The Tiber valley itself was one of the earliest highways from east to west and was in ancient times the natural division between the highly civilized Etruscans on the north and the Latins and the Greek colonies on the south. Here the varied life of ancient Italy met and mingled and the result was a virile race and a strong, aggressive civilization. Its centre was the Palatine hill, a low volcanic mound beside the Tiber, fourteen miles from its mouth. The uniformity of the Italian territory favored the union of its mixed population under the leadership of Rome its central city.

Reason Why Rome Went Forth to Conquer. Even more important in the development of its culture were the attacks from without to which it was constantly exposed. Even the lofty Alps did not prove impassable barriers to the barbarian hordes who were attracted by this fertile land. Ancient Italy, encircled by the sea and plentifully provided with open harbors on the east and south, was never free from the dread of foreign attack. Not until Rome had conquered the powerful nations living on even the most distant shores of the Mediterranean could she feel secure in her central position. It was this constant fear, as well as the influence of her commanding position, that made Rome in time the mistress of the Mediterranean. From the East she received a century or two later than Greece all that the old civilizations could give, both of good and evil. This inheritance she in turn gave to the western world toward which she faced and to which she belonged. Thus Rome was the great connecting link between the East and the West, between the ancient and the modern world.

Résumé. The biblical world was, both in extent and point of time, identical with the ancient civilized world. The outlook of the biblical writers was at first limited to the eastern Mediterranean, but was gradually broadened until it included practically all the peoples living about the great inland sea. Similarly the life and faith of the Hebrews, at first local, became in time world-wide. Each of the ancient races followed the lines of development marked out by their geographical environment. Two civilizations—that of the Hebrews and that of the Greeks—lacking a suitable background for local growth and expansion, went forth to conquer and transform the life and thought and faith of all the world.

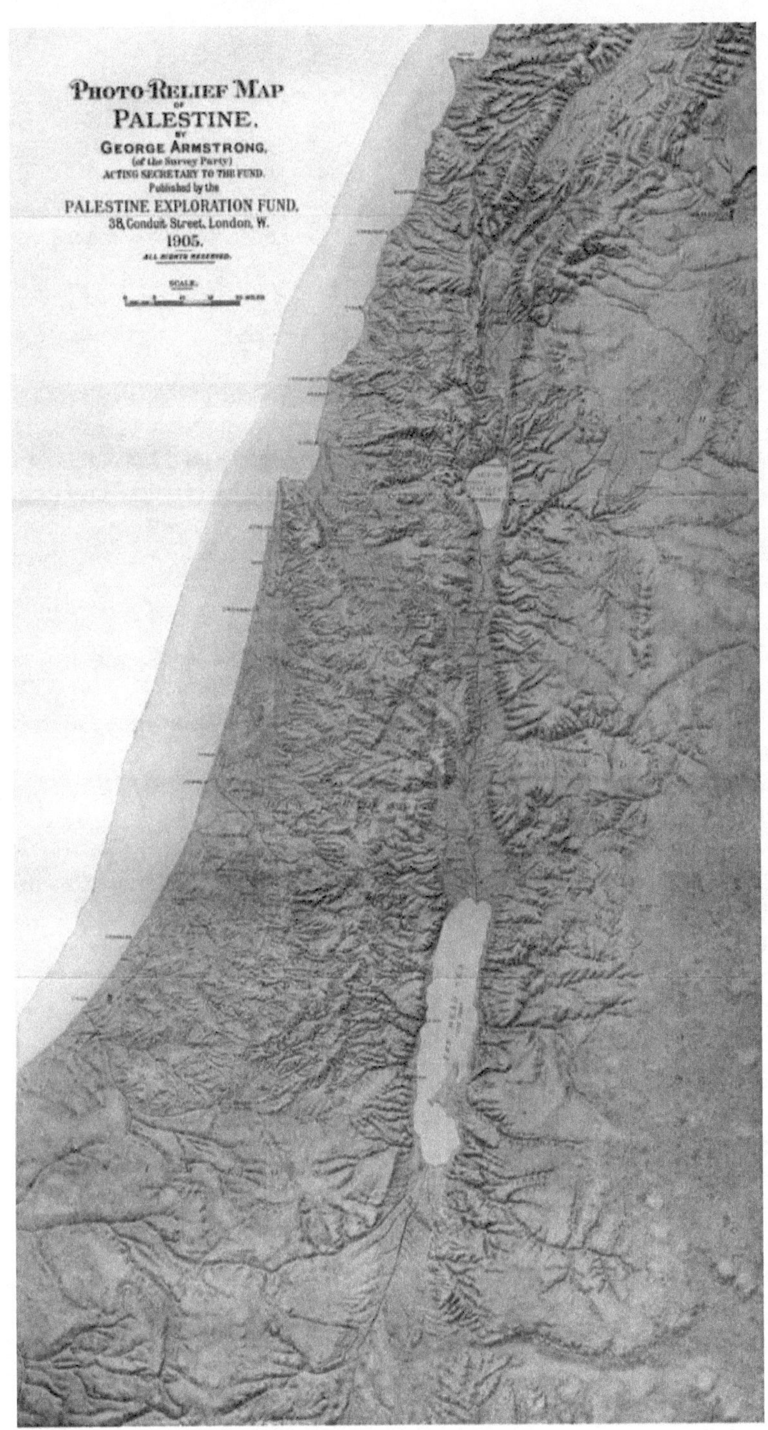

Photo-relief Map of Palestine

II

THE GENERAL CHARACTERISTICS
OF PALESTINE

History of the Terms Palestine and Canaan.—Bounds of Palestine.—
Geological History.—Alluvial and Sand Deposits.—General Divisions.—Variety in Physical Contour.—Effects of This Variety.—
Openness to the Arabian Desert.—Absence of Navigable Rivers
and Good Harbors.—Incentives to Industry.—Incentives to Faith
and Moral Culture.—Central and Exposed to Attack on Every
Side.—Significance of Palestine's Characteristics.

History of the Terms Palestine and Canaan. The term Palestine, originally
applied to the home of Israel's foes, the Philistines, was used by the Greeks as a
designation of southern Syria, exclusive of Phœnicia. The Greek historian Herodotus was the first to employ it in this extended sense. The Romans used the same
term in the form Palestina and through them the term Palestine has become the
prevailing name in the western world of the land once occupied by the Israelites
and their immediate neighbors on the east and west. The history of the older name
Canaan (Lowland) is similar. In the Tell el-Amarna Letters, written in the fourteenth century B.C., Canaan is limited to the coast plains; but as the Canaanites,
the Lowlanders, began to occupy the inland plains the use of the term was extended until it became the designation of all the territory from the Mediterranean to
the Jordan and Dead Sea valley. It does not appear, however, to have ever been
applied to the east-Jordan land.

Bounds of Palestine. Palestine lies between the eastern shore of the Mediterranean Sea and the Arabian desert. Its northern boundary is the southern slope of
Mount Hermon and the River Litany, as it turns abruptly to flow westward into
the Mediterranean. Palestine begins where the Lebanons and Anti-Lebanons break
into a series of elevated plateaus. Its southern boundary is the varying line drawn
east from the southeastern end of the Mediterranean a little south of the Dead Sea
at the point where the hills of Judah and the South Country descend to the desert.
Palestine therefore lies between 33° 30′ and 31° north latitude and 34° and 37° east
longitude. Its approximate width is about a hundred miles and its length from
north to south only about a hundred and fifty miles. It is, therefore, about the size
of the State of Vermont.

Geological History. The geological history of Palestine is somewhat complex,
but exceedingly illuminating. The underlying rock is granite. This is now almost

completely concealed by later layers of sandstone (which appears in Edom and the east-Jordan), dolomitic and nummulitic limestone and marl. During the earlier geological periods the land was entirely covered by the waters of the sea. Probably at the close of the Pliocene period came the great volcanic upheaval which gave to Syria and Palestine their distinctive character. It left a huge rift running from north to south throughout Syria. This rift is represented to-day by the valley between the Lebanons and its continuation, the valley of the Jordan and Dead Sea. Further south it may be traced through the Wady Arabah and the Gulf of Akaba. This vast depression is the deepest to be found anywhere on the earth's surface. The same great volcanic upheaval gave to the mountains along the western coast their decided northern and southern trend and the peculiar cliff-like structure which characterizes their descent to the western shore. Through the centuries frequent and severe earthquakes have been felt along the borders of this ancient rift, and they are still the terror of the inhabitants, even as in the days of the Hebrew prophets.

Alluvial and Sand Deposits. Until a comparatively late geological period the sea came to the foot of the mountains. The coast rose gradually and has later been built up by the process of erosion that has cut down the mountains, especially on the western side, where the rainfall was heaviest. The plains along the shore have thus been enriched by vast alluvial deposits. Very different was the deposit of Nile sediment, which was blown in from the sea by the western winds, leaving a wide border of yellow sand along the coast of Palestine.

General Divisions. Palestine is sharply divided by nature into four divisions or zones, which extend in parallel lines from north to south.[1] Along the Great Sea lie the narrow coast plains which broaden in the south into the plains of Sharon and Philistia. The second zone is the central plateau, with hills three to four thousand feet in height in the north, which sink by stages to the large Plain of Esdraelon. South of this great plain lie the fertile hills of Samaria which in turn merge into the stern hills of Judah. These again descend into the low, rocky, rolling hills of the South Country. The third zone is the Jordan and Dead Sea valley which begins at the foot of Mount Hermon and rapidly sinks, until at the Dead Sea it is one thousand two hundred and ninety-two feet below the surface of the ocean. The fourth zone includes the elevated plateaus which extend east of the Jordan and Dead Sea out into the rocky Arabian desert.

Variety in Physical Contour. The first striking characteristic of Palestine is the great variety in physical contour, climate, flora, and fauna to be found within its narrow compass of less than fifteen thousand square miles. Coast plains, inland valleys, elevated plateaus, deep, hot gorges, and glimpses of snow-clad mountains are all included within the closest possible bounds. In a journey of from two to three days the traveller from west to east passes from the equable, balmy climate of the Mediterranean coast to the comparatively cold highlands of the central plateau and then down into the moist, tropical climate of the hot Jordan and Dead Sea valley. Thence he mounts the highlands of Gilead or Moab, where the sun beats

---

[1] The numbers in parentheses refer to the stereographs or stereopticon pictures that illustrate the section in which the reference is found. Cf., for detail descriptions, Appendix II.

down hot at noonday, while the temperature falls low at night and deep snows cover the hilltops in winter. The hills of the central plateaus, covered with the trees of the temperate zone, overhang the palms and tropical fruit trees of the coast plains and Jordan valley.

Effects of this Variety. The different zones touch each other closely, and yet their wide differences in physical contour, climate, flora and fauna constitute invisible but insuperable barriers and produce fundamentally diverse types of life and civilization. To-day, as in the past, inhabitants of cities, tent dwellers, merchants, and peasants live in this narrow land within a few miles, yet separated from each other by the widest possible difference in culture and manner of life. The character of the land made impossible a closely knit civilization. It could never become the centre of a great world-power. It was rather destined to be the abode of many small tribes or nations, with widely differing institutions and degrees of culture. The great variety of scenery, climate, and life, however, made Palestine an epitome of all the world. It was pre-eminently fitted to be the home of a people called to speak a vital message in universal terms to all the races of the earth. Its striking contrasts and its marvellous beauty and picturesqueness also arrested the attention of primitive men and explain the prominence of nature worship among the early inhabitants of Palestine and the large place that its rocks, brooks, hills and meadows occupy in Israel's literature.

Openness to the Arabian Desert. The second marked peculiarity of Palestine is its openness to the desert. As Principal Smith has aptly said, Palestine "lay, so to speak, broadside on to the desert." With its comparatively fertile fields, it has proved a loadstone that for thousands of years has attracted the wandering Arabian tribes. These came in, however, not as a rule in great waves, but as families, or small tribes. Up through the South Country they penetrated the hills of Judah. There in time they learned to cultivate the vine, although they still retained their flocks. East of Moab and Gilead the arable land merges gradually into the rocky desert and the Arabs to-day, as in the past, claim as their own all the land to the Jordan and Dead Sea valley, except where the settled population successfully contests their claim by arms. Palestine, therefore, has always been powerfully influenced by the peculiar life and centralized government and fierce rivalry between tribes and petty peoples—these are but a few of the characteristics of Palestine's history that are primarily due to its openness to Arabia.

Absence of Navigable Rivers and Good Harbors. Palestine, on the other hand, is shut off from close commercial contact with other peoples. No great waterway invited the trader and warrior to go out and conquer the rest of the world. Instead, in the early periods when men depended chiefly upon communication by river or sea, Palestine shut in its inhabitants and tended to develop an intensive rather than an extensive civilization. Its one large river, the Jordan, flows, not into the ocean, but into a low inland sea, whose only outlet is by evaporation. The coast line of Palestine is also characterized by the lack of a single good harbor. At Joppa, at the northwestern end of Carmel, and at Tyre the otherwise straight shore line curves slightly inland; but at each of these points there is no natural protection from the severe western gales. The Phœnicians, shut in by the eastern mountains, dared the perils of the deep; but to the early peoples of Palestine the Great Sea was, on the whole, a barrier rather than an invitation to commerce and conquest.

Incentives to Industry. The physical characteristics of Palestine were well fitted to develop active, industrious inhabitants. The constant pressure on their borders by Arabs, who could be held back only by a strong, organized civilization, was a powerful spur. The natural division of the land among independent and usually hostile races made eternal activity and watchfulness the price that must be paid for life and freedom. Popular tradition, based on a fact that pre-eminently impresses every traveller in the land to-day, states that the fabled Titan, who was sent to scatter stones over the face of the earth, distributed them equally over Europe and Africa, but that when he came to Asia and was passing through Syria, his bag broke, depositing its contents on Palestine. Throughout most of its territory the rich soil can be cultivated only as the stones are gathered either in huge heaps or fences. The fertility of the plains can be utilized only as the waters of the mountain brooks are used for irrigation. It is, therefore, a land that bred hardy men, strong of muscle, resourceful, alert, and, active in mind and body.

Incentives to Faith and Moral Culture. Another still more significant characteristic of Palestine was the powerful incentive which it gave to the development of the faith of its inhabitants. The constant presence of Arab invaders powerfully emphasized their dependence upon their God or gods. The changing climate of Palestine deepened that sense of dependence. No great river like the Nile or the Euphrates brought its unfailing supply of water, and water was essential to life. The waters came down from heaven, or else burst like a miracle from the rocky earth. If the latter rains failed to fill the cisterns and enrich the springs and rivers, drought, with all its train of woes, was inevitable. Little wonder that the ancient Canaanites revered nature deities, and that they, like the Greeks, worshipped the spirits of the springs, and especially those from which came their dashing rivers. Locusts, earthquakes, and pestilence in the lowland frequently brought disaster. In all of these mysterious calamities primitive peoples saw the direct manifestation of the Deity. In the fourth chapter of his prophecy, Amos clearly voiced this wide-spread popular belief:

> "I also it was who withheld from you the rain,
> And I sent rain upon one city,
> While upon another I did not let it rain,
> Yet ye did not return to me," is the oracle of Jehovah.

> "I smote you with blight and mildew,
> I laid waste your gardens and vineyards,
> Your fig and your olive trees the young locust devoured;
> Yet you did not return to me," is the oracle of Jehovah.

> "I sent among you a pestilence by the way of Egypt,
> I slew your youths by the sword, taking captive your horses,
> And I caused the stench of your camps to rise in your nostrils,
> Yet ye did not return to me," is the oracle of Jehovah (Am. 4:7-10).

Hence in a land like Palestine it was natural and almost inevitable that men should eagerly seek to know the will of the Deity and should strive to live in accord with it. It was a fitting school in which to nurture the race that attained the deepest sense of the divine presence, the most intense spirit of worship and devotion, and the most exalted moral consciousness.

Central and Exposed to Attack on Every Side. Palestine, in common with the rest of Syria, held a central position in relation to the other ancient civilizations. Through it ran the great highways from Babylon and Assyria to Egypt. Along its eastern border passed the great road from Damascus and Mesopotamia to Arabia. It was the gateway and key to three continents—Africa, Asia, and Europe. From each of these in turn came conquerors—Egyptians and Ethiopians, Babylonians and Assyrians, Greeks and Romans—against whom the divided peoples of Palestine were practically helpless. Palestine, because of its physical characteristics and central position was destined to be ruled by rather than to rule over its powerful neighbors. And yet this close contact with the powerful nations of the earth inevitably enriched the civilization and faith of the peoples living within this much contested land. It produced the great political, social, and religious crises that called forth the Hebrew prophets. It made the Israelites the transmuters and transmitters of the rich heritage received from their cultured neighbors and from their inspired teachers. In turn it gave them their great opportunity, for repeated foreign conquests and exile enabled them in time to go forth and conquer, not with the sword of steel, but of divine truth, and to build up an empire that knew no bounds of time or space.

Significance of Palestine's Characteristics. Thus the more important characteristics of Palestine are richly suggestive of the unfolding of Israel's life and of the rôle that Judaism and Christianity were destined to play in the world's history. Palestine is the scene of the earlier stages of God's supreme revelation of himself and his purpose to man and through man. The more carefully that revelation is studied the clearer it appears that the means whereby it was perfected were natural and not contra-natural. The stony hills and valleys of Palestine, the unique combination of sea and plain, of mountain and desert, placed in the centre of the ancient world, were all silent but effective agents in realizing God's eternal purpose in the life of man.

III

THE COAST PLAINS

Extent and Character.—Fertility.—Divisions.—Plain of Tyre.—The
Plain of Acre.—Carmel.—Plain of Sharon.—The Philistine Plain.—
The Shephelah or Lowland.

Extent and Character. The eastern shore of the Mediterranean is skirted by a series of low-lying coast plains, from one to five miles wide in the north to twenty-five miles wide in the south. At two points in Palestine the mountains come down to the sea; the one is at the so-called Ladder of Tyre, about fifteen miles south of the city from which it is named. Here the precipitous cliffs break directly over the sea. The other point is at Carmel, which, however, does not touch the sea directly, but is bounded on its western end by a strip of plain about two hundred yards wide. The soil of these coast plains consists of alluvial deposits, largely clay and red quartz sand washed down in the later geological periods from the mountains of the central plateau and constantly renewed by the annual freshets.

Fertility. Because of the nature of the soil and their position, these plains are among the most fertile spots in all Palestine. Numerous brooks and rivers rush down from the eastern headlands. Some of these are perennial; others furnish a supply of water, which, if stored during the winter in reservoirs on the heights above, is amply sufficient to irrigate the plains below. The average temperature of these coast plains is sixty-eight degrees. The cool sea-winds equalize the climate so that the temperature changes little throughout the year and there is but slight variation between the north and the south. Under these favorable conditions the soil produces in rich abundance a great variety of tropical fruits. Here grow side by side oranges, lemons, apricots, figs, plums, bananas, grapes, olives, pomegranates, almonds, citrons, and a great variety of vegetables, as well as the cereals of the higher altitudes.

Divisions. The coast plains of Palestine fall naturally into four great divisions, broken by two mountain barriers. The northern is the Plain of Tyre, which is the southern continuation of the rich plains about Sidon. The second division is the Plain of Acre, which lies directly south of the Ladder of Tyre and extends to Carmel. The third is the Plain of Sharon, which begins at the south of Carmel and merges opposite Joppa into the ever widening Plain of Philistia.

Plain of Tyre. Throughout the Plain of Tyre the low foot-hills come down within a mile of the sea; but for five or six miles back from the coast they must be reckoned as a part of the same division, for their natural and political associations are all with the coast rather than with the uplands. The city of Tyre was originally built on an island[2] and was supplied with water from the Spring of Tyre, near the shore about five miles to the south. The four great perennial rivers of Phœnicia were the Litany (the present Nahr el-Kasimiyeh, a few miles north of Tyre), the Zaherâni, south of Sidon, the Nahr el-Auwali, which was the ancient Bostrenus that watered the plain to the north of Sidon, and the Nahr ed-Damur which was the Tamyras of the ancients. Many springs in the plain and on the hillsides contribute to the fertility of this land, which was the home of the Phœnicians. At the best the narrowness of the territory, which supported only a very limited population, made it necessary for this enterprising race to find an outlet elsewhere. Long before the days of the Hebrews their colonies had extended down the coast plains to Joppa and northward to the Eleutherus (the present Nahr el-Kebir, north of Tripoli). The nineteenth chapter of Judges refers to the Sidonian colony at Laish (later the Hebrew Dan) at the foot of Mount Hermon; but, with this exception, there is no evidence that they ever attempted to plant colonies inland. Instead they found their great outlet in the sea to the west. Launching their small craft from the smooth sands that extend crescent-shaped to the north and to the south of their chief cities, Tyre and Sidon, they skirted the Mediterranean, colonizing its islands and shores until a line of Phœnician settlements extended from one end of the Great Sea to the other. Thus they were the first to open that great door to the western world through which passed not only the products of Semitic art and industry, but also in time the immortal messages of Israel's inspired prophets, priests, and sages, and of him who spoke as never man spoke before.

The Plain of Acre. For ten miles to the south of the Plain of Tyre the coast plain is almost completely cut off by the mountains, which at Ras el-Abjad, the White Promontory of the Roman writers, and at Ras en-Nakurah push out into the sea. The great coast road runs along the cliffs high above the waters in the rock-cut road made by Egyptian, Assyrian, and Roman conquerors. The Plain of Acre, less than five miles wide in the north, widens to ten miles in the south. Four perennial streams water its fertile fields. On the west the sand from the sea has swept in at places for a mile or more, blocking up the streams in the south and transforming large areas into wet morasses. In ancient times, however, most of the southern part of the plain (like the northern end at present) was probably in a high state of cultivation. Many large tells or ruined mounds testify that it once supported a dense population. During most of its history this plain was held by the Phœnicians or their Greek and Roman conquerors, but at certain times the Hebrews appear to have here reached the sea.

Carmel. The most striking object on the western side of central Palestine is the bold elevated plateau of Carmel. Except for the little strip of lowland on its seaward side, it completely interrupts the succession of coast plains. Its formation is the same as that of the central plateaus. Viewing Palestine as a whole, it would seem that Carmel had slipped out of its natural position, leaving the open Plain of Esdraelon and destroying the otherwise regular symmetry of the land. Its long, slightly waving sky-line, as it rises abruptly above the plains of Acre and Esdraelon, commands the landscape for miles to the north[3] and adds greatly to the picturesqueness of Palestine. It is about eighteen hundred feet in height and slopes gradually downward to the southeast and northwest. The ascent on the north is more abrupt than on the south, where it descends slowly to the Plain of Sharon. As its name Carmel, The Garden, suggests, it is by no means a barren, rocky mountain. Instead, where the thickets and wild flowers have not taken possession of the soil, it is still cultivated, as was most of its broad surface in earlier times. The ruins of wine and olive presses and of ancient villages testify to its rich productivity. On its top the western showers first deposit their waters, so that in the Old Testament Carmel is a synonym for superlative fertility. Like the uplands of central Palestine, it was held by the Hebrews, who from its heights gained their clearest view of the Great Sea.

Plain of Sharon. South of Carmel, beginning with an acute angled triangle between the mountains and sea, rolls the undulating Plain of Sharon. Opposite the southern end of Carmel it is six or seven miles wide. Thence the plain broadens irregularly until, at its southern end, opposite Joppa, it is twelve miles in width. From north to south it is nearly fifty miles long. Groups of hills from two to three hundred feet high dot this undulating expanse of field and pasture. Five perennial streams flow across it to the sea. Of these the most important are the Crocodile River (the modern Nahr el-Zerka) a little north of Cæsarea, and the Iskanderuneh in the south. Here again a wide fringe of yellow sand bounds the sea and at several points holds back the waters of the streams, making large marshes. In the north there are a few groves of oaks, sole survivors of the great forest, mentioned by Josephus and Strabo, which once covered the Plain of Sharon. To-day the southern part of the plain is a series of cultivated, fruitful fields and gardens,[4] but the northern end is covered in spring by a wealth of wild flowers, among which are found anemones, brilliant red poppies, the narcissus, which is probably the rose of Sharon, and the blue iris, which may be the lily of the valley. Rich soil and abundant waters are found on this plain; but its resources were never fully developed, for it was the highway of the nations. Across it ran the great coast road from Egypt to Phœnicia in the north and to Damascus and Babylonia in the northwest. Phœnician, Philistine, and Israelite held this plain in turn, but only in part and temporarily, for having no natural defences, it was open to all the world.

The Philistine Plain. The only natural barrier that separates the plains of Sharon and Philistia is the river which comes down in two branches from the eastern hills, one branch leading westward past the Beth-horons and the other through the Valley of Ajalon. After much twisting and turning, and under many local names, this, the largest river south of Carmel, finds the sea a little north of Joppa. Southward the Plain of Philistia, about forty miles in length, broadens until it is twenty miles wide. The low hills of the Plain of Sharon change first into long, rolling swells and then throughout much of the distance settle into an almost absolutely level plain. In the southwest the sands of the sea have come in many miles. Ashkelon now lies between a sea of water and a sea of sand. At many other points the yellow waves are steadily engulfing the cultivated fields. Three perennial streams, with sprawling confluents, cut their muddy course across this rich alluvial plain. It is one of the important grain fields of Palestine, for the subsoil is constantly saturated with the moisture which falls in abundance in the winter and spring. No barns are necessary, for the grain is thrashed and stored out under the rainless summer skies. It is a land well fitted to support a rich and powerful agricultural civilization. Like all the coast plains, it is wide open to the trader and to the invader. Its possessors were obliged to be ever ready and able to defend their homes from all foes. Its inhabitants necessarily dwelt in a few strongly guarded cities. Here in ancient times, especially on the eastern side, were found the city-dwelling Canaanites. Later the valiant, energetic Philistines established their title to these fruitful plains and maintained it for centuries by sheer enterprise and force of arms. The chief Philistine cities were Ekron and Ashdod in the north, Askelon by the shore, quite close to the Judean foot-hills and Gaza[5] in the southwest. Except during the heroic Maccabean age, the Israelites never succeeded and apparently never seriously attempted to dispute this title. Lying on the highway that ran straight on along the coast to Egypt, this part of Palestine was most exposed to the powerful influences that came from the land of the Nile. The oldest Egyptian inscriptions, as well as the results of recent excavations, all reveal the wide extent of this influence.

The Shephelah or Lowland. Along the eastern side of the Philistine plain, from the valley of Ajalon southward, runs a series of low-lying foot-hills, which are separated from the central plateau of Palestine by broad, shallow valleys running north and south.[6] This territory was called by the biblical writers, the Shephelah or Lowland. These low chalk and limestone hills, with their narrow glens, their numerous caves and broken rocks, was the debatable ground between plain and hill country. Sometimes it was held by the inhabitants of the plain, sometimes by those of the hill country; always it was the battle-field between the two. Even to-day it is sparsely inhabited, the haunt of the Bedouin tribes, whose presence is clearest evidence of the difficulties that the local government experiences in controlling this wild border land. Like the Scottish lowlands, this region is redolent with the memories of ancient border warfare. It is also richly suggestive of one phase of that severe training which through the long centuries produced a race with a mission and a message to all the world.

IV

THE PLATEAU OF GALILEE
AND THE PLAIN OF ESDRAELON

Physical and Political Significance of the Central Plateau.—Natural
and Political Bounds.—Its Extent and Natural Divisions.—Physical Characteristics of Upper Galilee.—Its Fertility.—Characteristics of Lower Galilee.—Situation and Bounds of the Plain of Esdraelon.—Plain of Jezreel.—Water Supply and Fertility of Plain of
Esdraelon.—Central and Commanding Position.—Importance of
the Plain in Palestinian History.

Physical and Political Significance of the Central Plateau. The backbone of
Palestine is the great central plateau. It was in this important zone that the drama
of Israel's history was chiefly enacted. Here was the true home of the Hebrews.
By virtue of its position this central zone naturally commanded those to the east
and west. For one brief period the Philistines from the western coast plain nearly
succeeded in conquering and ruling all Palestine; but otherwise, until the world
powers outside began to invade the land, the centre of power lay among the hills.
This significant feature of Palestinian history is due to two facts: (1) that in war the
great advantage lies with the people who hold the higher eminences and so can
fight from above; and (2) that the rugged uplands usually produce more virile,
energetic, liberty-loving people. At the same time it may be noted that, while the
centre of power lay among the hills, the hill-dwellers never succeeded in conquering completely or in holding permanently the zones to the east and west. So firmly
were the invisible bounds of each zone established that the dwellers in one were
never able wholly to overleap these real though intangible lines and to weld together the diverse types of civilization that sprang up in these different regions, so
near in point of distance, yet really so far removed from each other.

Natural and Political Bounds. A part of the northern plateau bore even in
early Hebrew days the name of Galilee, the Circle or the Region (I Kings, 9:11,
II Kings, 15:29, Josh. 20:7). At first this region appears to have been confined to a
small area about Kedesh, where the Hebrew and older Gentile population met and
mingled. Gradually the name was extended, until in the Maccabean and Roman
period Galilee included all of the central plateau north of the Plain of Esdraelon
as far as the Litany itself. Its western boundary lay where the central plateau descends to the foot-hills and coast plains of Tyre and Acre, and its eastern was the
abrupt cliffs of the Jordan valley. These were its natural boundaries; but Josephus,

whose knowledge of Galilee was peculiarly personal, includes in it the towns about the Lake of Gennesaret (commonly designated in the New Testament as the Sea of Galilee), the Plain of Esdraelon and even Mount Carmel (*cf. Jewish Wars*, II, 3:4, 8:1, III, 3:1).

Its Extent and Natural Divisions. Defined by its narrower natural bounds, Galilee is about thirty miles wide from east to west, and nearly fifty miles long from north to south. It comprises an area, therefore, of a little less than fifteen hundred square miles. It falls into two clearly marked divisions: (1) Upper Galilee with its rolling elevated plateaus, bounded on the east and west by hills which rise rapidly to the height of between two thousand and four thousand feet; and (2) Lower Galilee, lying to the south of an irregular line drawn westward from the northern end of the Lake of Gennesaret to Acre on the shore of the Mediterranean. This division line is marked by the Wady Amud and the Wady et-Tuffah, which flow into the northwestern end of the Lake of Gennesaret, and the series of plains which cut from east to west through Galilee to a point opposite Acre. This second division includes the lower hills, which extend southward from the high plateaus of northern Galilee, making an irregular terrace, never over nineteen hundred feet high and gradually sloping to the Plain of Esdraelon, which sends out several low valleys to meet and intersect the descending hills. This clear-cut line of division was recognized both by Josephus and the Talmudic writers.

Physical Characteristics of Upper Galilee. The elevated hills of upper Galilee constitute, therefore, the first terrace that flanks the southern part of the Lebanons. The deep clefts between the higher Lebanons and Anti-Lebanons to the north here disappear. Even the Litany turns abruptly westward on the northern border of Galilee, leaving a broad mass of rounded limestone hills, greatly weathered by frost and rain. At a distance this mass looks like a mountain range, but it consists in reality of a high rolling plateau, cut by irregular valleys. This plateau of upper Galilee reaches its highest elevation in a line drawn northwest from Safed, which was probably "the city set on a hill" of the Gospel record.[7] The mountain on which Safed stands is two thousand seven hundred and fifty feet above the sea, while to the northwest Jebel Jermak, the highest mountain of Galilee, rises to the height of three thousand nine hundred and thirty-four feet. From this point many fertile upland valleys radiate to the northwest, the north, the northeast, and the east, but none to the south. Thus upper Galilee presents its boldest front to the south, towering high above lower Galilee and sloping to the north until it meets the mountains of the southern Lebanons. On the southeast it slopes gradually down to the Jordan and Lake Huleh, where two brooks come down from the plain of Hazor. Farther north the hills rise very abruptly from the Jordan and present a front unbroken by any important streams. At many points on this eastern slope lava streams have left their bold deposit of trap-rock. On the northwest the descent to the coast plains is very gradual and regular, but farther south the hills jut out abruptly to the sea. Upper Galilee is an open region with splendid vistas of the blue coastline of the Mediterranean on the west, of Carmel and the Samaria hills on the south, of the lofty almost unbroken line of the plateau of the Hauran and Gilead on the east; while the Lebanons tower on the north, and above them all rises the massive peak of Hermon, long into the springtime clad in cold, dazzling whiteness. Galilee, as a whole, was a land well fitted to breed enthusiasts and men of vision, intolerant alike of the inflexible rule of Rome and of the constricting priestcraft of Jerusalem. The Talmud states that the Galileans were ever more anxious for honor than for money.

Its Fertility. Upper Galilee was also a land of great fertility. The one limitation was the profusion of rocks strewn especially over the northern part. But if the Lebanons have poured their stones over northern Galilee, they have compensated with the wealth of waters which run through the valleys and break out in springs or else are scattered in dashing showers and deposited in heavy dews upon its rich soil. Where wars and conquest have not denuded the land, trees grow to the summits of the hills and grass and flowers flourish everywhere in greatest profusion. It is a land of plenty, sunshine, beauty, and contentment. Significant is the fact that it figures so little in Israel's troubled history, for happy is the land that has no history. Josephus's statement that in his day Galilee had a population of nearly three millions is undoubtedly an exaggeration. Even though, as in some parts of the land, to-day, the villages almost touched each other and no part of the land lay idle, Galilee could not have supported more than four or five hundred thousand inhabitants (*cf.* Masterman, *Studies in Galilee*, 131-134).

Characteristics of Lower Galilee. Lower Galilee possesses the fertility of upper Galilee in even greater measure. With a lower elevation and slightly warmer climate it bears a large variety of trees and fruits. Its valleys are also broader and lower and enriched with the soil washed down from the hills. The broad, low plain of Asochis (the present Sahel el-Buttauf) lies a little north of the heart of lower Galilee and from it valleys radiate to the northeast, southwest, and southeast. Another broad plain runs northeast from the Plain of Esdraelon to the neighborhood of Nazareth and Mount Tabor, and east of Tabor still another extends down to the Jordan River. The rounded top of Mount Tabor commands a marvellous view of lower Galilee. Across the fertile fields to the northeast lies the Sea of Galilee, shut in by its steep banks, and beyond it the mountain plateau of the Jaulan. [8] Across the valley to the south is the Hill of Moreh and the Samaritan hills beyond. [9] Two perennial brooks, the Wady Fejjas and the Wady el-Bireh, flow down through southeastern Galilee into the Jordan. The result is that lower Galilee is made up of a series of irregular hills (of which the Nazareth group, a little south of the centre, is the chief) separated by a network of broad, rich, intersecting plains. It combines the vistas and large horizons of the north with the fruitfulness of the plains. Here many different types of civilization meet and mingle. Instead of being remote and provincial, as is sometimes mistakenly supposed, lower Galilee is close to the heart of Palestine and open to all the varied influences which radiate from that little world. It is also intersected by a network of little wadys running in every direction from its open valleys and through its low-lying hills. Thus it was bound closely not only to the rest of Palestine, but also to the greater world that lay beyond.

Situation and Bounds of the Plain of Esdraelon. The Plain of Esdraelon is the last of the great terraces by which the Lebanons descend on the south to the sea-level. The plain itself lies only about two hundred feet above the level of the Mediterranean and to the east sinks toward the Jordan to below the sea-level. Its shape is that of an equiangular triangle. Its base lies close under the northeast side of Mount Carmel and is twenty miles long running from Tell el-Kasis to Jenîn. Its northern line runs along the foot of the Nazareth hills for fifteen miles to a point opposite Mount Tabor. The eastern boundary, from Tabor to Jenîn is also about fifteen miles in length but less regular. Moreh or Little Hermon and Mount Gilboa jut out into the plain, which sends down toward the Jordan two broad valleys, of which the most important is the plain of Jezreel to the north of Gilboa.[10] The watershed between these two plains is near the modern village of Zerin which stood not far from the ancient Jezreel.

Plain of Jezreel. The Plain of Jezreel extends like a great broad valley almost due east for about fifteen miles until it reaches the Jordan. Through it runs the Nahr Jalûd with its perennial parallel streams. Where the Plain of Jezreel joins the low-lying Jordan valley stands the guardian of the gateway, the town of Beisan, which represents the ancient Bethshean, later known as Scythopolis. This Plain of Jezreel, together with the narrow valley through which the Kishon now finds its way to the Mediterranean, completes the link between the Great Sea and the Jordan Valley and for a brief space separates the hills of Galilee from those of Samaria.

Water Supply and Fertility of the Plain of Esdraelon. Originally the Plain of Esdraelon appears to have been a shallow inland lake. Viewed from the top of Mount Gilboa it appears to be completely shut in by a circle of mountains on the north, west, and south.[11] Its elevation toward the east is so slight and its outlets to the east and west so imperfect that during the rainy season much of it is practically a morass. Into it drain the waters from the surrounding hills. Some of the drainage is on the surface, but most of it is underground, with the result that at many points on the plain rushing springs pour forth their waters, which run for a time as a dashing brook and then sink again into the porous soil. Springs of this character are found especially on the northeastern and southern sides of the plain. Some of them ultimately send their scattered waters down the Plain of Jezreel to the Jordan, but more of them find their outlet through the low, muddy Kishon, which, with many turnings, ploughs its way through the middle of the Plain of Esdraelon to the shadow of Mount Carmel and then finds a narrow outlet into the Mediterranean past the Galilean foot-hills, which here are scarcely one hundred yards from the spurs of Mount Carmel. As a result of its peculiar position and formation, the Plain of Esdraelon is one of the best watered areas in all Palestine. In certain places, indeed, it suffers from an excess of water. Its loamy, basaltic soil is also richly fertile and its alluvial deposits are free from stone. By nature it is fitted to be the great grain field of central Palestine. The hills that jut out into this garden land were naturally the first centres of a developed agricultural civilization. Here on the southern border are found the large mounds which were once the sites of teeming Canaanite cities.

Central and Commanding Position. The Plain of Esdraelon, like the Plain of Sharon, was a great highway of the nations. Through the broad valleys which lead into it came from every quarter the invaders, whether for peaceful or violent conquest, for here all the important roads converged. On its western border ran the great coast road from Egypt to Phœnicia. The eastern branches of the road also entered the plain from the south through three different avenues. The one was through the valley which led from the Plain of Sharon to the southeastern end of Mount Carmel. Still more direct and easy was the approach through northwestern Samaria along the Wady Arah, past the famous old fortress of Megiddo. The third was farther east along the broad Plain of Dothan to Engannim, the present Jenîn, and thence along the eastern side of the Plain of Esdraelon. These highways in turn connected with those which ran past Mount Tabor to the populous cities on the Lake of Gennesaret and thence to Damascus and the East. Another important artery of trade ran along the wide, level Plain of Jezreel, past Bethshean that guarded its eastern gateway[12] to the Jordan and thence northward to Damascus or directly eastward to Gilead and the desert (*cf.* chap. IX).

Importance of the Plain in Palestinian History. The Plain of Esdraelon was both the door and the key to Palestine. Through it came the ancient conquerors to possess the land. The Midianites in the days of Gideon were but a part of that ever-advancing Arab horde, which surged up through the Plain of Jezreel whenever the government of central Palestine was weak. On its gently sloping hills from the days of Thotmes III to Napoleon were waged the great battles that determined the possession of the land. Here, under the leadership of Deborah, the Hebrews fought the valiant fight that left them masters of Canaan and free to pass over the barrier of plain that had hitherto kept apart the tribes of the north from those of the south.

V

THE HILLS OF SAMARIA AND JUDAH

Character of the Hills of Samaria.—Northeastern Samaria.—Northwestern Samaria.—The View from Mount Ebal.—Bounds and General Characteristics of Southern Samaria.—Southwestern Samaria.—The Central Heights of Judah.—Lack of Water Supply.—Wilderness of Judea.—Western Judah.—Valley of Ajalon.—Wady Ali.—Valley of Sorek.—Valley of Elah.—Valley of Zephathah.—Wady el-Jizâir.—Significance of These Valleys.—The South Country.—Its Northern and Western Divisions.—Its Central and Eastern Divisions.—The Striking Contrasts between Judah and Samaria.—Effect upon Their Inhabitants.

Character of the Hills of Samaria. The hills of Samaria and Judah are the southern extension of the central plateau of Palestine, and yet, like Galilee and Esdraelon they constitute an independent natural unit. No sharply defined boundary separates them; rather the one gradually merges into the other. The heights of Samaria and Judah are commonly called mountains and the term is not entirely inappropriate when applied to the range as a whole; but the individual peaks are in reality little more than rounded hills. None of them rise over three thousand four hundred feet above the sea-level. The highest rest upon elevated plateaus, so that only two or three of them convey the impression of towering height and majesty that is ordinarily associated with the word mountain. Rather they are a chain of hills which, viewed from the shore of the Mediterranean or from the heights east of the Jordan, give the impression of a bold mountain range. This is especially true as one looks up toward them from the deep depression of the Jordan and Dead Sea valley, for they completely fill the western horizon. The water-shed lies on the eastern side of the range. The result is that the western hills have been worn down into gradually descending terraces; while on the east the deep Jordan valley is exceedingly abrupt, becoming more so in the south. At certain points the descent is over twenty-eight hundred feet in nine miles, and down by the western side of the Dead Sea there is often an almost sheer fall of between fifteen hundred and three thousand feet.

Northeastern Samaria. The hills of Samaria fall naturally into two great divisions. The first extends from the plains of Esdraelon and Jezreel to the one great valley which, following the Wady el-Ifzim, cuts through Samaria from the northwest to the southeast, running between Mount Ebal and Mount Gerizim. The territory north of this line resembles lower Galilee in many ways. On the east it consists of four ranges of hills, divided by a series of broad valleys filled with rich basaltic soil and plentifully supplied with water. These valleys and ranges of hills, like Mount Carmel, have a general trend from northwest to southeast. The northernmost is Mount Gilboa which rises with a broad gradual slope on every side, to a height of between one thousand two hundred and one thousand six hundred and fifty feet. The bare limestone rock crops out at many points, but villages and cultivated fields are found on its broad top. Viewed from this point the hills of Samaria rise gradually in great terraces.[13] To the east and south of Gilboa the wide plain about Bethshean cuts far into central Palestine. Farther south the hills of Samaria, as bold rocky headlands, jut far out into the Jordan valley. The next great valley south of the Plain of Jezreel is that through which the Wady Farah[14] discharges its plenteous waters into the Jordan. This stream and the Nahr Jalud are the chief western confluents of the lower Jordan.

Northwestern Samaria. In the northwest the hills of Samaria descend gradually and are intersected by wide valleys which open into the Plain of Sharon on the west and Esdraelon on the north. None of its hills are over twenty-five hundred feet in height. Verdure and often trees crown their summits, while in the valleys are the rich fields of grain or olive orchards, watered by springs and rivulets. The chief of these valleys is the Plain of Dothan,[15] which is connected by low passes with the Plain of Sharon on the west and the Plain of Esdraelon on the north. Farther south are the moist upland meadows known to-day as the "Meadow of Sinking in." These in turn are connected by an easy pass with the network of plains that run southward past Ebal and Gerizim and on the southwest to the city of Samaria and the Wady esh-Shair.[16]

The View from Mount Ebal. The one real mountain of northern Samaria is Ebal, which rises to the height of three thousand and seventy-seven feet. It is a broad rounded mass of limestone rock running from east to west parallel to Gerizim, its companion on the south. Its sides, almost to the top, are covered with gardens and olive orchards, enclosed by picturesque cactus hedges. It commands the most comprehensive view of any point in Palestine. Immediately to the south is the broad cultivated back of Mount Gerizim, which lies only a few feet lower than Ebal, while down in the narrow valley between the two mountains is Nablus, the ancient Shechem. In the more distant horizon is the ascending mass of the southern Samaritan and Judean hills.[17] On the east the Gilead hills present a lofty, bold sky-line. Nearer but concealed by the rapidly descending cliffs, is the deep valley of the Jordan; while in the foreground following the sky-line to the northeast lies the level plateau of the Hauran, which extends to the east of the Sea of Galilee, and beyond, if the air is clear, the broad peak of Mount Hermon towers, seventy-five miles away. In the immediate foreground[18] to the north is the network of open valleys of northern Samaria intersected by the ridges of hills which sweep down from the northwest toward the Jordan. Beyond is the depression where lies the Plain of Esdraelon, while still farther to the north rise in regular terraces lower and upper Galilee. The broad low line of highlands in the northwest is Carmel running out to the sea. In the west the irregular Samaritan hills, with their many intersecting valleys, descend leisurely to the coast plains. Beyond, only about twenty-five miles away, is the blue Mediterranean with its fringe of yellow sands.

Bounds and General Characteristics of Southern Samaria. Southern Samaria, which lies to the south and west of Mount Ebal, extends as far as the Wady Kelt and its northern confluent, the Wady es-Suweinit, which comes up from ancient Jericho to the vicinity of Michmash and Geba. On the southwest it reaches to the Wady Malakeh, which, a little north of the pass of Beth-horon, under the name Wady 'Ain 'Arîk, penetrates nearly to the top of the watershed. In many ways southern Samaria resembles northern Galilee. It is an elevated plateau rising gradually from the western coast plains and culminating in the southeast. Baal-Hazor, five miles north of the pass of Michmash, rising to the height of three thousand, three hundred and eighteen feet, is the highest point in Samaria, and lacks only a few feet of being the highest point south of the Plain of Esdraelon.

The descent in the east to the Jordan valley is exceedingly steep and rocky. Two or three rushing brooks have cut deep channels through the barren limestone rocks, which are covered with only a scanty herbage. Northwest of Jericho rises, as a terrace leading up to the heights above, the semi-detached mass of barren rock known as the Quarantana (Jebel Kuruntul), and still higher up to the west lies the wilderness of Bethaven, and beyond the rocky hills of Mount Ephraim.[19] On the high central plateau north of Baal-Hazor are a network of small but open plains, which run up past Shiloh to the east of Mount Gerizim. These are fringed by rocky hills, but are themselves exceedingly well-watered and fruitful and are covered to-day with waving grain fields.

Southwestern Samaria. The western part of southern Samaria is the land of deep but open valleys. Trees and grass, with many well-tilled fields, cover the hills and valleys. Chief of these valleys which lead up from the plain are the Wady esh-Shair (the Barley Vale), west of Shechem,[16] the Brook Kanah, the Wady Jib, which first flows south and then westward into the Wady Deir Ballut, and the Wady ez-Zerka, which, like the Wady Malakeh, finds its outlet into the sea a little north of Jaffa. Prosperous villages, some capping the summits of rounded hills, and others far down in sheltered spots in the deep valleys, are scattered throughout this entire region. The site of each was evidently chosen with a view to defence against the many foes that, from earliest times, have passed up through the valleys which stand wide open to the west. Like the rest of Samaria, it was a land where peace could be secured only by the sword and by strong battlements. It was also a land where nature gave rich gifts to those who were strong enough to maintain themselves against all invaders.

The Central Heights of Judah. The central plateau of southern Palestine culminates in Judea. It is a mass of rounded hills averaging only about fifteen miles wide and not more than forty miles long. Here erosion has worn away all bold, imposing peaks. The highest points, Mizpah,[20] the modern Neby Samwil (two thousand, eight hundred and thirty-five feet high), in the north and the heights immediately north of Hebron (three thousand, three hundred and seventy feet), where the southern plateau reaches its maximum elevation, are but rounded hills on the top of a great plateau. Between these are narrow, rocky valleys, dry during most of the year and strewn with stones laid bare by the winter freshets. The landscape lacks distinctive character. The prevailing impression is that of gray and yellow limestone;[21] and yet these fields of Judah are not altogether unproductive, as is amply demonstrated by the verdant fields in the vicinity of Jerusalem, Bethlehem,[22] and Hebron. Occasionally the native soil has been retained in a little upland plain,[23] as that east of Bethlehem or at Maon and Carmel, south of Hebron, or in certain favored valleys, such as Hinnom, to the south of Jerusalem. The soil, which is held upon the hillsides by the terraces or piles of stone, is exceedingly fruitful and supports patches of grain, or luxurious vines, or verdant olive trees, which stand out in striking contrast to the grim, rocky background.

Lack of Water Supply. Even greater than the lack of soil is the lack of water in Judah. Not a single perennial stream is found within its immediate boundaries. Ezekiel's vision of the broad stream running from the temple and irrigating the entire land clearly indicates what he recognized to be its great need. Throughout the entire land not a dozen copious springs burst from the dry rock. Jerusalem and Hebron are thus blest and, as a result, are still the chief cities of the land. Southwest of Bethlehem are the so-called Pools of Solomon, the plenteous waters of which are treasured in huge, ancient, rock-cut reservoirs, from which, in Roman times, they were conducted by high and low level aqueducts to Jerusalem. No snow-clad Lebanons tower above the parched hills of Judah to supply the much needed waters. To-day the rains of winter rush down the rocky hills and valleys, where there is little soil and vegetation to absorb and retain the moisture, leaving the land more denuded than before. Undoubtedly, when the hills of Judah were properly cultivated, as the presence of ruined terraces and watch-towers even in the most deserted places indicate they once were, the aspect of the landscape was very different; and yet, compared with other parts of Palestine, it was ever barren. Its inhabitants have always had to struggle for soil and water. In the past, as at present, the chief water supply was from the rocky cisterns. These were cut on the inside in the shape of a huge Oriental water-jug and placed in a depression in the rock so that they would be filled by the wash from the winter rains, which are usually very copious throughout Palestine.

Wilderness of Judea. The eastern slope of the southern plateaus of Palestine is rightly called a wilderness. Like the Shephelah or lowland on the west it is a distinct physical division of the west-Jordan land. The cultivated fields extend only four or five miles east of the central watershed. Near Jerusalem the barren wilderness comes up and touches the fertile fields about Bethany.[24] The descent on this eastern side of Judea to the low-lying Dead Sea is so precipitous that the water from the winter rains runs off rapidly and has cut deep channels through the soft clay and limestone cliffs so that irrigation is impossible.[25] No important villages are found in this desolate region except at Engedi, where a beautiful spring bursts out of the cliffs overhanging the Dead Sea and transforms the barren desert into what seems by contrast a little paradise of trees and gardens. Otherwise it is a land of dry, rocky, rounded hills which descend in a series of three great terraces to the depths below. Some vegetation is found between the rocks on the higher uplands. It is the land of the shepherd and of the Arab invaders[26] who here press in from the desert and contend, as they have for thousands of years, with the shepherds of the outlying villages for the possession of the barren land. The dominant features in the landscape are the rocky, rounded bluffs, the great gorge of the Dead Sea, usually enveloped in mists, and the dim outlines of the massive Moabite hills beyond. This wilderness of Judea exercised two powerful influences upon the life and thought of the people of the south: (1) it brought to their doors the atmosphere and peculiar customs and beliefs of the desert; and (2) it kept before them the might and destructive power of Jehovah, as exemplified by the Dead Sea and by the grim traditions that were associated with this remarkable natural phenomenon.

Western Judah. In contrast to the barren wilderness of eastern Judah, the western hills slope gradually down to the Philistine plain. The chief characteristic of this western slope is the series of valleys which lead up from the lowlands, piercing almost to the watershed in the great central plateau of Judah. Most of these valleys are broad and fertile as they enter the hills, but become ever more tortuous and wild as they ascend the rocky heights. In the rainy season (December to February) they are frequently swept by rushing torrents, which, undeterred by soil or vegetation, soon run their course, leaving the stream, during the greater part of the year, dry and rocky. At many points the ascent is abrupt, between steep rocks, clad with low bushes and wild flowers. In some places the path is so narrow that it is impossible for a horse to turn with comfort.

Valley of Ajalon. Six important valleys thus lead up from the plain to the central highlands. The northernmost, and in many ways the most important, is the Valley of Ajalon. It marks the northwestern boundary of Judah. It is a great, broad, fertile plain, lying between five hundred and a thousand feet above sea-level. The stream which ultimately finds its way into the sea a little north of Joppa, here makes a broad curve to the northeast, receiving four or five small tributary streams from the highlands of Judah and southern Samaria. From this valley several roads lead up to the plateau north of Jerusalem. Of these the most important is the one that ascends the pass of the Upper and Lower Beth-horons, along which ran the most direct and, in early times, the main highway from Jerusalem to Joppa.[118]

Wady Ali. A little south of the Valley of Ajalon is the narrow Wady Ali, along which runs to-day the carriage road from Jerusalem to Joppa. Apparently because of the deepness and narrowness of this valley it does not figure in biblical history until the Maccabean period.

Valley of Sorek. The third important gateway to Judah was the Valley of Sorek, the present Wady es-Surar. Here the modern railway from Joppa to Jerusalem penetrates the central plateau. Just before the Valley of Sorek reaches the steep ascent to the highlands it receives two important confluents, the Wady el-Ghurab, from the northwest, and the Wady en-Nagil from the south. Here the valley opens into a broad fertile plain, closely connected with the larger Plain of Philistia and yet encircled by the hills of the Shephelah. Immediately to the north was the home of the Danites and about this picturesque point gather the Samson stories. Along a winding and steep ascent the narrow pass thence runs directly eastward toward Jerusalem, approaching the city across the Valley of Rephaim from the southwest.

Valley of Elah. The fourth valley is that of Elah, the Valley of the Terebinth, which is known to-day as the Wady es-Sunt. This valley abounds in memories of David's earlier exploits.[88] Its eastern branch, the Wady el-Jindy leads through a narrow defile up toward Bethlehem. Its more important branch, the Wady es-Sur, runs directly southward past what are probably to be identified as the ancient Adullam and Keilah, and thence turning eastward, reaches the uplands near the famous Maccabean fortress of Bethzur, a little north of Hebron.

Valley of Zephathah. The fifth valley is that of Zephathah, which is known to-day in its upper course as the Wady el-Afranj. Its western gateway is guarded by the present important city of Beit-Jibrin, the Eleutheropolis of the Greek and Roman period. Recently opened caves near by reveal the importance of the Egyptian influence which, at a very early period entered Palestine along this important highway. The valley itself leads up through winding, narrow walls past the Plain of Mamre, directly to Hebron. Along it ran the great road from Jerusalem to Philistia and Egypt.

Wady el-Jizâir. The southernmost valley of western Judah is a continuation of the Wady el-Hesy, which runs past the frontier town of Lachish and is to-day known in its extension into the Judean highlands as the Wady el-Jizâir. Passing the ancient city of Adoraim, it also led to Hebron and ultimately to Jerusalem.

Significance of These Valleys. Of these six western valleys, unquestionably the three most important were the Valley of Ajalon, with its main gateways opening toward Jerusalem, the Valley of Sorek, with its broad entrance, also leading straight up to the capital city, and the Valley of Elah, rich with historic memories. Each of these, however, could be easily defended at certain strategic points by a few determined men on the heights above. When these natural gates were closed, Judah was practically unassailable on the west and could look with a strong sense of security down from its frowning heights upon the hostile armies which swept along the broad coast plains.

The South Country. The central plateau of Palestine extends south of Judah fully seventy miles. At first it gradually descends in a series of terraces, and then breaks into a confusion of barren, rocky, treeless ridges, running for the most part from east to west and cut by deep waterless gorges. As in Judah, the eastern hills which overhang the Wady Arabah are more abrupt and the winter torrents have cut deep channels in the gray limestone rocks. On the west the descent is more gradual, running out into the level wilderness, bounded on the west by the Wady el-Arish, known to the biblical writers as the Brook of Egypt. This wild, desolate region, fifty miles wide and seventy long, is the famous South Country, which figured so largely in early Israelite history. Its name, *Negeb*, Dry Land, well describes its general character.[1]

Its Northern and Western Divisions. The hill country immediately to the south of Judah is fairly fertile. Cultivated fields are found in the valleys and terraces on the hillsides, even as far as the Wady Sheba and the famous desert sanctuary of Beersheba. To the south and west of Beersheba are found the ruins of many cities, which evidently enjoyed high prosperity during the later Roman period. Here, as throughout most of the South Country, rain falls during the winter season, so that where the water is stored, irrigation is possible. A few springs also furnish a perennial supply of water. Thus under a strong stable government, the northern and northwestern portions of the South Country are capable of supporting a large, semi-agricultural population. By nature, however, it is the land of the nomad. Throughout most of its history, the Bedouin have dominated it as they do to-day. When undeveloped by irrigation, its hills and valleys are covered in springtime by a green herbage, which disappears, except in some secluded glens, before the glaring heat of summer. To the south, the Negeb at last descends to the great barren desert of Tîh, across which ran the highways to Egypt, to Arabia, and to Babylonia.

Its Central and Eastern Divisions. The central and eastern part of this South Country is dry and barren and occupied only by fierce Bedouin tribes. The absence of water, the ruggedness of its mountain ranges, and the fierceness of its population have rendered it almost impassable throughout most of its history. Many portions of it are still unexplored. Thus, on its southern boundary, Judah was thoroughly protected from the advance of hostile armies. At the same time, from this South Country there came a constant infiltration of the population and ideas of the desert, which left a deep imprint upon the character of the southern Israelites.

The Striking Contrasts Between Judah and Samaria. The contrasts between the hills of Judah and Samaria are many and significant. The hills of Samaria are a collection of distinct groups, divided by broad valleys, which intersect the land in every direction. The hills of Judah, in contrast, constitute a great, elevated, solid plateau, cut by no great valleys running throughout the land from east to west or from north to south. Judah is a mountain fortress, with strong natural barriers on every side. Samaria, on the contrary, stands with doors wide open to the foreign trader and invader. Its inhabitants are compelled to resort to the hilltops, or else to build strong fortresses for their defence. The great highways of commerce pass on either side of Judah, while they ran through the heart of Samaria. Judah was secure, not only because of its natural battlements of rock, but because of its barrenness. Its grim limestone hills, its stony moorlands, and its dry valleys offered few attractions to the invader. On the other hand, the rich fields of Samaria and its opulent cities were a constant loadstone, drawing toward them conquerors from the north, south, and east.

Effect Upon Their Inhabitants. Judah, with its few springs and its rock-strewn fields, offered a frugal livelihood to men who were willing to toil and to live without the luxuries of life. It bred a sturdy, brave race, intensely loyal to their rocks and hills, tenacious of their beliefs, even to the point of bigotry and martyrdom. Like their limestone hills, they were grim and unattractive, but capable of resisting the wearing process of the centuries. In contrast, the fertile hills of Samaria, with their plentiful springs and rushing streams, bred a luxury-loving, care-free, tolerant race, who were ready, almost eager, for foreign ideas and cults, as well as customs. Thus that great schism between north and south, between Jew and Samaritan, was not merely the result of later rivalries, but found its primal cause in the physical characteristics that distinguished the land of Judah from that of Samaria.

VI

THE JORDAN AND DEAD SEA VALLEY

Geological History.—Evidences of Volcanic Action.—Natural Divisions.—Mount Hermon.—Source of the Jordan at Banias.—At Tell el-Kadi.—The Two Western Confluents.—The Upper Jordan Valley.—The Rapid Descent to the Sea of Galilee.—The Sea of Galilee.—Its Shores.—From the Sea of Galilee to the Dead Sea.—Character of the Valley.—The Jordan Itself.—Fords of the Lower Jordan.—Ancient Names of the Dead Sea.—Its Unique Characteristics.—Its Eastern Bank.—The Southern End.—The Western Shores.—Grim Associations of the Dead Sea.

Geological History. The great gorge of the Jordan and Dead Sea valley is the most striking natural phenomenon in Palestine. No place on the face of the earth has had a more dramatic geological history. As has already been noted (p. 8), this great rift which runs from northern Syria to the Red Sea was probably formed in the latter part of the Pliocene Age. At the northern end of the Dead Sea its bed reaches a depth of nearly one-half a mile beneath the ocean level. It is thus by far the deepest depression on the face of the earth. During the Pluvial period this huge rift was filled with water, making a large inland sea, fully two hundred miles long, with its surface nearly one hundred feet above the ocean level. Apparently the higher land to the south of the present Dead Sea cut off the ocean, so that at the first it was a fresh-water lake. During the Interglacial period, possibly in part as the result of volcanic changes, it fell to a level of not more than three hundred feet above the present surface of the Dead Sea. It was during this period and the ice age that followed that the deposits were made on the side of the valley, which have given it its present terraced form.

Evidences of Volcanic Action. From the Pluvial period to the present the valley has been the scene of frequent volcanic disturbances. The water, sinking through the great rifts and subterranean passages, and being transformed by the heat into steam, forced up great masses of lava, which may be traced at many points on the heights both to the east and to the west of the Jordan valley. Earthquakes, many of them severe, are still common in this volcanic region. That of 1837 destroyed the city of Safed, killing one thousand of its inhabitants. In recent years severe shocks were felt in June, 1896, January, 1900, March and December, 1903. Many copious, hot, mineral springs still bear testimony to the presence of volcanic forces. Those near Tiberias, on the eastern side of the Sea of Galilee and in the Wady Zerka Ma'in, east of the Dead Sea, have a temperature of about 144°, while the waters of El-Hammeh in the Yarmuk Valley vary in temperature from about 93° to 110.° These springs are strongly impregnated with mineral salts and it is from these and similar sources that the salts have come that make the waters of the Dead Sea what they are to-day, heavy and far more saline than the ocean itself.

Natural Divisions. The Jordan and Dead Sea valley falls into four natural divisions: (1) the upper Jordan, from Mount Hermon to the Sea of Galilee, (2) the Sea of Galilee, (3) the lower Jordan, and (4) the Dead Sea. At its northernmost point rises Mount Hermon, called by the natives Jebel es-Sheik, that is, Mountain of the White-haired.

Mount Hermon. Hermon is in reality a massive mountain plateau, twenty miles long from northeast to southwest. Like most of the mountains of Palestine, it is of hard limestone, covered at places with soft chalk. On its northern side the vineyards run up to a height of almost five thousand feet.[27] Above are found scattered oaks, almond and dwarf juniper trees. The mountain rises to the height of nine thousand and fifty feet and is crowned by three peaks.[28] The northern and southern peaks are about the same height, while the western, separated from the others by a depression, is about one hundred feet lower. Mount Hermon commands a marvellous view of almost the entire land of Palestine. From the masses of snow which cover its broad top far into the summer and lie in its ravines throughout the year, come the copious waters of the upper Jordan. Its sources spring from the western and southern bases of Mount Hermon fully developed streams. Three-fourths of the waters of Mount Hermon thus find their way down the deep gorge of the Jordan.

Source of the Jordan at Banias. One of the two main sources of the Jordan is at Banias, the Cæsarea Philippi of New Testament times. About one hundred feet beneath an ancient grotto in the side of a sheer cliff, the stream pours forth from the rocks and goes rushing down through thickets of trees and the gardens which are irrigated by its waters.[29] By Josephus and other ancient writers the springs at Banias were regarded as the true source of the Jordan. Here the ancient Canaanites apparently reared a sanctuary to the god of the stream and later the Greeks built a temple to Pan, from whence comes, with the change of the initial letter, the modern name of Banias, or City of Pan. Here also Herod reared a temple which was one of the glories of the Roman city.

At Tell el-Kadi. The largest source of the Jordan is on the western side of the mound now known as Tell el-Kadi. A stream about ten feet wide flows directly from the rock and is joined by a smaller confluent a little to the south, forming the so-called El-Leddan. The imposing mound of Tell el-Kadi, lying at the head of the Jordan Valley and commanding the highway that leads to Banias, and thence across the eastern spurs of Mount Hermon to Damascus, is probably the site of the Canaanite Laish, later the Hebrew Dan.

The Western Confluents. A mile and a half further to the south the two eastern sources of the Jordan are joined by the Hasbany. This stream springs from a pool on the western side of Mount Hermon and thence flows southward through the broad plain on the west of the mountain from which it sprang. The fourth source of the Jordan, the Nahr Bareighit, the least important of the four, rising not far from the River Litany, comes down through a valley to the northwest.

The Upper Jordan Valley. During the first part of its descent to the Dead Sea, the Jordan winds leisurely through a valley about five miles wide, flanked by hills rising to between fifteen hundred and two thousand feet.[30] Its northernmost part, under the shadow of Mount Hermon, is plentifully strewn with stones, but a few miles below Tell el-Kadi fertile grain fields appear, watered by copious springs. The Jewish colonists on the northwestern edge of the Jordan valley, are beginning to cultivate these meadows, again demonstrating how fertile they are. Six miles above Lake Huleh the river loses itself in reedy marshes[31] and finally empties into the lake through six different channels. Here the papyrus grows in great profusion. Lake Huleh itself, four miles long, is little more than a great malarial marsh, formed by the temporary stopping of the river by the eastern and western hills, which here approach within three or four miles of each other.

The Rapid Descent to the Sea of Galilee. From Banias to Lake Huleh the Jordan descends over one thousand feet and in the eleven miles from the lake to the Sea of Galilee it plunges downward six hundred and ninety feet. These occasional pauses, followed by sudden plunges, have given the river its name, the Jordan, which means the Descender. A little below Lake Huleh, the valley of the Jordan narrows into a rocky gorge. Through this rocky chasm, hemmed in by steep cliffs on both sides, the Jordan plunges in continuous cascades until it reaches the delta which it has formed at the northern end of the Sea of Galilee.

The Sea of Galilee. At Lake Huleh the waters of the Jordan are seven feet above the ocean level, but at the Sea of Galilee six hundred and eighty-two feet below. The Sea of Galilee is a pear-shaped lake, twelve and one-half miles in length and eight in width, encircled by bold limestone cliffs.[32] Its greatest depth, which is in the north, is seven hundred and fifty feet. Its blue, clear waters, bathed in sunshine, and the soft, warm breezes that blow across the lake, make it in spring-time, and even in winter, one of the most delightful spots in all the world. In the summer, however, its atmosphere is hot and sultry, and at many points malarial. Ordinarily, the ocean winds blow high above the Sea of Galilee without affecting its hot, tropical climate, but occasionally they pour down through the valleys, especially to the north and northwest, suddenly transforming these quiet waters into a tempestuous sea.

Its Shores. On the east rise the steep, now barren but probably once tree-clad, limestone hills of the Jaulan, capped by vast layers of black basalt, towering in the distance like huge battlements. They stand back, however, from the lake, leaving a shore averaging one-half mile in width. On the north the Jordan has worn down the hills, which here descend gradually in wild, stony moorlands, covered with thorns and rough grasses. To the northwest opens the fertile plain of Gennesaret,[33] four miles wide, watered by dashing mountain brooks and flanked by the high hills of upper Galilee. The industry of German colonists is again beginning to demonstrate the marvellous fertility of this fair plain, where the fruits and grains of tropical and temperate climes grow side by side. On the western side of the lake the hills descend in terraces, leaving a narrow strip of shore, connected with the uplands by one or two shallow valleys. To the south the shore broadens and the hills recede until they are four miles apart at the southern end,[34] where the Jordan leaves the Sea of Galilee.

From the Sea of Galilee to the Dead Sea. The distance from the Sea of Galilee to the Dead Sea in a straight line is only sixty-five miles, but, owing to its constant turnings, the actual course of the river measures nearly two hundred miles. In this last plunge the river descends more than one thousand feet. Its descent is more rapid in the upper part of its course. A little below the Sea of Galilee it receives its largest confluent, the River Yarmuk, which breaks through the heights of the Hauran to the east. The volume of the water thus poured in nearly equals that of the Jordan itself at this point. Further south the Brook Jalûd comes down on the west from the Plain of Jezreel past Bethshean. About twenty miles from its mouth, the Jordan receives the waters from the Jabbok, which descends from the heights of Gilead on the east, and from the Wady Farah, which comes from the vicinity of Shechem on the west.

Character of the Valley. Below the Sea of Galilee the Jordan valley, at first but four miles wide, gradually broadens until it is eight miles in width opposite Bethshean, where the valley of Jezreel joins that of the Jordan. Most of the land in this part of the Jordan valley, immediately below the Sea of Galilee, is tillable. The ruins of ancient aqueducts indicate that the streams that come down from the hillsides were once used for irrigation. The valley is again being in part reclaimed by Jewish colonists. Ten miles south of Bethshean the Samaritan headlands crowd close to the Jordan, so that the valley is only three miles in width. Where the Jabbok and Wady Farah join the Jordan the valley again broadens until, opposite Jericho, it is fourteen miles in width.[35] Most of this lower Jordan valley is a parched desert covered by low bushes and desert plants, except where the streams from the highlands are used for irrigation. Fertile fields are thus reclaimed where the Wady Nimrin and the Wady el-Kefrein come from the eastern hills opposite Jericho. At Jericho itself the waters of the Wady Kelt and those of the famous Fountain of Elisha are utilized to-day as they were in ancient times. South of Jericho, however, the soil is heavily impregnated with saline and alkaline salts, so that it extends in an almost barren waste to the northern end of the Dead Sea.

The Jordan Itself. Through this broad valley the Jordan winds, frequently changing its course, and ploughing a great furrow, called by the natives the Zôr.[36] In flood time the river is from five hundred feet to a mile wide, while in the summer it is at places not more than seventy-five or a hundred feet in width and varies in depth from three to twelve feet. At all times it is a muddy, coffee-colored stream, partaking of the color of the slimy, alluvial soil through which it flows. Its banks are covered by thickets of trees, bushes, and reeds, in which are found many wild beasts and birds. This flood channel of the Jordan is a scene of wreckage and ruin, mingled with tropical luxuriance. The lowest bed of this ancient inland lake is given up to-day, as it always was in the past, to wild beasts, to occasional fugitives, to squalid Bedouin, and to the muddy, sprawling river which here rules supreme.

Fords of the Lower Jordan. The lower course of the Jordan is now spanned by four bridges. In ancient times the dwellers in Palestine were obliged to depend entirely upon its fords, of which there are between twenty and twenty-five. One of the more important is at the point where the river leaves the Sea of Galilee and is still used as a ferry. Another is the famous ford of Abarah, a little northeast of Bethshean. The third is a little farther south, opposite the ancient Pella. Another, the Dâmieh ford, is at the mouth of the Jabbok. The fifth is northeast of Jericho just below the point where the Wady Nimrin enters the Jordan. The most famous is the Pilgrim Ford, southeast of Jericho, just below the place where the Wady Kelt joins the Jordan. Owing to the alluvial character of its banks, its rapid current, and the frequency of the floods, fed by the melting snows from the Lebanons and by the heavy storms of the winter and spring, the Jordan has always proved a river difficult to cross. Its rôle throughout all of its history has been that of a divider rather than that of a binder together of tribes and races. Throughout its course of one hundred and seven miles it is rarely navigable. Flowing, as it does, into the barren waters of the Dead Sea, the Jordan was, therefore, a check upon rather than an encouragement to commerce.

Ancient Names of the Dead Sea. The residue of the ancient inland lake is represented by the present Dead Sea. This name is comparatively modern. In the Bible it is called by various names, such as simply the Sea, the Sea of the Plain, the Eastern Sea, or the Salt Sea. To-day it is known among the Arabs as the Sea of Lot.

Its Unique Characteristics. The Dead Sea lies one thousand two hundred and ninety-two feet below the surface of the ocean.[37] It is forty-seven and a half miles long and ten miles across at its widest point. At its northeastern end, under the heights of Moab, the lake reaches to the vast depth of one thousand two hundred and seventy-eight feet. In striking contrast, the southern end of the sea is only ten to fifteen feet in depth. Its waters are so thoroughly impregnated with poisonous chemicals that no fish can live in them and only the lowest organisms survive. Its bitter taste is due to the presence of chloride of magnesium and the oily feeling is produced by the chloride of calcium, which it holds in solution. As is well known, the density is so great that it is practically impossible for man or beast to sink beneath its waters. In time of storm the waves beat on the shore with a heavy, metallic sound. The waters of the sea are frequently lashed by heavy thunder-storms, which linger here sometimes for hours, held in by the high, towering cliffs on either side. With few exceptions the shores of the Dead Sea are barren and strewn at places with the wreckage of trees. Its water, however, is limpid, varying from light blue to green. Owing to the proximity of the desert and the intense heat—the temperature rising in summer as high as 118°—it is the scene of a stupendous process of evaporation. It is computed that between six and eight million tons of water rise in vapor from this great natural caldron each day. Often the vapor is so dense that it obscures the landscape, but at other times it imparts a marvellous prismatic color to the huge cliffs that encircle the lake,[38] so that the combination of the blue waters, the cloudless skies, and the rich, blended reds, grays, and purples of the opalescent landscape make it one of the most sublime views in all the world.

Its Eastern Bank. On the eastern side the cliffs of Moab rise at some points almost sheer to the height of between twenty-five hundred and three thousand feet.

These limestone hills are mottled with huge blotches of black limestone and basalt and are frequently capped with white, chalky rocks. They are cut by several important streams, which have worn deep canyons that extend back many miles into the Moabite hills. A few miles south of the northeastern end the Wady Zerka Ma'in flows into the sea. On its northern bank, near the sea, the famous baths of Callir-rhöe burst from the rock. Farther south the River Arnon, cutting a canyon three thousand feet deep through the plateau of Moab, reaches the sea through a broad opening. Here a few scattered palms and acacias relieve the utter desolation of this eastern wall of rock. Still farther south the promontory of El-Lisan, The Tongue, as it is called by the natives, pushes out into the sea, extending to within three miles of the western shore. It is a bold mass of calcareous marl, forty to eighty feet in height, treeless and barren. In pleasing contrast with this barrenness is the oasis lying behind it, watered by the Wady el-Kerak. Here are found the four Bedouin villages which are the only towns along the coast of this desolate sea.

The Southern End. At the southern end of the Dead Sea is a slimy mud marsh, low and malarial, covered with tropical thickets which are filled with the birds and the beasts of the southern clime. Farther south is the fertile Ghôr es-Safieh. In this little oasis, lying between the sea and the wilderness, a little wheat, barley, and tobacco are grown and a dense tropical vegetation abounds. Southward for a hundred and twelve miles to the Gulf of Akaba extends the Arabah,[39] the continuation of the great rift of which the Jordan and the Dead Sea valleys are a part. Low sand-hills lie across the centre of this broad, shallow valley, making direct travel impossible. Sixty-five miles to the south the watershed is reached. This is six hundred and sixty feet above the level of the ocean, that is, nearly two thousand feet above the level of the Dead Sea. It is a land of stones, gravel, and sand,[40] with only a few trickling springs—a lonesome, forbidding region where heat, dust, and the Bedouin rule supreme to-day as they have for thousands of years.

The Western Shores. The hills on the western side of the Dead Sea, except at two points, do not come close to the margin of the water. A beach from a hundred yards to a mile in width fringes the sea on this western side. Beyond this shore the hills rise in terraces to the height of from two thousand to two thousand five hundred feet. These are white, rounded, and barren, except at Engedi, where the waters of its famous spring have developed an oasis,[41] which marks the side of the plateau with a pleasing mass of dark green. Many small wadies cut down through these western hills. In their beds are found a few trees and bushes, but otherwise the landscape is as bold and unrelieved by vegetation as on the east. On the southwest, at Jebel Usdum, there is a remarkable range of salt cliffs, six hundred feet high, three and three-fourth miles in length and a half mile in width. Here local tradition fixes the scene of the death of Lot's wife. Along this western shore are also found deposits of bitumen. Frequently portions of it are found floating in the waters; sometimes they catch on fire, adding to the lurid impressiveness of this mysterious valley.

Grim Associations of the Dead Sea. These are a few of the many reminders that fully justify the modern name of the Dead Sea. Its historic associations, the destruction of the wicked cities of the plain, the murder of John the Baptist at

Machærus on the eastern heights, and the later massacre at Masada are all harsh and appalling. In common with the Jordan valley, this region is richly suggestive of the destructive forces of nature. Life is here grim, severe, and relentless. It is not difficult to detect in Jewish character the deep impressions made by this constant contact with the symbols of death and with these suggestions of the presence of a stern, austere God.

VII

THE EAST-JORDAN LAND

Form and Climate of the East-Jordan Land.—Well-Watered and Fertile.—The Four Great Natural Divisions.—Characteristics of the Northern and Western Jaulan.—Southern and Eastern Jaulan.—Character of the Hauran.—Borderland of the Hauran.—Gilead.—The Jabbok and Jebel Ôsha.—Southern Gilead.—Character of the Plateau of Moab.—Its Fertility and Water Supply.—Its Mountains.—Its Views.—The Arnon.—Southern Moab and Edom.—Significance of the East-Jordan Land.

Form and Climate of the East-Jordan Land. The east-Jordan land of biblical history is in form an irregular triangle, with its base skirting the Jordan Valley, its northern angle at the foot of Mount Hermon, its southern a little beyond the southern end of the Dead Sea, while its third angle lies in the Druse Mountains, about seventy miles east of the Sea of Galilee. Damascus,[42] to the northwest, is just beyond the bounds of Palestine. This famous ancient city lies in the midst of a verdant oasis made by the waters of the Abana River,[43] which breaks through the eastern Lebanons and finally loses itself in the Arabian desert. The heart of the east-Jordan land is the wide, level plain watered by the tributaries of the Yarmuk River. The east-Jordan territory is a great elevated plateau, averaging fully two thousand feet in height. This southern continuation of the Anti-Lebanon mountains is a land that lies open to the sunshine and to the strong breezes that blow from the dry desert or fresh from the western sea. Its temperature, as a whole, is much colder than that of western Palestine. Frosts at night begin as early as the first of November and continue into March. Deep snows cover a large portion of it in winter. I myself have travelled in the middle of March for hours through blinding snows, two or three feet deep, up among the highlands of Gilead. In summer frequent mists sweep over the heights. At night the temperature often falls very low, and, as a result, heavy dews are deposited. Even during the day cool sea-breezes make the air thoroughly invigorating. Thus it richly deserved the reputation which it enjoyed in antiquity of being one of the most healthful regions in all the world.

Well Watered and Fertile. In contrast to western Palestine, the east-Jordan land is well supplied with springs and perennial rivers. Grass grows almost everywhere in rich profusion, even far out toward the desert. Great forests are still found in Gilead, and fruit trees that yield abundantly. East of the Jordan are the chief grain fields of Palestine, but it is pre-eminently the home of the herdsman and shepherd. Herds of cattle and flocks of sheep and goats dot the landscape almost everywhere from the foot of Hermon to the southern end of Moab.

The Four Great Natural Divisions. The east-Jordan land falls into four great natural divisions. The first is the Jaulan or Golan, the Gaulanitis of the Roman period, which extends from the foot of Mount Hermon to the Yarmuk River and from the Jordan and the Sea of Galilee to the Nahr el-Allân, a northern tributary of the Yarmuk. To the east and southeast of the Jaulan is the second great division, the Hauran. It extends northward to the vast lava-beds of El-Lejah, and eastward to the Druse Mountains, which look out upon the desert. In certain passages of the Old Testament the term Bashan seems to have been applied to the entire region north of the Yarmuk, but its exact bounds are not clearly defined. The third division includes the mountains of Gilead, which extend from the Yarmuk to the Wady Heshbân at the northern end of the Dead Sea, and from the Jordan out to the desert beyond the territory of ancient Ammon. The fourth division is the plateau of Moab, which extends from the Wady Heshbân to the Wady el-Hesa, southeast of the Dead Sea, and from the Salt Sea to the great pilgrim road on the borders of the desert.

Characteristics of the Northern and Western Jaulan. The Jaulan slopes southward to the Yarmuk and westward to the Jordan. Its characteristic features are two parallel ranges of isolated volcanic mountains between two and four thousand feet in height extending southward from Mount Hermon.

In some of these bold peaks the outlines of the ancient craters are still visible. Tell Abu Neda, of the western range, rises to the height of nearly four thousand feet. Its crater is broken at one side and its ulterior is cultivated, producing a variety of vegetables and grains. Another peak farther south, Tell el-Faras, about three thousand one hundred feet high, has a well-preserved, round crater, which inclines to the north. From these craters in early times successive waves of lava flowed toward the Jordan valley, covering this entire region. The northern part of the Jaulan is a great rocky pasture land, strewn with black basaltic boulders. In the spring it is a mass of green, which attracts thousands of Bedouin with their flocks. In the summer it becomes dry and desolate except where a few perennial springs develop little oases. The villages are small and far apart. Inland a few wadies supply water for irrigation, but as they run westward toward the Jordan they soon cut deep torrent beds through the rocks and thus become practically useless for purposes of agriculture.

Southern and Eastern Jaulan. The southern part of the Jaulan, from a point opposite the northern end of the Sea of Galilee, is a lofty plateau. Here the volcanic rock is more broken. In this rich, dark red soil much grain is raised, especially wheat and barley. Two important streams, the Wady Semakh and the Wady Fîk, here descend to the Sea of Galilee through long deep gorges. The southeastern Jaulan is pierced by two parallel streams, the Nahr er-Rukkad and the Nahr el-Allân, which run almost due south. In their upper courses they flow on the surface of the ground, but soon sink into deep gorges which lead to the Yarmuk. The Yarmuk itself is the most commanding river of all the east-Jordan land. Its tributaries water the fertile lands of the Hauran. Like all the great rivers east of the Jordan, it has cut a deep channel through the basaltic rocks. To-day the railroad from Damascus to Haifa twists along its tortuous course between walls of rock five hundred to one thousand feet in height. The climate in this deep gorge is that of the Jordan valley itself. Oleanders, palms, and figs grow here, overshadowed by the pines and oaks of the upland plateau. The variety of twisted and tilted limestone and volcanic rocks laid bare on its rugged sides makes it one of the wildest and most picturesque valleys in all Palestine.

Character of the Hauran. The most productive grain fields of the eastern Mediterranean are found in the Hauran or Hollow.[1] With the exception of an occasional low hill, this region is as level as a floor. The soil is a rich volcanic loam, well watered and superlatively fruitful. Unlike the Jaulan, which was once largely wooded, it is treeless, except among the mountains to the east. It is also one of the few spots in Palestine practically free from stones. Here wheat and barley and the other grains of Palestine grow in rankest profusion. The landscape is comparatively monotonous except as an occasional wady furrows its way down toward the Yarmuk or some of its tributaries. Like many regions in Palestine it is dominated by the snowy heights of Hermon, which stand out in brilliant contrast to the monotony of the plain.

Borderland of the Hauran. To the north rises, thirty or forty feet above the plain, the great lava plain of El-Lejah. It is a solid, gently undulating mass of lava, containing an area of three hundred and fifty square miles. No rivers, and only occasional springs, are found throughout this barren waste, which is penetrated only by a few footpaths. It is the ancient Trachonitis, the refuge of outlaws and robbers to-day as in the past. To the east the plain of the Hauran rises to Jebel Hauran, also known as the Druse Mountains. Three of the peaks of these eastern sentinels are between four and six thousand feet high. On the south, the Hauran gradually merges into the yellow steppes of El-Hamâd and farther west into the limestone hills of Ez-Zumleh.

Gilead. South of the Yarmuk the black basalt of the Jaulan yields to the light limestone of the west-Jordan. The entire territory of Gilead more closely resembles the western hills of Palestine than does any other part of the east-Jordan region. On the broad rolling uplands of eastern Gilead there are large grain fields and the soil is cultivated at many other points. In the Roman period great cities, of which Gerasa[44] was the chief, testified to the rich productivity of this region, but for the most part it is the paradise of the herdsmen and the shepherd. It is a land of deep valleys, rounded hills, and frequent springs. On the northwest many small streams cut their way to the Jordan valley. The roads run up and down steep inclines where the flocks and the herds cling to the sloping hillsides. Groves of noble oaks cover the hilltops and reveal the strength inherent in the soil.

The Jabbok and Jebel Osha. The dominant factor in southern Gilead is the River Jabbok.[45] It rises among the hills not far from the Moabite border, only eighteen miles from the Jordan, and then flows northeast, past the old Ammonite capital. Thence it completes the half circle, cutting its way through the Gileadite hills to the Jordan. At some points its channel is between two and three thousand feet below the level of the plateau. It is a joyous river, rippling in flashes of sunlight over the rocks, through green glades and tangles of oleanders and rushes, a type of this happy, picturesque land of the shepherd. The centre of the half circle described by the Brook Jabbok is the Jebel Osha, the highest peak in Gilead. From its height of three thousand five hundred and ninety-five feet, practically all of Gilead is spread to the north and south and east like a great variegated carpet.

Southern Gilead. In southern Gilead the trees become fewer and fewer until south of Jebel Osha they almost disappear. In spring-time the fields are green with grass and grain, but in summer they become parched and brown. The wadies in the south, such as Wady Nimrin and Wady Heshbân, avail little for irrigation, since their channels are far beneath the level of the surrounding plateau. The region as a whole begins to take on something of the sombre color of the Dead Sea region which lies in the depths below.

Character of the Plateau of Moab. In its largest bounds Moab is a territory sixty miles long and thirty miles wide. From across the Dead Sea it looks like a high mountain range, but in reality it is simply a lofty upland plateau[46] towering above the deep gorge of the Dead Sea. Throughout most of its extent it is between two thousand five hundred and three thousand three hundred feet above the ocean level, and therefore from three thousand eight hundred to four thousand six hundred feet above the blue waters of the Dead Sea. It is a gently rolling, treeless plain; its low hilltops are crowned with the ruins of ancient cities. Only a few bushes are to be found upon these bare moors. The prevailing rock is soft cretaceous limestone, which crops out at many points. The soil of the central zone, however, which runs from north to south, averaging about ten miles in width, is exceedingly fertile. Many grain fields are found throughout this territory; but like Gilead, Moab is pre-eminently the land of the herdsman and the shepherd. In the wadies which run down to the Dead Sea thousands of camels are bred, while on the hills above are seen at every point flocks of cattle, sheep, and goats.

Its Fertility and Water Supply. In the spring-time the upland fields are masses of green, which almost conceal the stones and outcrop of rock. The marvel is that any vegetation is found in a land thus bounded, on the west by the Sea of Death and on the east by the rocky desert. Most of the streams run through deep glens and no springs are found on the surface. The explanation of the marvel is found in the high elevation of the plateau and the great process of evaporation which is ever going on in the Dead Sea basin below. The west winds from the Mediterranean and the Dead Sea come laden with moisture, which they deposit in the winter and spring in drenching rains, and throughout the year in heavy dews at night.

Its Mountains. The mountains of Moab are little more than hills rising a few hundred feet above the rolling upland. The so-called mountains of the Abarim are simply the wild, rocky hills and promontories which rise rapidly from the Dead Sea.[47] Seen from across the Dead Sea they have the appearance of mountains. They skirt the eastern side of the lower Jordan and Dead Sea, running eastward nine or ten miles to meet the fields of Moab on the heights. This region corresponds to the wilderness of Judea across the sea on the west. Mount Nebo, which now bears the name Neba, is a flat tongue of land two thousand six hundred and forty-three feet above the ocean level, running out two miles westward from the main plateau. It overlooks the northern end of the Dead Sea, which is nearly four thousand feet below. It commands a marvellous view up the Jordan valley, between the lofty heights of Gilead on the right and the hills of Samaria and Judah on the left. Farther inland and to the south is the loftier peak of Jebel Attarus. The chief mountain south of the Arnon is Jebel Shihan, which rises to the height of two thousand seven hundred and eighty feet above the ocean level.

Its Rivers. The most striking features in the landscape of Moab are the deep canyons which plough from east to west across the plateau. Those in the north run back only a few miles, leaving northeastern Moab a comparatively unbroken plateau, but in the south they cut deep furrows eastward even to the borders of the desert. The Wady Zerka Ma'in has worn a broad channel through the limestone, basaltic, and sandstone rocks of northwestern Moab, so that ten miles from the point where it flows into the Dead Sea it is fully two miles across. Along the bottom of this great chasm runs a limpid brook, winding through beautiful groves of oleanders and beside fertile patches of land, which are in marked contrast to the utterly barren and desolate cliffs above.

The Arnon. Farther south the Arnon, the chief river of Moab, rises on the border of the desert. Rapidly cutting its way down into the plateau, it receives its first important confluent from the south, and farther on the Wady Waleh from the north. At the point where the central highway through Moab from the north crosses the Arnon the canyon is three thousand feet deep and two miles from bank to bank. It is by far the most stupendous and picturesque chasm in all Palestine.[48] The steep red cliffs, variegated and richly colored by white, gray, and yellow strata, extend in wavy billows east and west as far as the eyes can reach. The descent is almost sheer into the depths below, where the river, easily fordable at many points and with an actual channel only a few feet wide, rushes over the smooth rocks or winds leisurely through its fringe of oleanders and green bushes. Where the tributary wadies have cut down the soft limestone, nature's castles stand out, guarding the broad natural highway from the desert to the sea. The Arnon only in a lesser degree separated the land of Moab and destroyed its political unity, even as did the Jordan the land of Israel.

Southern Moab and Edom. Farther south the Wady el-Kerak, narrow and deep, runs past both sides of the natural citadel, whose name it bears,[49] and finds its way to the Dead Sea back of the barren promontory of El-Lisan. Thus the three zones of Moab, the western promontories, the central fields, and the dry pasture lands on the east, are repeatedly intersected by the deep gorges that make it a land easy to approach from the desert and difficult to defend. Farther south the plateau of Moab merges into the wild, picturesque mountains of Mount Seir, the home of the Edomites. The valley becomes narrower and the mountains bolder, more jagged, and abrupt. The culmination of these natural wonders is the Wady Mûsa, which cuts a deep, narrow channel through the heart of the mountains.[50] In the midst of this valley, surrounded by gorgeously colored sandstone cliffs, out of which have been carved homes, streets, tombs, theatres, temples,[51] and well-preserved high places,[52, 53] stands that most astonishing and marvellous of all oriental cities—Petra.

Significance of the East-Jordan Land. Health, beauty, and fertility have ever been the three rich possessions of the east-Jordan land. It was effectually cut off, however, from contact with the teeming, highly civilized life of the Mediterranean seaboard by the deep chasm of the Jordan and Dead Sea valley and by the barren hills that flanked this great gorge on its southern end. It was a land that faced the desert and the east rather than the west. It was itself the loadstone that constantly attracted the wandering dwellers of the desert. The life and institutions of the desert have here prevailed through all the centuries. Here the wandering nomads first tasted and learned to appreciate the advantages of settled agricultural life and made the gradual and natural transition from the nomadic to the agricultural state. Here also the mighty energies of the powerful western nations were put forth in a mighty effort to conquer and to hold this land, for they realized that it was their natural eastern outpost against the desert. It was here, therefore, that the militant civilization and life of the East and West met, struggled, and mingled. Here the same conflicts and processes are going on to-day as in the past. This close contact with the desert has always been the strength, the significance, and the weakness of the east-Jordan land.

VIII

THE TWO CAPITALS: JERUSALEM AND SAMARIA

Importance of Jerusalem and Samaria.—Site of Jerusalem.—The Kidron Valley.—The Tyropœon Valley.—The Original City.—Its Extent.—The Western Hill.—The Northern Extension of the City.—Josephus's Description of Jerusalem.—The Geological Formation.—The Water Supply.—Jerusalem's Military Strength.—Strength of Its Position.—Samaria's Name.—Its Situation.—Its Military Strength.—Its Beauty and Prosperity.

Importance of Jerusalem and Samaria. Two cities of ancient Palestine, Jerusalem and Samaria, towered above all others, both in size and in importance. Each was for a long period the capital of an important kingdom. Each represented a distinct type of civilization and religion. Their topography throws much light upon their development and history.

Site of Jerusalem. At first glance the site of Jerusalem seems one of the most unpromising places in all the land of Palestine for a great city. It lies on two or three low hills, projecting from the irregular plateau, which extends southward from the watershed of central Judah. It is overshadowed by higher hills near by and has no lofty, commanding acropolis. The Wilderness of Judea bounds it on the east and the hills and valleys about are rocky and comparatively barren. The reason why a city originally sprang up on this forbidding site was the presence of a spring, now known as the Virgin's Spring, on the side of the Kidron Valley[54] to the southeast of the present Jerusalem. It is the one perennial spring in this region and fixes at once the site of the old pre-Israelite town. (*Cf.* map op. p. 143.)

The Kidron Valley. The Kidron is a characteristic Palestinian wady. It runs almost due north past the city and then gradually bends to the west. It is about two hundred yards in width and is flanked by hills, which rise four to six hundred feet on either side. During the winter and spring rains a brook rushes down this ravine, but in the summer it is waterless, although many olive trees find sufficient moisture in the bottom and on sides of the valley. At its southern end the Kidron is joined by the broad valley of Ben Hinnom,[55] which runs due west nearly half a mile and then turns northward, thus, with the Kidron, enclosing on three sides a nearly regular rectangle half to three-quarters of a mile in width.

The Tyropœon Valley. The southern promontories or hills thus enclosed were in ancient times divided by a small shallow valley, the Tyropœon or Cheesemongers' Valley, which ran northward from the Valley of Hinnom, separating the rectangle into two unequal parts. The city has been so often besieged and razed to the ground that its original site has been largely obscured by the masses of débris scattered everywhere and especially in the Tyropœon Valley. At many points the native rock lies from forty to one hundred feet beneath the present level. East of the temple area a shaft was sunk one hundred and twenty feet before the virgin rock was reached. Hundreds of such shafts have been sent down at different points throughout the city so that the exact site of the ancient town is now well known. The Tyropœon Valley, which cuts through the heart of Jerusalem, is the key to the understanding of the ancient city. From the point where it joins the Kidron and Hinnom valleys in the south to its northern end, a little outside the present Damascus Gate, this valley is about sixteen hundred yards in length. The hills on either side originally rose to the height of between one hundred and one hundred and fifty feet above the bottom of the valley, which becomes broader and shallower toward the north. Opposite the present temple area a western branch extends about three hundred yards, nearly cutting off the southwestern hill from the northern plateau.

The Original City. The rounded ridge of rock between the Tyropœon and Kidron valleys was clearly the original site of Jerusalem. It is the so-called Ophel, on which the ancient Jebusite fortress was reared. The southern end rises rapidly from the valley below where the Tyropœon and Kidron join. Its northern continuation is the temple area. Excavations have shown that immediately north of the present temple area there was a rock cutting, from the Tyropœon Valley on the west to the Kidron Valley on the east, leaving a precipice of native rock twenty-five feet high as a barrier against attack from the north. At the southeastern corner of the temple area traces have also been found of the well-built wall which ran along the edge of the Kidron Valley, probably encircling the ancient Jebusite city. Thus it was surrounded on three sides with rapidly descending valleys from one to three hundred feet deep, while immediately below was the perennial spring, essential to the life of its early inhabitants. It is easy, therefore, to understand why the early Jebusites regarded their city as impregnable.

Its Extent. The hill Ophel contains an area of between sixteen and eighteen acres, which was amply sufficient for a crowded village of ancient times. This was also, without reasonable doubt, the site of David's city. As the Israelite city grew it probably extended almost to the level of the valley in the south, near the modern Pool of Siloam. At present the northern end of the hill Ophel is higher than the southern. It also broadens into the temple area, which is two thousand four hundred and forty feet above the sea-level. It is not improbable, however, that the site of the old Jebusite fortress was once higher than the temple rock to the north. If the fortress of Akra, which figures prominently in Maccabean history, was identical with the ancient citadel of Ophel, then, according to the testimony of Josephus (*Jew. Wars*, V, 4:1), Simon the Maccabean ruler cut down this southern eminence to make it lower than the adjoining temple area.

The Western Hill. It is not clear when the western hill was included within the bounds of Jerusalem; possibly in the days of Solomon; certainly some time before the Babylonian exile. On the south and west this hill descends rapidly to the Valley of Hinnom, on the east to the Tyropœon Valley; while on the north it is connected by a narrow neck of rock with the northern hill of Jerusalem. It is about seven hundred yards long from north to south and four hundred from east to west. It is highest on the west, where it is two thousand five hundred and twenty feet above the sea-level. It is therefore about eighty feet higher than the temple area to the east.

The Northern Extension of the City. As the city grew in later times, it extended naturally to the north and included the little hill or knob directly north of the so-called western hill, with which it was connected by a neck of rock. This northern hill was bounded on the west by a depression running from the Hinnom Valley and on the south and east by the upper Tyropœon. On the north it had no natural defence.[56] Its highest point, about two thousand four hundred and ninety feet, was nearly on the same level as the temple area. The northern extension of the city also included another section of the ridge of rock which runs northward from the temple area, parallel to the Kidron Valley. A scarp twenty feet deep was cut across this ridge from east to west and to-day forms the northeastern limits of the city. In contrast to the ancient city, which extended far down into the valleys to the south, the modern city has climbed up the plateau toward the north.

Josephus's Description of Jerusalem. The late Jewish historian, Josephus, has given the most graphic description of the topography of Jerusalem. In the light of the preceding study of its site, his vivid picture becomes clearly intelligible. While he had in mind the city of his own day (the middle of the first Christian century) his words describe equally well the ancient town: "The city of Jerusalem was fortified with three walls, on such parts as were not surrounded with impassable valleys; for in such places it had but one wall. The city was built upon two hills, which are opposite to one another, and have a valley to divide them asunder, at which valley the corresponding houses on both hills end. Of these hills, that which contains the upper city is much higher, and in length more direct. But the other hill, which was called the Acra, and sustains the lower city, is of the shape of a moon when it is horned; over against this there was a third hill, but naturally lower than the Acra, and parted formerly from the other by a broad valley. However, in those times, when the Asmoneans reigned, they filled up that valley with earth, and had a mind to join the city to the temple. They then took off part of the height of Acra and reduced it to a less elevation than it was before, that the temple might be superior to it. Now the Valley of the Cheesemongers, as it was called, which separated the hill of the upper city from that of the lower, extended as far as Siloam; for that is the name of a fountain which has sweet water in it, and this also in great plenty. But on the outside these hills are surrounded by deep valleys, and by reason of the precipices belonging to them, they are on both sides everywhere inaccessible."

The Geological Formation. The geological formation of the hills of Jerusalem also throws much light upon its history. The strata is inclined toward the southeast at an average angle of ten or twelve degrees. The surface rock is hard, silicious limestone with bands of flint. This crops out on the top of the temple mount, on the west side of the Kidron Valley, and in the quarries to the north of Jerusalem. Below is a bed of soft, white limestone, easy to cut and good for building, since it hardens with exposure. The presence of this underlying rock made possible the extensive system of cisterns and underground passages with which Jerusalem is honeycombed and which has played such a large part in the tragic history of the city. Beneath this layer is a hard, dolomitic limestone, white but streaked with pink. While the upper layers of rock are porous, this lower stratum holds the water, with the result that at the one point where it comes to the surface on the western side of the lower Kidron Valley there is a spring. The southern inclination of this hard rock also carries the drainage of the city to the south, to the point where the Kidron and Hinnom valleys meet.

The Water Supply. Jerusalem, like most of the cities of Judah, was inadequately supplied with springs. The Virgin's Spring, which is in all probability identical with the ancient spring of Gihon, is intermittent. Its waters issue from a natural siphon in the rock, flowing according to the local rainfall, sometimes for only an hour or more, and at others for several days. It is entered by steps which lead into a natural cave, half way down the side of the Kidron Valley. From this point, in early times, the waters were conducted through the ridge of rock on which the city rested by a rock-cut tunnel, which is one of the wonders of ancient engineering. Thence they were carried to a point at the southern end of the Tyropœon Valley, where was once the famous Pool of Siloam, which was probably inside the ancient city walls. Here was built in later times a great basin, fifty-two feet square, from which the inhabitants of the city drew their chief supply of water.[112] Still another conduit carried the overflow from this pool to the so-called Job's Well, four hundred and fifty yards to the southeast, where the Kidron and the Hinnom valleys meet. West of the temple area there was apparently in ancient times a pool which received the waters from the upper basin of the Tyropœon, but there is no clear geological or historical evidence of a living spring in the northern or western part of the city. Aside from their one perennial spring and these pools the inhabitants of ancient Jerusalem were wholly dependent upon rock-cisterns for their water supply. Modern excavations have revealed the remains of the aqueducts, by which the plentiful waters of the so-called Pools of Solomon, southwest of Bethlehem, were later conducted through the valleys and along the hillsides to Jerusalem. The water was then distributed by means of high and low level aqueducts in different parts of the city, but especially in the temple area, for use in connection with the sacrificial ritual. From the same Pools of Solomon water is still brought by pipes to the southwestern side of the city.[57]

Jerusalem's Military Strength. Jerusalem's strength consisted not in its elevation, but in the deep ravines which encircled it on the east, south, west, and in part on the north. The native rock lay only a few feet beneath the surface, and the soft limestone could be cut with comparative ease. A vertical cutting of twenty or twenty-five feet into the steep side of the hill gave a precipitous rampart of native rock, indestructible and difficult to scale. The weakness of Jerusalem was the lack of natural defences on the north.[56] This natural defect was partially overcome by the deep cuttings in the natural rock, which at certain points left a sheer descent of twenty or twenty-five feet. These artificial defences were supplemented in the more level places by broad, strong walls that made Jerusalem, throughout most of its history, the strongest citadel in Palestine.

Strength of Its Position. The city shared with the rest of Judah the protection of natural barriers on every side. It could be approached on the east only over the rough headlands that arose above the Jordan and the Dead Sea. While it was on the great highway which led along the central plateau from northern Israel to Hebron and the South Country, large invading armies never advanced against Jerusalem by this difficult mountain road. On the west the valleys which led up from the coast plains converged at Jerusalem, making it comparatively easy for the Hebrews in command of these upland passages to descend rapidly upon their foes in the plain. These passes were also easily guarded from above against advancing armies. The comparative barrenness of the territory about Jerusalem was another important source of its strength, for the land furnished insufficient sustenance for a large besieging army. Thus Jerusalem, although close to the great currents of the world's civilization, stood apart and aloof, secure because of its poverty and comparative insignificance, secure behind its bold western headlands and its walls of gray limestone.[58] It was the fitting capital of an austere race, who jealously and bravely guarded their freedom and their faith. Shut in among the limestone hills, it was typical of the land of Judah.

Samaria's Name. Samaria, situated in the midst of a broad, fertile plain, opening toward the sea and commanding far-reaching, glorious vistas, was equally representative of northern Israel. Both capitals were raised to the commanding position which they enjoyed, not as the result of chance, but through the deliberate choice of a strong and able sovereign. In I Kings 16:24 it is stated that Omri, the founder of the most powerful military dynasty of northern Israel, "bought the hill of Samaria from Shemer for two talents of silver; and he built on the hill and named the city Samaria, after Shemer, the owner of the hill." Whatever be its historical derivation, the name Shomeron, or Samaria, is eminently appropriate, for it means watch-tower.

Its Situation. The hill lies on the eastern side of the Wady esh-Shair or Barley Vale, a wide and beautiful valley, which comes up from the Plain of Sharon. Opposite Samaria it broadens out and unites with several shallow valleys, which come down from the north and northeast. Along the Barley Vale runs the great highway which leads northwest from Shechem and central Israel to the Plain of Esdraelon and Phœnicia. Another highway runs directly north, past the Plain of Dothan to northern Israel and Damascus. Samaria lay near the border line between the powerful tribes of Ephraim and Manasseh. It was, however, a little south and east of the centre of northern Israel. Its gates were wide open to the civilization and commerce which swept up and down the coast plains. From the city's heights there was a fine view of the Mediterranean, which represented that larger world into close touch with which Omri aimed to bring his people.

Its Military Strength. The city was built on an elongated, isolated hill,[59] rising on the west between three and four hundred feet above the plain. The hill descends precipitously on three sides; on the east it is connected with the hills by a neck of land which lies about two hundred feet above the surrounding plain. As in the case of Jerusalem, these surrounding valleys were the source of its military strength. The hill is about three-fourths of a mile in length. On its top rises a large acropolis,[60] nearly round and about a third of a mile in diameter. In the Roman period this acropolis was surrounded by a wide terrace, with a colonnade about one and one-half miles in circumference. On the top of this rounded hill there was ample space for a large and powerful city. Surrounded, like Jerusalem, by a strong wall, it was practically impregnable.

Its Beauty and Prosperity. The view from Samaria is one of the most picturesque and attractive in all Palestine. Isaiah well describes this city as "the splendid ornament which crowns the fertile valley." Green fields, olive and vine-clad hills delight the eye on every side. Between the hills may be seen glimpses of green, peaceful valleys. Plenty and prosperity are in evidence at every turn. Samaria itself lies one thousand four hundred and fifty-four feet above the sea-level and is surrounded by higher hills on nearly every side. Two miles to the north is a hill between nine hundred and a thousand feet higher than that of Samaria, while to the southeast other hills lead up to the rocky heights of Mount Ebal, over three thousand feet above the sea-level. Thus Samaria was a symbol of the beauty, the prosperity, the openness to foreign influence, the inherent strength and the fatal weakness of northern, as contrasted with southern Israel.

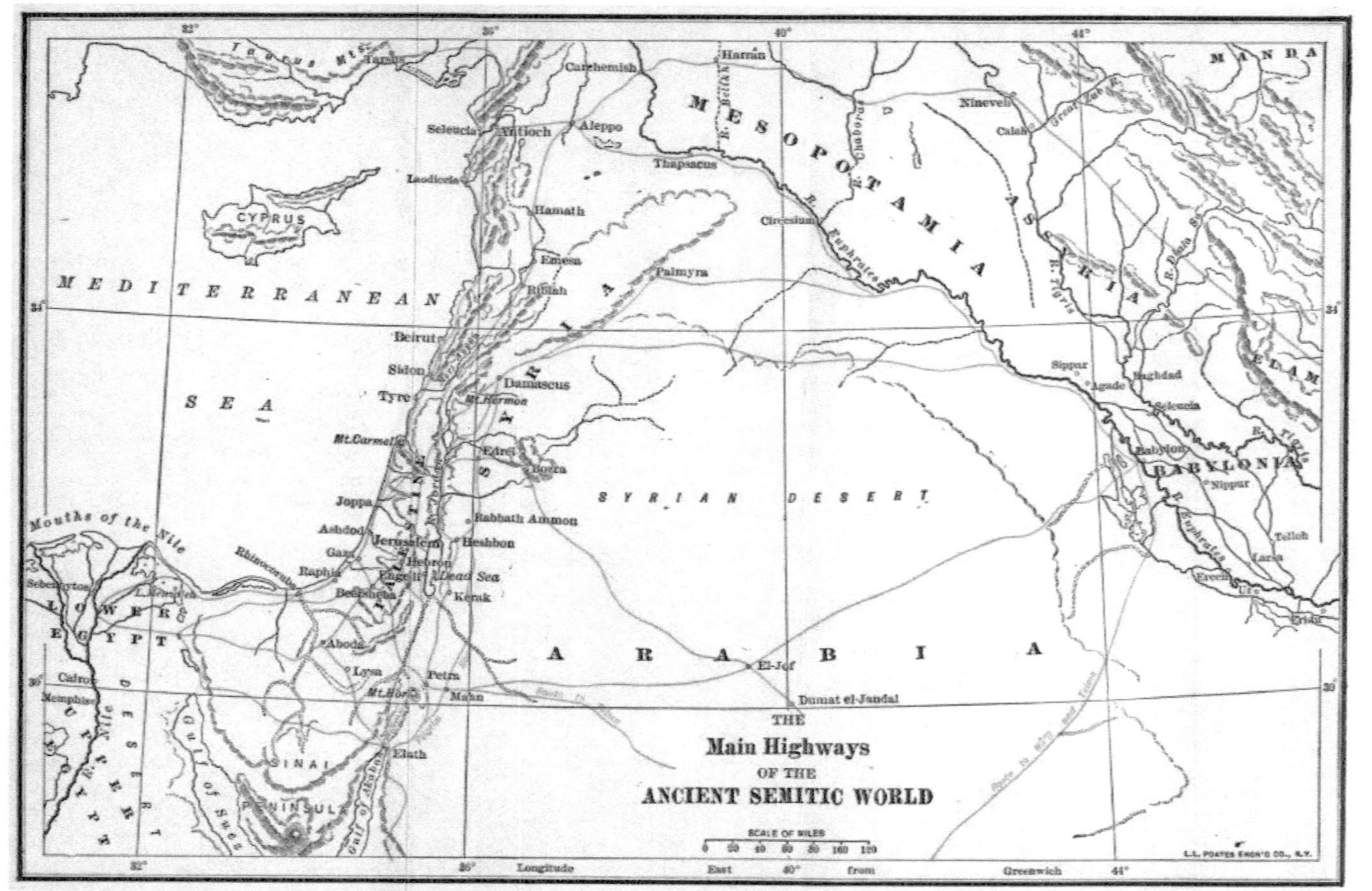

The Main Highways of the Ancient Semitic World

L.L. Poates Engr'g Co., N.Y.

IX

THE GREAT HIGHWAYS
OF THE BIBLICAL WORLD

Importance of the Highways.—Lack of the Road-building Instincts
among the Semites.—Evidence that Modern Roads Follow the Old
Ways.—Ordinary Palestinian Roads.—Evidence that the Hebrews
Built Roads.—The Four Roads from Egypt.—Trails into Palestine
from the South.—Highway Through Moab.—The Great Desert
Highway.—Character of the Southern Approaches to Palestine.—
The Coast Road.—The "Way of the Sea."—Its Commercial and
Strategic Importance.—The Central Road and Its Cross-roads in
the South.—In the North.—The Road Along the Jordan.—Roads
Eastward from Damascus.—The Highway from Antioch to Ephe-
sus.—The Road from Asia Minor to Rome.—From Ephesus to
Rome.—From Syria to Rome by Sea.—From Alexandria to Rome
by Sea.—Significance of the Great Highways.

Importance of the Highways. Upon the direction and character of the highways depend to a great extent the growth and history of early civilization. By the
great roads which entered Palestine the Hebrews came as immigrants. Along the
same roads those later waves of both hostile and peaceful invasion swept in upon
them that largely shaped their history. These highways were to them the open
doors to the life and civilization of the outside world. Over these same roads the
Hebrews later fled as fugitives or were dragged as captives. Along these channels
of communication and commerce the missionaries and apostles at a still later day
went forth to their peaceful conquest of the Roman empire. Thus, next to the land
itself, the highways of the ancient world have exerted the most powerful influence
upon biblical history, literature, and religion.

Lack of the Road-building Instincts among the Semites. The Semitic races, as
a rule, were not road-builders. Their earlier nomadic experiences had accustomed
them to long and arduous marches over rough, rocky roads. The ox, the camel,
the horse, and the donkey furnished the common means of transportation. Most
of the people went from place to place on foot, and in Palestine the distances were
so short that this mode of travel was easy and practical. To-day in well-travelled
roads large boulders lie in the middle of the way, worn smooth by the hoofs of
pack-animals and by the feet of countless passersby, who through the centuries
have stumbled over them rather than put forth the effort of a few moments in

removing them. The Aryans were the first to develop good roads in southwestern Asia. The royal Persian post-roads, that connected remote parts of the vast empire, introduced a new era in road-building. The greatest road-builders of antiquity were the Romans; but most of the superb highways, which to-day arouse the wonder and admiration of the traveller, were constructed by them in the second and third Christian centuries, later, therefore, than the biblical period.

Evidence that Modern Roads Follow the Old Ways. There is strong evidence that the later roads usually followed the ancient paths. Both were connecting links between the same important centres. Both necessarily crossed the same fords and the same mountain passes. The later roads were held within the same limits by natural barriers and by that tendency to follow established traditions which has ever characterized the East. In riding over the roads of Palestine to-day the traveller is constantly reminded that he is following in the footsteps of the early inhabitants of the land. Often the path, instead of following the most direct course, climbs over a pass or steep hill, past a rocky ruin once a famous city, but now a mere chaos of scattered rocks. The road still follows this awkward détour simply because a thousand years ago it led to a populous town. Where the roads have changed their course it has been because the centre of population or of political ascendancy has changed, or else because the Romans, disregarding old traditions or physical obstacles, flung their mighty highways over the mountains and across the deep valleys.

Ordinary Palestinian Roads. The common Hebrew word for road is *derekh*, which means literally *a trodden path*, made by the feet of men and animals. It well describes a majority of the roads of Palestine to-day. It suggests to the experienced Palestinian traveller in most cases a narrow path, so thickly strewn with rocks that it is to him a never-ceasing wonder that his horse or mule is able, without mishap, hour after hour to pick its way over these rough piles of stone. Sometimes the path runs over a steep mountain hillside, where the animal is obliged to lift itself and rider by sheer strength up rocky steps a foot and a half to two feet in height or to hold itself with marvellous skill on the sloping side of a slippery rock. Often the horse flounders blindly among scattered boulders while it braces itself against the rush of a mountain stream. At times the traveller must balance himself on his horse as it struggles and often swims through fords whose waters reach almost to the top of its back.

Evidence that the Hebrews Built Roads. There are indications, however, that road construction was not entirely unknown to the ancient Hebrews. *Mĕsillāh*, another common Hebrew term for road, means literally *that which is heaped up*, that is, *a raised way*. The common translation, *highway*, is exact. In Judges 20:31, 32 there are references to highways which ran to Bethel and to Gibeah. In I Samuel 6:12 is an incidental reference to the road which ran from the Philistine city of Ekron up through the Valley of Sorek toward Jerusalem. Along this road the ark was sent, drawn on a cart by two cows. The ancient narrative alludes, however, to the roughness of the road. From I Kings 12:18 it is clear that in the days of the united kingdom a highway for chariots ran from Shechem to Jerusalem. The allusions in II Kings 7 also indicate that in the later days of the northern kingdom there was a road from Damascus to Samaria, over which the chariots of the Arameans passed. As early as the reign of David royal chariots became common in Israel (*e. g.*, I Kings 1:5). This fact does not prove the existence of great highways like those built by the Romans, for the ancient charioteers were able to drive over roads which would seem to a westerner utterly impassable; but it does imply the rude beginnings of road construction, probably under royal supervision. Apparently the Israelites inherited from the more highly civilized Canaanites a few well-worn highways and a certain knowledge of the art of road-making.

The Four Roads from Egypt. Four great roads led eastward from the land of Egypt. The northernmost, which was called "the way of the land of the Philistines" (Ex. 13:17), issued from the northern end of the Nile delta and passed north of the marshy Lake Menzaleh. Thence it ran along within a few miles of the coast of the Mediterranean, through Raphia to Gaza. There it met the great coast road to the north and the local roads running through the heart of Palestine. The second road was called "the way to Shur" (Gen. 16:17, I Sam. 15:7). It seems to have first passed through the present Wady Tumilat, thence turning northward to the southern end of Lake Menzaleh, to have run past the Egyptian fortress of Taru, now Tell Abu Sefeh. Taru may be identical with the word Shur, which appears in the Hebrew name of this highway.

From this point the road struck almost directly across the undulating desert to Beersheba and thence along the Wady es-Seba and the Wady el-Kulil to Hebron. The third highway led from the eastern end of the Wady Tumilat almost due east until it crossed the Brook of Egypt. Then one branch turned northeast past the ancient Rehoboth, to join the second road at Beersheba. The other branch went on eastward across the Arabah to Petra and thence across the Arabian Desert to Babylonia. The fourth road from Egypt also started from the Wady Tumilat, thence past the Bitter Lakes directly across the northern end of the Sinaitic peninsula to the ancient Elath, at the end of the northeastern arm of the Red Sea.

Trails into Palestine from the South. Five roads led up into Palestine from the south. One, "the way of the Red Sea" (*Yam Suph*, Nu. 14:25, 21:4, Dt. 1:40), starting from Elath, ran northwest, until at Aboda it joined the third highway from Egypt, which ran northeast to Beersheba and Hebron. A second more arduous and less used trail ran directly north from Elath through the Arabah to the southwestern end of the Dead Sea. Thence the traveller might proceed to Jerusalem by a western détour through El-Fôkâ and Hebron, or else keep along the shore of the Dead Sea and then turn inland at Engedi. A third trail led from Elath along the desert to the old Edomite and later Nabatean capital of Petra. With camels and a sufficient supply of water it was possible thence to cross the Arabah and the heart of the South Country in a northwesterly direction to Beersheba.

Highway Through Moab. The fourth road ran directly north from Petra across deep gorges and over rocky roads through Shôbek, et-Tufileh, Kerak and northward, following a straight course about eighteen miles to the east of the Dead Sea. This was the main highway through the heart of Moab. Farther north it ran past the famous Moabite towns of Dibon and Medeba. At Heshban, opposite the northern end of the Dead Sea, a branch turned westward to the lower ford of the Jordan, while the main road ran north along the eastern side of the Jordan until it joined the Damascus road south of the Sea of Galilee. At Heshban another important branch turned to the northeast and, passing through Rabbath-Ammon, joined the desert road to Damascus. In later times the Romans, to protect their east-Jordan border cities, built a magnificent road from Rabbath-Ammon to Petra, following the ancient highway through the heart of Moab. Mile-stones, great rock-cuttings, ruins of stone bridges, and miles of stone pavement still remain to bear testimony to Rome's strength in the distant provinces even during the period of the empire's decline.

The Great Desert Highway. The chief highway from the south to the north was the present pilgrim road from Damascus to Mecca, along which now runs the modern Turkish railway. This road was the main connecting link between Arabia and the lands of the eastern Mediterranean. Making a wide détour westward to touch the port of Elath, it then turned to the northeast of Petra and ran along the desert highland between thirty and forty miles to the east of the Jordan and Dead Sea valley. It crossed the dry, open desert, strewn at many points with débris of black basaltic rocks. Like most desert roads it sprawled out over the hot plains, unconfined by fields or mountain passes. The stations were simply stopping-places for travellers and traders, for it everywhere avoided the cultivated land, except where its western branch passed through the heart of the Hauran on its way to Damascus. Here it ran close to the important cities of Edrei, the famous fortress on the upper Yarmuk, and Ashteroth-Karnaim. A little northeast of Rabbath-Ammon one branch, deflected to the northeast, and passing through the desert town of Bozrah, and thence skirting the eastern side of the lava tract of El-Lejah, reached Damascus. From Edrei and Bozrah a caravan route ran southeast to the ancient Duma, the present Dumat el-Jandal, and on to the oasis of Tema.

Character of the Southern Approaches to Palestine. It is significant that the chief entrances to the west-Jordan land from the south are not through the South Country but by the way of Moab. The roads which lead directly into Judah are deflected by the grim, barren ranges of the South Country either to Beersheba on the southwest or to the Arabah on the southeast. The roads themselves lie through a rough, wild, dry, Bedouin-invested country, over which it is impossible for large tribes or armies to advance. Of the two east-Jordan highways, that through the heart of Moab passes over steep mountains and down into deep wadies, and in ancient times led through a thickly populated and well-guarded region. The great and easy highway is along the borders of the desert, and it was probably by this way that most of the invaders from the south found their way to the west-Jordan land.

The Coast Road. In western Palestine four main highways, connected by cross-roads, led from the south to northern Syria and eastward to Assyria and Babylonia. The first was the direct coast road which connected Egypt with Phœnicia and Asia Minor. Throughout its course it kept close to the sea. Only in Philistia was it driven inland by the drifting sands. Along an artificially constructed causeway it rounded the end of Mount Carmel and proceeded northward along the Plain of Acre over the difficult cliffs of the Ladder of Tyre to the plains of Phœnicia. Thence it ran along the open way past Beirut, until it reached the difficult pass of the Dog River. There the bas-reliefs and inscriptions on the rocks indicate not only that from the days of Ramses II the great conquerors of antiquity had passed along this highway of the nations, but also that many of them shared in the task of cutting the road across these difficult cliffs.

The "Way of the Sea." The second great northern highway, the famous Via Maris of the Romans, branching from the coast road either at Ashdod or Joppa, ran on the eastern side of the Plain of Sharon, close to the foothills of Samaria. Near where it was joined by the important road which came down through the Barley Vale from Shechem and Samaria, this great highway divided into three branches. One ran to the north along the eastern and northern side of Mount Carmel and joined the coast road. Another, apparently the main branch, turned to the northeast, passed through the Wady Arah, and emerged upon the Plain of Esdraelon beside the famous old fortress of Megiddo. From here it ran directly across the plain, past Mount Tabor through Lubieh and down the steep decline from the plateau to the northwestern end of the Sea of Galilee. Owing to the soft, loamy character of the Plain of Esdraelon, this was often impassable in the winter and spring. Caravans and armies would then take the third branch from the Plain of Sharon, which at first ran almost due east over the Plain of Dothan and past the old Canaanite city of Ibleam. Thence it crossed the Plain of Esdraelon at Jezreel and joined the direct road that ran past Mount Tabor to the Sea of Galilee. From the northwestern end of the Sea of Galilee this much traveled Way of the Sea ascended the heights to the north and crossed the Jordan a little below Lake Huleh at the ford now spanned by the old stone bridge known as the "Bridge of the Daughters of Jacob." From the Jordan the road followed an almost straight line northwest, past El-Kuneitra in eastern Jaulan, across the desert to Damascus.

Its Commercial and Strategic Importance. From the point where it crossed the Jordan a branch of this main highway went westward through the valley between upper and lower Galilee, to ancient Accho, the chief seaport of Damascus. Thus across Galilee, with its open roads, poured the commerce of Damascus and the desert world of which it was the outlet. From Damascus to Egypt this second great highway of Syria ran almost entirely over broad deserts or open plains. It was the main road through the heart of northern Israel, along which passed not only the merchants, but also the conquering armies of Babylonia and Assyria.

The Central Road and Its Cross-Roads in the South. The third great northern highway was connected with Egypt and the south by the way of Beersheba. It followed close to the watershed of central Judah, along the line of the present carriage-road from Hebron to Jerusalem. It ran past Bethzur and Beth-zecharias, famous in Maccabean warfare. From Bethzur an important highway deflected to the northwest, following the Wady es-Sur and the eastern side of the Shephelah, or Lowlands, as far as the Valley of Ajalon on the borders of the Philistine Plain. From Jerusalem several roads ran through the valleys to the west and northwest, connecting with the highways on the Plain of Sharon. Of these the chief went northwest past Gibeon, down the deep descent of the upper and lower Beth-horons to Joppa. Another ran still farther to the northwest to Gophna, to join the second great highway at Antipatris.

In the North. The main highway continued directly north from Jerusalem to Shechem. Then turning a little to the northwest it passed through the city of Samaria over the open plains to Ibleam, where it joined the eastern branch of the famous Way of the Sea, which led past the northwestern end of the Sea of Galilee to Damascus. Opposite Mount Gerizim a branch of the central road turned northeast and ran through Thebez, Bethshean, and the western side of the Sea of Galilee. An extension of the central highway ran north over central Galilee through the valley of Merj Ayun to the great valley between the Lebanons and Anti-Lebanons. Thence this central highway continued through Riblah and Hamath, crossing the upper Euphrates at Carchemish. Turning eastward at this point it ran through northern Mesopotamia past Harran and across the level plains between the Tigris and the Euphrates to Nineveh and Babylon. It was along this broad highway that the Assyrian and Babylonian conquerors repeatedly advanced against Palestine and later carried away Hebrew captives from both northern and southern Israel.

The Road Along the Jordan. The fourth main highway to the north, starting from Jerusalem, passed northeast through the barren, picturesque wilderness of Judea to Jericho. Thence it followed the western side of the Jordan Valley and the Sea of Galilee to Khan Minyeh, where it joined the other great roads which led to northern Syria and Damascus. From this fourth highway many cross-roads led eastward and westward. From Jericho a western road ran up the Wady Suweinit to Michmash and thence across southwestern Samaria. Farther north, three others led up from the Plain of the Jordan to Shechem and thence by the Barley Vale to the Plain of Sharon. At Bethshean the road to the north was crossed by another highway, which ran from Gilead westward across the Plain of Jezreel. Thence a highway crossed the northwestern side of the Plain of Esdraelon, reaching the great coast road at Haifa and Accho. Also from the southwestern end of the Sea of Galilee another important road ran northwest past the Plain of Asochis to Accho. From the upper Jordan valley a highway led northeast past ancient Dan and Banias along the eastern spurs of Mount Hermon to Damascus.

Roads Eastward from Damascus. From Damascus a great caravan route struck off due east across the northern end of the Arabian Desert, reaching the Euphrates in the vicinity of Sippar. Thence it turned southward to Babylon and the cities of lower Babylonia. Another route, popular in later times and probably also in use during the Assyrio-Babylonian period, made a larger circle to the north, touching at Palmyra and other desert stations. Palestine, and especially the central plain of Esdraelon, was therefore the focus of the great highways which connected all points in the ancient world.

The Highway from Antioch to Ephesus. The main highway which skirted the coast of the eastern Mediterranean crossed the Amanus Mountains through the Syrian Gates a little north of Antioch. At this point one branch ran northward to connect with the great trade routes which came from Babylonia and the East. The main road to the west, however, after touching at Alexandria (the present Alexandretta) rounded the eastern end of the Mediterranean, where it was joined by one of the great trade routes which came from the Euphrates Valley. After passing through Tarsus, it abruptly turned almost due north, crossing the Taurus Mountains by the Cilician Pass, and then with much twisting and winding went westward, following in general the dividing line between the central plateau of Asia Minor and the rugged southern mountains. At Kybistra it forked, the northern branch crossing the plateau directly to Laodicea. The southern and more commonly used branch made a long détour through the important cities of Derbe and Iconium. At Julia to the northwest the great western highway again parted. One main branch ran in a southwesterly direction through Apameia, Colossæ, and thence by the broad and fertile valley of the River Mæander to Ephesus, the commercial and later the political capital of Asia Minor. Another straighter but less used highway followed the valley of the Cayster to Ephesus.

The Road from Asia Minor to Rome. The other great branch of the main highway from Julia westward was the old overland route to Rome. It ran first due east. Two important branches came down from Dorylaion in the north, connecting it with Nicæa and Constantinople. The old overland route continued eastward through Philadelphia and Sardis. From Sardis a branch ran straight to Smyrna, the commercial rival of Ephesus. The main road, however, turned to the northwest from Sardis, passing through Thyatira, Pergamus, the earlier capital of Asia Minor, to Troas, from whence the traveller could take ship directly to Neopolis and Philippi. A highway, however, passed northward across the Hellespont and thence through southern Thrace to Philippi. From this point the great Via Egnatia led due west through Thessalonica and Pella to Aulonia and Dyrrachium. From these Adriatic ports a short sea voyage brought the traveller to Brundisium, whence a well-worn highway led directly across southern Italy to Rome. This long and arduous road through southern Europe and central Asia Minor was the main thoroughfare for travel, trade, and official communication between Rome and her eastern provinces.

From Ephesus to Rome. Travellers who preferred a shorter land and a longer water journey took ship from Ephesus to Corinth. Thence they were transferred across the isthmus to a ship which skirted the shores of Epirus and landed them at Brundisium. If they preferred a still longer water journey, they could take ship at Ephesus around the southern end of Greece, either to Brundisium or else through the straits of Messina; thence to Puteoli, or to Ostia, the port of Rome itself.

From Syria to Rome by Sea. Travellers or merchants making the journey from Palestine wholly by water had before them the choice of two ways. The most common course was to take ship at some one of the ports of Syria: Cæsarea, Accho, Tyre, or Sidon. Thence they skirted the shores of Syria and Asia Minor to Rhodes, seeking a harbor each night or whenever the weather was unfavorable. From Rhodes the ordinary course was to the eastern end of Crete and thence along its southern shores, where favorable harbors could be found. From the western end of Crete the ancient mariners skirted the southern shores of Greece, and then, with the aid of the northern winds, which came down through the Adriatic, made their way to the eastern shores of Sicily and thence through the straits of Messina. From here they sailed to Puteoli or else to the mouth of the Tiber.

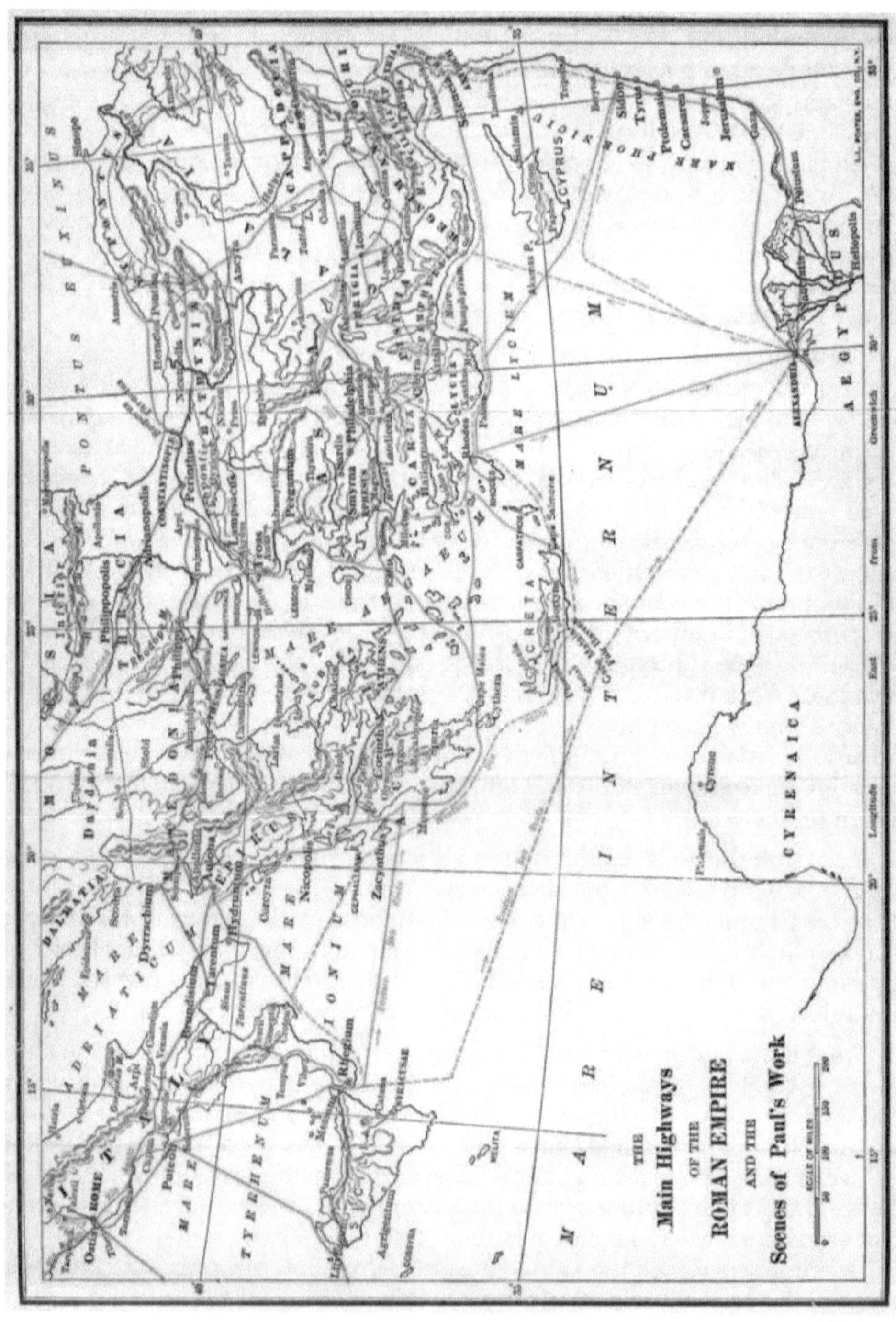

The Main Highways of the Roman Empire and the Scenes of Paul's Work

L.L. Poates Engr'g Co., N.Y.

From Alexandria to Rome. The second method of reaching Rome from Syria by sea was by way of Alexandria, which could be reached either by local ship or by the coast road. From this great seaport of Egypt, during the Roman period, fleets of large grain vessels made frequent trips, bearing Egyptian grain to the capital city. According to the Latin writer, Vegetius (IV, 39, V, 9) the open season for navigation on the Mediterranean extended from March tenth to November tenth, although the favorable season was limited to the four short months between May twenty-sixth and September fourteenth. From about the twentieth of July to the end of August the famous Etesian winds ordinarily blew steadily from the west. These winds made it possible for the fleets of east-bound merchantmen to make the trip from Rome to Alexandria in what seemed to the ancients the marvellously short period of from twenty to twenty-five days. The west-bound trip, however, was much more difficult. Owing to the prevailing west winds the mariners were obliged to cross the Mediterranean to some point on the southern shores of Asia Minor and thence to run westward from port to port along the usual route on the southern side of Crete and Greece.[2]

Significance of the Great Highways. Over these great highways across and around the eastern Mediterranean the civilization of the ancient world spread to the ends of the earth. These were the paths which the Jewish exiles followed in their western exodus. By the beginning of the Christian era Jewish colonies and groups of converts to Judaism were to be found in all the cities touched by these great arteries of commerce. Along these highways passed the armies and culture of the West to the conquest of the East, and the ideas and religions of the East to the conquest of the West. They were thus the natural bonds that bound together the human race in one common brotherhood.

---

[2] Cf. *Roads and Travel in the New Testament*, by Ramsay, in Extra Vol., Hastings's *Dictionary of the Bible*, pp. 375-403.

PART II
HISTORICAL GEOGRAPHY

X

EARLY PALESTINE

The Aim and Value of Historical Geography.—Sources of Information
Regarding Ancient Palestine.—Evidence of the Excavations.—
The Oldest Inhabitants of Palestine.—The Semitic Invasions from
the Desert.—Influence of the Early Amorite Civilization Upon
Babylonia.—Probable Site of the Oldest Semitic Civilization.—
Remains of the Old Amorite Civilization.—Babylonian Influence
in Palestine.—Egyptian Influence in the Cities of the Plain.—Dif-
ferent Types of Civilization in Palestine.—Conditions Leading to
the Hyksos Invasion of Egypt.—Fortunes of the Invaders.—The
One Natural Site in Syria for a Great Empire.—Influences of the
Land Upon the Early Forms of Worship.—Upon the Beliefs of Its
Inhabitants.

The Aim and Value of Historical Geography. Historical geography deals primarily with the background of history rather than with the detailed historical facts
themselves. It aims to go back of events and movements and to study underlying
forces and causes. Primitive peoples are more subject to the influences of physical
environment than the more civilized races. Modern peoples are able with the aid
of art and science to rise superior in many ways to natural conditions and limitations. A knowledge, therefore, of the physical forces at work in early Palestinian
history is of especial value in reconstructing this important but little known chapter in the life of the race.

Sources of Information Regarding Early Palestine. The discoveries of the
past quarter century have revealed in a remarkable way the outlines, at least, of
the early history of the states along the eastern Mediterranean. The meagre biblical
references have been supplemented by the contemporary testimony of the Babylonian and Egyptian monuments. For this early period the Babylonian data are
still incomplete, being limited to the statements of certain early conquerors, such
as Lugalzaggisi and Sargon I, that they made expeditions to the West Country.
Beginning, however, with about 1600 B.C., the Egyptian records furnish rich and
in many cases detailed pictures of conditions in Syria and Palestine. Thotmose III,
who reigned between 1479 and 1447 B.C., has given a vivid account of his many
campaigns and conquests in the lands along the eastern Mediterranean. In his
lists inscribed on the great temple at Karnak he gives the names of three hundred
and eighty cities, of which one hundred and nineteen are in Palestine. From the

reign of one of his successors, Amenhotep IV, the great reforming king of Egypt, comes the famous collection of the Tell el-Amarna letters. These were found in ruins which lie on the east side of the Nile about one hundred and seventy miles south of Cairo. Nearly three hundred of these tablets, written in the Babylonian language and script, have been recovered. They represent the correspondence of Amenhotep IV and his predecessor with the kings of Babylonia, Assyria, and Mitanni, and especially with the Egyptian governors of Palestine.

Evidence of the Excavations. Recent excavations in Palestine at the ancient border town of Lachish and at Gezer on the coast plain, at Taanach and Megeddo on the southwestern side of the Plain of Esdraelon, and at Jericho in the Jordan valley, have greatly enriched our knowledge of early Palestine, for a large majority of the inscriptions and archæological remains that have been discovered at these sites come from the pre-Hebrew period. Of these the ruins of Gezer have been most thoroughly excavated (under the direction of the Palestine Exploration Fund) and have yielded by far the most detailed and valuable results. The ancient town lay on the borders of Philistia, on the line between Judah and northern Israel. It was built on one of the foot-hills which extend out into the plain beyond the Valley of Ajalon.[61] Thus, while it belonged to the hill country, it was almost entirely surrounded by the plain and open to all the influences which affected the Mediterranean coast cities. The original town rested on two hills, one on the east and the other on the west, and extended across the shallow intervening valley. Four or five distinct cities, built successively one upon another, have been unearthed.

The Oldest Inhabitants of Palestine. The remains found in the lowest stratum of the mound of Gezer introduce us to the earliest inhabitants of Palestine. They probably belonged to the Neolithic Age and to a non-Semitic race. From the skeletons thus far discovered it is clear that they were short in stature, averaging between five feet four inches and five feet seven inches in height. Already they had begun to cultivate the ground and to make rude flint implements. They kept cows, pigs, sheep, and goats. In certain caves, coming from this or an earlier age, rude attempts to picture these animals have also been discovered. Their pottery was shaped by hand and decorated with red or white lines. Their ancient town was surrounded by an earthen wall, ten feet thick, faced on the inside and out with stone. Gezer was evidently selected as the site of an ancient city because about it are many caves, the original dwelling-places of these primitive people. They apparently worshipped underground deities, in connection with sacred caves. Outside the entrance to such a cave at Gezer are found eighty or more cuplike cavities sunk in the rock and probably used for purposes of sacrifice.

The Semitic Invasions From the Desert. Situated, as was Canaan, on the borders of the desert, it was practically inevitable that in time great waves of nomadic invaders would sweep in through the broad valleys and down the coast plains. In the light of the excavations at Gezer and the testimony of the Egyptian inscriptions, this was precisely what occurred somewhere between 2500 and 2000 B.C. Undoubtedly the Semites had begun to find their way to Palestine before this period, but it is clear in the light of recent discoveries that this great movement from the desert toward the eastern shores of the Mediterranean antedated by several centuries another similar movement eastward, which carried from Syria or northern Arabia to Babylon the founders of its first dynasty. In the light of the latest discoveries, the rule of this dynasty must be dated between 2100 and 1700 B.C. The excavations at Gezer reveal the presence there at this period of a Semitic race from five feet seven inches to five feet eleven inches in height, sturdier than the preceding aborigines and possessed of relatively high civilization. The city was surrounded by a wall about ten feet thick, made of large hammer-trimmed stones, and guarded by towers at intervals of ninety feet. The approach on the south was through a huge gateway nine feet wide, forty-two feet long, and flanked by two towers, which were faced by sunburnt bricks. Bronze and copper implements are found and there are abundant evidences of an advanced culture.

Influence of the Early Amorite Civilization Upon Babylon. The recent work entitled *Amurru*, by Professor Clay of Yale, has raised anew the question of what was the centre of the oldest Semitic civilization. The attempt made by certain scholars to prove the Babylonian origin of all that is distinctive in the civilization, traditions, and religion of the early Semitic nations including Israel is extreme. The evidence adduced by Professor Clay to prove that in the earliest period Syria influenced Babylonia more than the Tigris-Euphrates valley influenced the westland is cumulative. Many of the familiar Babylonian traditions bear marks that suggest a western origin. Over one-tenth of the names in the large literature that comes from the reign of Hammurabi, the great king of the First Babylonian dynasty, are Amorite or western Semitic. The names and attributes of most of the Babylonian gods are best explained on the basis of a western origin. The Babylonian custom of rearing ziggurats or high places for their deities, even on the level plains of Babylonia, seems to reflect the western custom of worshipping the gods on the high places. Furthermore, Syria is pre-eminently the home of the sun worship that was especially prominent in the Babylonian cults.

The Probable Site of the Oldest Semitic Civilization. The many references to the Amorites in early Egyptian and Hebrew history indicates that they developed an ancient and high civilization. The original centre of their power appears to have been central Syria, and especially the broad, fertile plains between the Lebanons and the Anti-Lebanons, through which flowed the upper waters of the River Orontes. It is certain that from a geographical point of view conditions were here supremely favorable for an early and powerful civilization. The climate was warm and yet stimulating, the soil rich and easily cultivated. The lofty mountains on either side afforded natural protection, and yet did not ward off frequent thrusts that came from the Arab invaders that pressed in, like the ancestors of the Amorites, from the adjoining desert. Communication was also easy in every direction. Through this great plain ran the main highways of trade from north to south and east and west. Ample opportunity was offered for expansion on every side. The later appearance of the Amorites in Palestine and at other places along the eastern Mediterranean coastland is also best explained if the earliest home of their civilization was central Syria.

Remains of the Old Amorite Civilization. Large mounds, evidently the remains of ancient Amorite cities, dot the broad plain between the Lebanons. These have as yet been untouched by the spade of the excavator. They alone can tell the age, character, and history of the old Amorite civilization. They furnish the most promising field for excavations in all the Semitic world. On the neighboring mountain heights exquisite sun temples still remain. Although they may have been reared by the later Phœnicians they doubtless stand on the sites of older Amorite sanctuaries. As of old, the sun, as it rises and sends its first rays through a lofty mountain pass, shines through the open door of the temple and lights up the altar within. The ruins of the great temple at Baalbek, which stand in the middle of the plain between the Lebanons, are still one of the wonders of the world.[62] Although this vast temple was built late in the Roman period, it testifies to the rich productivity of the broad valley in which it lies and to the religious traditions that clung to this favored region.

Babylonian Influence in Palestine. Even though the origin of the earliest Semitic culture in the Tigris-Euphrates valley may, in the light of future excavations, be traced back to Syria, there is no doubt that from the days of Hammurabi, about 1900 B.C., Babylon exerted a powerful influence upon Syria and Palestine. The frequent references in the literature that comes from the reign of Hammurabi to the Amorite merchants and immigrants show how close were the relations between the westland and the Tigris-Euphrates valley. Hammurabi, in a recently discovered inscription, also calls himself "the king of the Amurru." The Babylonian language and method of writing was used in Palestine as late as the fourteenth century B.C. by the Egyptian governors of Syria and Palestine even in communicating with the kings of Egypt. Practically all of the pre-Hebrew literature thus far discovered in the mounds of Palestine was written in Babylonian characters. These facts are irrefutable evidence of the strength and duration of the influence that the highly developed civilization of Babylon in the five centuries after Hammurabi exerted upon the West Country.

Egyptian Influence in the Cities of the Plain. Thus far the results of the excavations in Palestine have revealed a preponderating Egyptian influence. At Gezer scarabs from the Twelfth Egyptian dynasty (between 2000 and 1788 B.C.) have been discovered. The method of burial here employed was identical with that of Egypt at the same period. The excavations at ancient Lachish and Taanach also indicate that along the coast plains and inland valleys which led from these plains, Egypt's influence was paramount. This condition is precisely what would be anticipated from the relative position of Egypt and Palestine. Two or three great open highways led around the southeastern end of the Mediterranean, binding these two countries closely together. Egypt, by virtue of its fertility and favorable physical conditions, developed a much higher and earlier civilization than did Palestine. Hence it was inevitable that these western and central cities of Palestine would sooner or later take on the complexion of the earlier civilization.

Different Types of Civilization in Palestine. The excavations in the old Canaanite city of Jericho, in contrast to those on the borders of the Philistine Plain, have disclosed only a few indications of Egyptian influence there at this early period. Evidently the natural barriers which separated the different parts of Palestine from each other were asserting themselves, with the result that the life and civilization of the various cities throughout the land already presented wide variations. Along the coast were strong Semitic cities, surrounded by thick walls and possessed of all that the mingled culture of ancient Amurru, Babylonia, and Egypt could give. Traces of the influence of Mycenæan and Ægean civilization are also found in the strata which come from this early period. In the north the Phœnician cities were approaching the zenith of their power. Up among the hills of the central plateau, however, the Shashu, or Bedouin, still pastured their flocks undisturbed, except near the large cities, where they were probably obliged to pay tribute.

Conditions Leading to the Hyksos Invasion of Egypt. About 1700 B.C. there came a marked change in the political situation in southwestern Asia. In Babylon the Kassites came down from the mountains to the northeast and conquered the valleys of the lower Tigris and Euphrates. About the same time Assyria asserted its independence and began to lay the foundations for its future greatness. Somewhat later an Aryan race, known as the Mitanni, descended from the north, seized the plains of Mesopotamia, and established there a strong kingdom. This new kingdom, as well as the weakness of Babylon itself, delivered Palestine from eastern invasions. Egypt was also torn by civil wars and dissensions between the nobles. Under these favoring conditions the Semitic peoples of Palestine, Syria, and probably also of Arabia, united for the invasion of Egypt.

Fortunes of the Invaders. The Egyptian records unfortunately give little information concerning this so-called Hyksos invasion. The fact, however, is established that northern Egypt, for about a century, until the earlier part of the sixteenth century B.C., was held by Asiatic conquerors bearing Semitic names. When finally expelled from Egypt by the Theban kings in the south, these foreign conquerors retired to Palestine and Syria. Thither they were pursued by the energetic warrior kings who arose at this critical period in Egypt's history. At first the Hyksos leaders made their stand at Sharuhen, a city probably situated somewhere in southern Judah. Later the Egyptian kings conquered the cities of Palestine, and finally, after a prolonged struggle, succeeded in capturing the powerful city of Kadesh on the Orontes, which was apparently the centre of the confederacy of Syrian states.

The One Natural Site in Syria for a Great Empire. The history of the Hyksos invaders by analogy throws light upon the older Amorite kingdom, of which it was perhaps a later revival, and demonstrates that the broad valley between the Lebanons and the Anti-Lebanons, of which Kadesh was the centre, was practically the only region in Syria fitted to become the seat of a strong civilization and a large empire. Entrenched among these northern plains and protecting mountain ranges, it was possible for an energetic people to extend their sway over practically all the coast lands of the eastern Mediterranean. Naturally, when a favorable opportunity offered for the conquest of Egypt, it would be eagerly improved; for the rich valley of the Nile has always been a tempting prey to outside peoples. The history of the later Hittite kingdom, the southern capital of which was also at Kadesh, illustrates the same principle. A still later and even more familiar analogy is the career of the Seleucidean kingdom, whose capital was at Antioch, a little farther north. Thus the only four kingdoms in the history of the eastern Mediterranean that conquered this entire territory and aspired to wider conquest sprang up, not in Palestine, but amidst the more favorable conditions in central Syria.

Influence of the Land Upon the Early Forms of Worship. The peculiar physical conditions of Palestine not only shaped to a great extent its early history, but also made a profound impression upon the religion of its inhabitants. The limestone rock of Palestine was especially favorable to the formation of caves. These caverns and passages in the rocks were not only the homes of the earliest inhabitants, but were also closely identified with the oldest forms of religious worship. Beneath the earlier sanctuaries at Gezer and Taanach were caves, clearly connected with the primitive cult which once flourished there. Probably the gods here worshipped were subterranean deities.

The prominence of the oracle in the early religions of Palestine may well be due to the ease with which a designing priesthood could deceive a credulous people by the skilful use of these subterranean chambers. The most striking features in the landscape of Palestine were the high peaks, the jagged rocks, the springs bursting from the hillside, and the green trees standing out in striking contrast to their gray, sombre background. Each of these occupied a prominent place in the early Canaanite religions. On the heights, commanding wide views over valley and plain, were reared the high places, or ancient rock-cut altars.[52, 53] Scores of these are still to be found among the rocky hills of Palestine. Certain rocks were regarded as sacred because it was believed that in them the deity dwelt. These sacred rock-pillars, or maççebôth, as they were called by the Hebrews, were found near every ancient Canaanite altar and even, as at Taanach, before the entrance to private houses. A row of nine such pillars has been discovered standing in the temple court at Gezer. At Taanach there was a double row. The most impressive examples are the two huge monoliths which guard the ascent to the famous high place at Petra. Frequently these sacred stones or pillars are worn smooth by the lips of worshippers or by the libations which have been poured upon them. Often there are cuttings on the top or side, where sacrifices were probably offered to the numen or deity, who was supposed to reside within. Beside or beneath each ancient sanctuary, as at Gezer and Taanach, was a spring or well, which apparently figured in the worship. Beside these ancient sanctuaries grew trees, symbols of life and the mystery of generation. Sometimes these trees were represented by the asherahs or sacred poles to which the Hebrew prophets often referred.

Upon the Beliefs of Its Inhabitants. More fundamental still was the impression which the diverse physical contour of Palestine made upon the beliefs of its ancient inhabitants. Where the contour of the land made political unity impossible there were necessarily many independent races and kingdoms, each worshipping their patron god or goddess. Hence the religions of Palestine were grossly polytheistic and the worship of one common God was a goal which the people would never have attained except under a strong compelling influence from without. The different cults of Palestine were also deeply influenced by the character of the land amidst which they developed. The deities of the Canaanites living on the fertile plains were either gods of fertility or else represented the mysterious principle of generation. Their worship naturally became voluptuous and licentious. The grim hills of central Palestine and the dark volcanic gorge of the Jordan and Dead Sea engendered a cruel and relentless type of religion and worship in which human sacrifice was an important feature. Thus, although the foundations of a nobler type of culture were being laid, the political and religious history of Palestine during this earlier period gave little promise of the supremely important rôle that it was destined to play in the life of mankind.

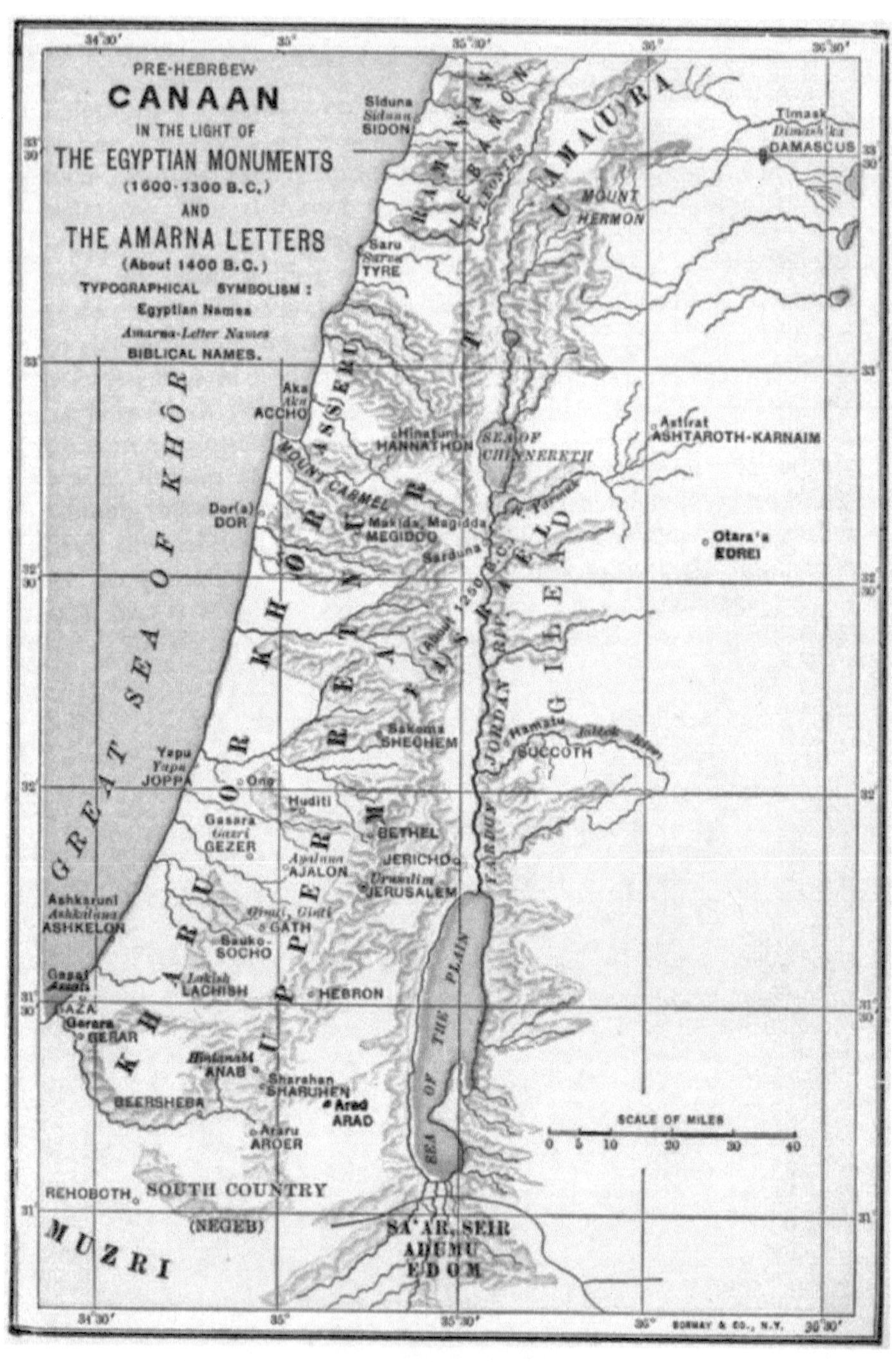

Pre-Hebrew Canaan in the Light of the Egyptian Monuments (1600 – 1300 B.C.) and the Amarna Letters (about 1400 B.C.)

Borway & Co., N.Y.

XI

PALESTINE UNDER THE RULE OF EGYPT

Reasons why Egypt Conquered Palestine.—Commanding Position
of Megiddo.—Its Military Strength.—Thotmose III's Advance
Against Megiddo.—The Decisive Battle.—Capture of Megiddo.—
The Cities of Palestine.—Disastrous Effects of Egyptian Rule.—
Lack of Union in Palestine.—Exposure to Invasions from the
Desert.—Advance of the Habiri.—Rise of the Hittite Power.—Pal-
estine between 1270 and 1170 B.C.—The Epoch-making Twelfth
Century.

Reasons Why Egypt Conquered Palestine. The Egyptian rule in Palestine was
established about 1580 B.C. and, with the exception of two long lapses, was maintained for nearly three centuries. Thotmose III, the greatest warrior and organizer in Egyptian history, after fifteen energetically fought campaigns, extended the
border of Egypt to the Euphrates and brought all the petty little rival kingdoms in
Palestine and Syria under his control. The reason for his intense activity was not
merely the lust for conquest and spoil, but the desire to deliver Egypt from the
danger of another attack similar to that of the Hyksos. From a very early period the
northeastern boundary of Egypt was guarded by fortresses, since there were no
natural barriers between it and Palestine. The population of northern Arabia was
too scattered to be a menace to the peace of Egypt; but Palestine and Syria, with
their fertile fields and growing population, were a just cause of anxiety and fear to
the peace-loving dwellers of the Nile valley. The powerful kingdoms on the Tigris
and Euphrates were also from the earliest times ever eager for western conquest.
Thus with the sixteenth century B.C. began the great struggle between the East
and the West for the possession of Palestine.

Commanding Position of Megiddo. Throughout the Egyptian period the city
of Megiddo, on the southwestern side of the Plain of Esdraelon, overshadowed
all others in importance. Here the united kings of Syria and Palestine made their
stand against Thotmose III, and after capturing this mighty fortress, the Egyptian
ruler was left master of Palestine. The reason why Megiddo had attained this prestige was partially because of its strategic importance and partially because of its
military strength. Recent excavations leave little doubt that this famous Canaanite
city is to be identified with the present Tell el-Mutesellim[63]. It is one of the three
or four most imposing mounds in all Palestine. It lies close to the Samaritan hills
and yet stands out in the plain, a huge, round plateau between fifty and seven-

ty-five feet in height. It commands a view of practically every part of the Plain of Esdraelon and far along the Plain of Jezreel toward the Jordan until the view is cut off by Mount Gilboa. It looks straight across the Plain of Esdraelon at its broadest point, through the valleys which lead past Mount Tabor to the Sea of Galilee. A little to the left rise the hills of Lower Galilee, while to the northwest it commands the view through the narrow pass to the Plain of Acre and the Mediterranean. Under its northeastern front ran the important road leading northwest from the Jordan and central Palestine and connecting with the main highway along the northern coast. On its southeastern side, through a broad, fertile valley, came the main highway from the southern coast plains and Egypt, which ran northeastward to Damascus. A northern branch passed through the wide plain between the Lebanons and the Anti-Lebanons.

Its Military Strength. The city is to-day a stately, deserted ruin, but its sides are so steep on the east and west that it is still impossible for even the hardy Arabian horses to mount to the top from these directions. For one on foot, accustomed to climbing, it is an exceedingly difficult scramble. A low saddle of land connects the mound with the Samaritan hills to the west, making the approach from this point somewhat easier. Recent excavations have further revealed the great strength of this fortress city. It was surrounded by a wall twenty-eight feet thick and guarded by towers of corresponding strength. On its level top was an area of several acres, ample room for a large Canaanite population, for the houses were little more than cubicles, and the streets narrow, intricate lanes, at many points scarcely wide enough for two people to pass comfortably. The public buildings, however, which included a palace and temple, were of a much stronger and more massive construction.[64]

Thotmose III's Advance Against Megiddo. Standing upon the mound of Megiddo it is not difficult to picture the great decisive battle, which the scribes of Thotmose III have recorded vividly and with great detail. His courage in rejecting the counsels of his generals to advance from the Plain of Sharon by a détour and his resolve to approach the city directly through the valley from the southwest command our admiration, for five miles to the south the valley narrows, affording a splendid opportunity for a determined enemy to attack an invading army with great advantage. Without opposition, however, the Egyptian army, with its gay oriental trappings, came up the valley. Its energetic king was in front, "showing the way by his own footsteps." Having reached the Plain of Esdraelon at the south of Megiddo, the king, late the same afternoon or in the night, threw out his left wing on the hills to the northwest of the city that he might command the roads leading along the western side of the Plain of Esdraelon. He thus both secured his line of retreat and was in a position to cut off fugitives in case he won the decisive battle. This position also gave him the easiest line of approach to Megiddo itself.

The Decisive Battle. The following morning the king rallied his forces for battle. While his left wing retained its strategic position his right wing was drawn up on a hill to the southwest of the city. He was thus able to descend upon the forces of the allied Canaanite kings, who were drawn up in a north and south line before the city. Riding in a glittering chariot of elektrum, the indomitable warrior led the onset. Before this army, already a victor on many hard-fought battle-fields, the Canaanites at the first attack fled headlong to Megiddo. Finding the gates closed against them, many of the fugitives were drawn up the wall by their friends within. Elated by their easily won victory and attracted by the rich spoils in the camp of the vanquished king of Kadesh, the victors fell to plundering and thereby lost a precious opportunity to capture the city at once.

Capture of Megiddo. Not daunted by its seemingly impregnable walls, Thotmose III at once gave orders to surround it. His servants he sent out to gather the ripening grain on the fields which stretched across the Plain of Esdraelon and to collect the great herds that were pasturing over the grass-covered hills and valleys on its border. Within the city no provision had been made for a siege, and the thousands shut up within its walls were soon reduced to starvation. After several weeks, the city was, therefore, compelled to surrender. The king of Kadesh had fled, but his family and the families of his nobles fell into the hands of the conqueror. The spoils found in the captured city reveals the almost incredible opulence of this early Canaanite civilization. Nine hundred and twenty-four chariots, two thousand two hundred and thirty-eight horses, two hundred suits of armor, the royal tent, with the sceptre of the king of Kadesh, an ebony statue of himself, inlaid with lapis-lazuli and gold, a silver statue, probably of some god, and vast quantities of gold and silver were among the spoils which the conqueror claims to have found in the captured city.

The Cities of Palestine. The contemporary literature already discovered indicates that by 1400 B.C. most of the cities that figured in Hebrew history were already established and that Palestine was almost, if not fully, as densely populated as in the days of the Hebrews. Among the chief Phœnician cities on the coast were Arvad in the north, Byblos and Beirut in central Syria, and Sidon, Tyre, and Accho in the south. The coast plains to the south of Mount Carmel, including the cities of Dor, Gezer, Ashdod, Altaku, Askalon, Gath, and Gaza, were at this period held by the Phœnicians or their kinsmen the Canaanites. Among the cities later captured by the Hebrews were Kadesh and Hanathon in Galilee, and Shechem, Bethel, Beth-horon, Ajalon, Jerusalem, and Beth-anoth in southern Palestine. As in the days of the Hebrew occupation, the Plain of Esdraelon was the centre of a strong Canaanite confederacy, which included Megiddo, Taanach, Shunem, Bethshean, and certain other cities whose sites have not yet been identified.

Disastrous Effects of Egyptian Rule. The Egyptian rule of Palestine put a stop for a time to the wars between the petty city states and brought them all into close contact with the life and culture of Egypt. But the fertile Nile valley, with its warm climate and luxurious atmosphere, was not a land to produce a great colonizing or organizing power. Egypt, because of its shut in position, was always selfish and provincial. None of the Egyptian rulers of Palestine sought to develop the interests and resources of the native peoples or to unite them under a common government. Their sole interest in Palestine was to protect themselves from the danger of invasion from that quarter and to extract the largest possible tribute from its inhabitants. Egypt willingly left the native chiefs of Palestine in control as long as they paid tribute and did not rebel, for the sharp contrast between the soft, equable climate of the Nile valley and the winter cold of the eastern Mediterranean coast lands made residence there exceedingly distasteful to the Egyptians. The few resident Egyptians were officials, whose chief duties were to collect the tribute and to report conditions to their king. Apparently the Pharaohs never attempted to establish a standing army in Palestine or Syria; but to maintain their rule they depended upon the rivalry of the local princes and upon intimidating the natives by campaigns characterized by the greatest severity and cruelty in the treatment of rebels. Thus Egypt took the wealth and life blood of Palestine and gave almost nothing in return.

Lack of Union in Palestine. On the other hand, the topography of Palestine was such that it furnished no basis for a broad patriotism that would unite all the petty kingdoms and races in its narrow bounds. This inability successfully to combine against the common foe, and the broad valleys that opened into central and northern Palestine from the south and west, made its conquest by an Egyptian army very easy.

Exposure to Invasions From the Desert. Another marked characteristic of Palestine is the key to the understanding of the next stage in its history. As has been noted before, "it lay broadside on to the desert." As surely as air rushes into a vacuum, so the tribes from the desert steppes irresistibly surged into Palestine through its eastern gateways the moment its internal strength was relaxed. The selfish, intermittent, destructive rule of Egypt not only repeatedly decimated the population of Palestine but weakened its outposts. In time they even goaded on the native princes to call in the Bedouin tribes to aid them in throwing off the conqueror's heavy yoke.

Advance of the Habiri. The Tell el Amarna letters and those discovered in Palestine reveal precisely this state of affairs. It was under the rule of Amenhotep IV, who was more intent upon religious reforms than on the ruling of his distant provinces, that Egyptian control of Palestine was first relaxed. A stream of letters poured in upon the king from the governors of the cities of Palestine, telling of each other's treachery and of the advance of bands of the Habiri, who at this time, about 1360 B.C., poured into Palestine from the desert. These new invaders possess a unique interest for the student of biblical history, for among them in all probability were Aramean as well as Arabian tribes, the ancestors of the later Hebrews. They seem to have been independent tribes under the leadership of their chiefs. They succeeded in capturing many of the weaker outlying cities. Often they were employed as mercenaries by the rival princes of Canaan, and they readily allied themselves with the native peoples in an endeavor to throw off the yoke of Egypt. The governors of such important cities as Megiddo, Askalon, and Gezer wrote beseeching the Pharaoh to send troops to aid them against these strong invaders. In the ruins of Taanach is found an interesting letter, sent to the governor of the town by an officer at Megiddo. It reads: "To Istar-washur from Aman-hashir. May Adad preserve thy life! Send thy brothers with their chariots, and send a horse, thy tribute, and presents, and all prisoners who are with thee; send them to Megiddo by to-morrow." In the ruins of Lachish was found a similar letter, written in Babylonian by its governor Zimrida, and stating that unless an Egyptian army was sent quickly the city must submit to the invaders. Jerusalem, under its governor, Abdhiba, was one of the last cities to resist the advance of the Habiri. At last, however, these people from the desert prevailed. An Egyptian officer, writing of the native peoples, states: "They have been destroyed, their towns laid waste.... Their countries are starving, they live like goats of the mountain."

Rise of the Hittite Power. This chapter in the history of early Palestine throws much light upon later Hebrew history. The invaders evidently soon coalesced with the older Canaanite inhabitants, infusing new blood and energy into the people; but they quickly adopted the older civilization. The conditions of Palestine remained practically the same as in the days before the Egyptian invasions. The geographical characteristics of the land reasserted themselves. The old rivalries and wars between the little states of Palestine quickly sprang up again, so that, when the energetic kings of the Nineteenth Egyptian Dynasty appeared, the land was once more ripe for conquest. Meantime, however, the Hittites, profiting by the more favorable physical conditions in northern Syria, had come down from Cappadocia and the mountains of eastern Asia Minor and had built up a strong kingdom, having for its southern capital Kadesh on the Orontes. From this centre they had extended their influence not only over Syria, but also over Palestine. When Ramses II, the great ruler of the Nineteenth Dynasty, set out in 1288 B.C. to conquer the eastern Mediterranean coast lands, he found himself, like Thotmose III, two hundred years before, confronted by a powerful foe, strongly intrenched in the broad valleys between the Lebanons. After an undecisive battle and many campaigns Ramses was glad to establish with this rival power a treaty which left the Hittites in possession of northern Syria and the Egyptians masters of Palestine.

Palestine Between 1270 and 1170 B.C. The period of half a century which immediately followed was one of peace and prosperity for Palestine. Ramses II and his son, Merneptah, kept the great empire intact by their indomitable energy and efficient organization. With the passing of the Nineteenth Dynasty there came a period of anarchy in which the Egyptian rule of Palestine was for a time relaxed. Ramses III, the great ruler of the Twentieth Dynasty, set about restoring the former bounds of the empire. For over a quarter of a century (1198-1167 B.C.) he succeeded in holding Palestine and in inflicting severe blows upon the Hittite power in the north; but his reign marked the end of Egypt's greatness. The Valley of the Nile was never fitted by nature to be the centre of a great world power. Its foreign conquests had been largely the result of the energy and personal ability of four or five great Pharaohs. Syria and Palestine, because of their central position, felt the effect of all the great world movements, not only in the south and east, but also in the west. During the beginning of the twelfth century B.C. there was a great upheaval among the Aryan peoples living along the northern coast lands of the Mediterranean. As a result, they were obliged to seek homes elsewhere and so came streaming down the coast of Syria in thousands both by land and by sea. They overran Syria and broke forever the power of the Hittites along the eastern Mediterranean. Hordes of them pressed into the Nile Delta, and were turned back only by the strong armies and activity of Ramses III. One branch, the Peleset, of the Egyptian inscriptions, overthrew the old Canaanite population and settled at this time on the coast plains south of Joppa. They were known in Hebrew history as the Philistines.

The Epoch-Making Twelfth Century. It was also during this transitional twelfth century that the cumbersome Babylonian language and system of writing ceased to be used in Palestine. Instead, a consonantal alphabet, derived by the Phœnicians from the Egyptians and also possibly in part from the Babylonians, came into use. The same alphabet, transmitted through the Ionian Greeks, became the basis of the one now in vogue throughout Europe and the western world. This same Phœnician alphabet was used by the later Hebrew priests, prophets, and sages in conveying their immortal messages to the world. Thus the twelfth century B.C. inaugurated a new and significant era in the intellectual as well as the political history of mankind.

XII

THE NOMADIC AND EGYPTIAN PERIOD
OF HEBREW HISTORY

The Entrance of the Forefathers of the Hebrews Into Canaan.—References to Israelites During the Egyptian Period.—The Habiri in Eastern and Central Palestine.—The Trend Toward Egypt.—The Land of Goshen.—The Wady Tumilat.—Ramses II's Policy.—Building the Store Cities of Ramses and Pithom.—Condition of the Hebrew Serfs.—Training of Moses.—The Historical Facts Underlying the Plague Stories.—Method of Travel in the Desert.—Moses' Equipment as a Leader.—The Scene of the Exodus.—Probability that the Passage was at Lake Timsah.

The Entrance of the Forefathers of the Hebrews Into Canaan. The biblical traditions regarding the beginnings of Hebrew history differ widely in regard to details, but regarding the great movements they are in perfect agreement. They all unite in declaring that the forefathers of the race were nomads and entered Palestine from the east. The fourteenth chapter of Genesis contains later echoes of a tradition which connects Abraham, the forefather of the race, with the far-away glorious age of Hammurabi (Amraphel) who lived about 1900 B.C. Interpreted into historic terms, this narrative implies that the Hebrews traced back their ancestry to the great movement of nomads toward Palestine which took place about the beginning of the second millennium B.C. It was about this time that the earlier non-Semitic population in Palestine was supplanted by the Semitic races, known to later generations as the Canaanites. In tracing their ancestry to these early immigrants, the Hebrews were entirely justified, for the mixed race, which ultimately occupied central Palestine and was known as the Israelites, in time completely absorbed the old Amorite and Canaanite population. The Jacob traditions point to a later movement of nomadic peoples toward Palestine. In the light of the contemporary history of Canaan it is exceedingly probable that this is to be identified with the incoming wave of the Habiri, among whom were undoubtedly to be found many of the early ancestors of the Hebrews. These successive waves of nomadic invasion were the inevitable result of the physical conditions already considered and were a part of that prolonged mixing of races which has gone on in Palestine through thousands of years and which contributed much to the virility and enduring power of the Israelites.

References to the Israelites During the Egyptian Period. The references to the

Habiri in the Tell el-Amarna letters and in the inscriptions found in the mounds in Palestine imply that the majority of the Habiri either conquered the older Canaanite population or else coalesced with them and thus found permanent homes in the land. This infusion of new blood was, in fact, an inevitable consequence of Egypt's cruel, destructive policy in the treatment of Palestine. Seti I and Ramses II, of the Nineteenth Egyptian Dynasty, in the record of their campaigns in Palestine, refer to a state called Asaru or Aseru in western Galilee. This was the region occupied by the Hebrew tribe of Asshur and would seem to indicate that by 1300 B.C., half a century after the invasion of the Habiri, this tribe was already firmly established in the land of Canaan. Merneptah, the son of Ramses II, refers to Israel in a connection which leaves no reasonable doubt that a people bearing this name were to be found in his day in Palestine. This is the earliest and only reference to Israel thus far found on the monuments prior to the ninth century B.C. That many if not a majority of the ancestors of the later Hebrews were already established in Palestine by the beginning of the thirteenth century B.C. must now be regarded as a practically established fact.

The Habiri in Eastern and Central Palestine. The bounds of Palestine were narrow and the ancient population numerous. Some of the Habiri appear to have found homes in the east-Jordan land, where they gradually acquired the habits of agriculturists and reappear in later history as the Moabites and Ammonites. Naturally, some of these invaders retained their flocks and herds and nomadic mode of life. This was possible because of the peculiar character of Palestine. In the uplands of the central plateau, and especially in the south, the traveller still frequently comes upon the flocks and black tents of the Bedouin. According to the earliest biblical narratives it was here that certain of the Hebrew tribes remained for a generation or more, with their flocks and tents, tolerated by the city dwellers who cultivated the plains even as are the Bedouin by the inhabitants of Palestine to-day.

The Trend Toward Egypt. The Hebrew narratives imply that some of these tribes lived in the South Country of Judah, beside the great highways which led to Egypt. The early Egyptian records contain frequent references to the movements of Semitic nomads from southwestern Asia toward the Valley of the Nile. In the tomb at Beni-Hassan there is a picture of thirty-seven Semitic warriors being received by a local Egyptian ruler. To-day, at certain seasons of the year, the visitor at Cairo may find encamped on the eastern side of the city hundreds of Bedouin, who after months of wandering in the Arabian desert find the banks of the Nile a desired haven of rest. All the highways from southern, eastern, and northeastern Arabia, as well as from Palestine, converge at the Wady Tumilat, the natural gateway of Egypt. When the pressure of population increased in Palestine and Egyptian rule was re-established, as it was by 1280 B.C., the nomadic ancestors of the Hebrews sought homes elsewhere. For them a change of abode to the attractive pasture land along the eastern delta of the Nile was easy. The biblical narratives state that they also went at the invitation of their powerful kinsman, Joseph.

The Land of Goshen. According to the oldest Hebrew records, the part of Egypt in which the Hebrews settled was the land of Goshen. The word has not yet been found on the Egyptian monuments, but there is little doubt regarding its general situation. In its broadest bounds, it apparently included the Wady Tumilat, and extended from the Crocodile Lake, the modern Lake Timsah, to the Pelusiac or the Tanitic branch of the Nile. It was a narrow strip of land thirty or forty miles long. On the west, where the Wady Tumilat opened into the Nile Delta, it broadened into an irregular triangle. Its angles were at the modern cities of Zigazig, in the northwest, Belbeis in the south, and Abu Hammâd at the beginning of the valley on the east. By many scholars this triangle is regarded as the original land of Goshen. Until the days of Ramses II the entire region, including the Wady Tumilat, was given up to the shepherds. Here, therefore, the Israelites could keep their flocks and maintain their tribal unity and practical independence.

The Wady Tumilat. The Wady Tumilat is a low-lying, shallow valley bounded on either side by the hot, rocky desert. In ancient times it was dry except when its narrow bed was occasionally flooded by the inundations of the Nile. On the west it opened into the Nile Delta. At an early period the Egyptians had established at the eastern part of the Wady Tumilat a fortress (known as the "Wall of the Prince"), for it was the most vulnerable spot on all the Egyptian frontier. Amidst these more favoring conditions on the borders of the Nile Delta it was inevitable that nomads, possessed of virile physiques, but hitherto restricted by lack of food and water, would rapidly multiply. The modern East presents many analogies. The alarm which, according to the biblical narrative, this increase aroused in the minds of the Egyptians is in perfect keeping with the fear with which the dwellers of the Nile always regarded the Bedouin.

Ramses II's Policy. The great change in the fortunes of the Hebrews was in all probability the result of the policy of Ramses II. To carry out his ambitious building enterprises it was necessary for him to enlist the services of vast bodies of workmen. Into this service he naturally pressed the foreigners resident in or on the borders of Egypt. In order to connect Egypt more closely with its Palestinian provinces, and above all to develop its resources to the full, this famous organizer conceived and carried through the plan of converting the eastern Nile Delta and the Wady Tumilat into tillable land. To this end he probably repaired and enlarged the canal that had been constructed as early as the days of the Twelfth Dynasty. It was about fifteen yards in width and sixteen to seventeen and a half feet in depth, and ran eastward from the Nile Delta through the Wady Tumilat into the Crocodile Lake. According to Pliny, it was sixty-three miles in length. It is paralleled to-day throughout most of its course by the fresh-water canal, which irrigates this region and supplies the towns on the Suez Canal with drinking water. The ancient canal was constructed primarily for navigation, but it was also essential in reclaiming the land on either side.

Building the Store-Cities of Ramses and Pithom. To effect the transformation of this region, Ramses II built two important cities. One of them bore his name and became the designation of the surrounding territory, which was known as the country of Ramses. It probably stood at the western end of the Wady Tumilat. The other, the Pithom[65] of the biblical records, has been proved in the light of modern excavation to have been the ancient P-atum, that is, the House of the God Atum.

This city was situated near the eastern end of the Wady Tumilat, at the present Tell el-Maskhutah, ten or twelve miles west of Lake Timsah. This was probably also the site of the older fortress known as the "Wall of the Prince." Several inscriptions have been found here containing the name P-atum. In later Egyptian geographical lists this was also the name of a local province. Here Naville discovered what appear to have been great store chambers with walls two or three yards in thickness, made of crude, sun-dried bricks. These chambers were not connected and the grain was put into them through openings in the top. Here, apparently, Ramses II gathered the vast supplies of grain necessary for his Palestinian campaigns, for these cities were built during the earlier, warlike period of his reign.

Condition of the Hebrew Serfs. In the light of the well-established facts of Egyptian history and of the geographical background, it is easy to appreciate the condition of the nomadic Israelites. Their pasture lands were transformed into cultivated fields and occupied by Egyptian colonists. The sons of the desert, ever restive under the restraints of civil authority, were put at forced labor and compelled to build the border fortresses which made their bondage the more hopeless. Palestine was in the control of their royal Egyptian task-master. The wilderness that stretched almost from their doors far out into the wild, rocky desert, offered the one possible place of escape; but under the iron rule of Ramses II and his successor, Merneptah, the escape of large bodies of fugitives was practically impossible.

Training of Moses. The one Hebrew, however, who dared raise his hand against the oppression of the Pharaoh, succeeded in escaping beyond the border fortresses and found a home among the nomadic kinsmen of his race in the rugged mountains that lie between southern Judah and the Sinaitic peninsula. Here, amidst the dangers and solitudes of the desert, Moses, the great prophet, leader, and founder of the Hebrew nation, received his training. Here he learned to trust the Power that guides the destinies of men and nations, and to despise the boasted strength of Egypt. In guiding the flocks of Jethro, his father-in-law, through the trackless wilderness filled with wild beasts and hostile Bedouin, he had also become skilled in leading men.

The Historical Facts Underlying the Plague Stories. Moses' work in leading the Hebrews from Egypt is a familiar chapter in biblical history. In the break-down of the Egyptian government and in the period of anarchy which followed the fall of the Nineteenth Dynasty, a supremely favorable opportunity was offered for the escape of the serfs. An Egyptian writer states that at this time "the Egyptians had no chief ruler for many years. The land of Egypt was in the hands of the nobles and rulers of towns; each slew his neighbor, great and small." A certain Syrian also proclaimed himself king and made the entire land tributary to him, plundering the people. To these evils were added the horrors of foreign invasion. Even under a good government the sanitary conditions in Egypt are far from satisfactory. In the time of anarchy and bloodshed the hot valley of the Nile is ravaged by disease and plagues. The seven plagues described in the oldest biblical narrative were not miracles, but the natural catastrophes which, from time to time, have afflicted the land of Egypt. Most of them are characteristic of the Nile Valley and can only be fully understood in the light of its physical and climatic peculiarities. Certain of these plagues also stand in a close casual relation to each other, as well as to the historical events recorded by the contemporary Egyptian historians. Foreign invasion and civil war, with the attendant slaughter, would inevitably lead to the contamination of the waters of the Nile. Upon this one river depended the health and life of the inhabitants of Egypt. Unsanitary conditions and the defilement of the waters would breed frogs and flies. The flies would in turn spread abroad the germs of the disease which attacked the flocks. Hail and swarms of locusts are exceedingly rare in Egypt, but they are not unknown, as careful observers have attested, and their rarity would make their appearance all the more impressive. The identification of these remarkable plagues with the anger of the god or gods was accepted by the Egyptian as well as by the biblical writers.

Method of Travel in the Desert. The peculiar topography of the territory of eastern Egypt, which was the scene of the exodus, throws much light upon the historic event which lies back of the different biblical narratives. As in the account of the plagues, the later versions, which unfortunately are the most familiar, have magnified the miraculous element. The older version, however, is clearly the one which should be followed. Apparently the scattered Hebrew tribes were rallied and later guided in their marches by the means still employed by the caravans through the same wastes of sand and rock. A brazier of coals is carried before the leader of the caravan to show where he is and the direction of the march, so that those who straggle sometimes many miles behind will not be lost in the wilderness. By day there rises from these coals a column of smoke which, in the clear atmosphere of the desert, may be seen many miles away. By night the glowing coals are lifted aloft so that all may be guided by their light. In this manner the Hebrews were reminded of Jehovah's presence and guided by his prophet, Moses.

Moses' Equipment as a Leader. The distance from the eastern side of the land of Goshen to the wilderness was only a few miles. What the Hebrew serfs most needed was a courageous, energetic, and trained leader, able to command their confidence and inspire them to quick and decided action. These qualities Moses had acquired largely as a result of his desert experience. Above all, he was able to appeal to their faith in the God of their fathers, and thus, like the great prophet of Islam, to rule his followers through their religious as well as through their selfish impulses.

The Scene of the Exodus. Of the two ways which led eastward from Egypt, the Israelites chose the southern, that ran directly into the desert. The northern route, the Way of the Philistines, was already guarded by strong, warlike peoples. Unfortunately, the oldest biblical account of the exodus contains no geographical data, and none of the three or four places mentioned in the late priestly narrative have been identified. The interpretation which places the scene of the exodus near the present port of Suez, at the northern end of the western arm of the Red Sea, is based wholly on the biblical reference to the Sea of Reeds, which is commonly translated Red Sea. That this term is frequently used in the Old Testament as the designation of the Red Sea is unquestioned; but there is no place in the vicinity of the present Port of Suez which satisfies the conditions implied by the biblical narrative. Furthermore, it is difficult to see what would have led the Hebrews to make this long and difficult détour to the south rather than escape to the desert directly east of the Wady Tumilat. The biblical narrative implies that the latter was the course followed. The significant term, Sea of Reeds, points not to the Red Sea, in whose saline waters reeds would not thrive, but to the marshy shores of the Crocodile Lake, the modern Lake Timsah, which lay directly east of the Wady Tumilat. Into it poured the fresh waters from the Nile, which were conducted thither by the canal that ran along the wady. Even though the modern Suez Canal, which runs through it, has transformed conditions, Lake Timsah is still surrounded by a thicket of vegetation. Inasmuch as the Hebrews frequently used the word sea (for example, the Sea of Galilee) as the designation of an inland lake, the name Sea of Reeds was exceedingly appropriate.

Probability That the Passage Was at Lake Timsah. According to the earliest biblical narrative deliverance came to the Hebrews as they were pursued by the Egyptians because "Jehovah caused the sea to go back, by a strong east wind all the night, and made the bed of the sea dry." The shallow southeastern end of Lake Timsah satisfies most fully the physical conditions implied by this ancient narrative. At its southern end it opens out into a broad bay, but between this point and the main body of the lake was a shallow, marshy strait, not more than a quarter of a mile across. A strong wind driving it from the level desert would force back the waters into other parts of the lake, leaving this passage comparatively dry. A close and significant parallel is recorded by Major-General Tulloch, who states that the shallow waters of Lake Menzaleh, which lies only a short distance to the north and is subject to the same conditions, were driven back by the wind for seven miles, leaving the bottom of the lake dry (*Journal of the Victorian Institute*, vol. XXVIII, p. 267, and vol. XXVI, p. 12). The biblical narrative also states that "Jehovah bound the chariot wheels of the Egyptians so that they proceeded with difficulty." This is precisely what would follow, not on a hard, sandy shore, but in the marshy, muddy depths of a body of fresh water like Lake Timsah. While the exact scene of that incident, which, more than any other in their history, impressed upon the consciousness of the Israelites Jehovah's power and willingness to deliver them, will never be exactly identified, the southeastern end of Lake Timsah is the most probable site.

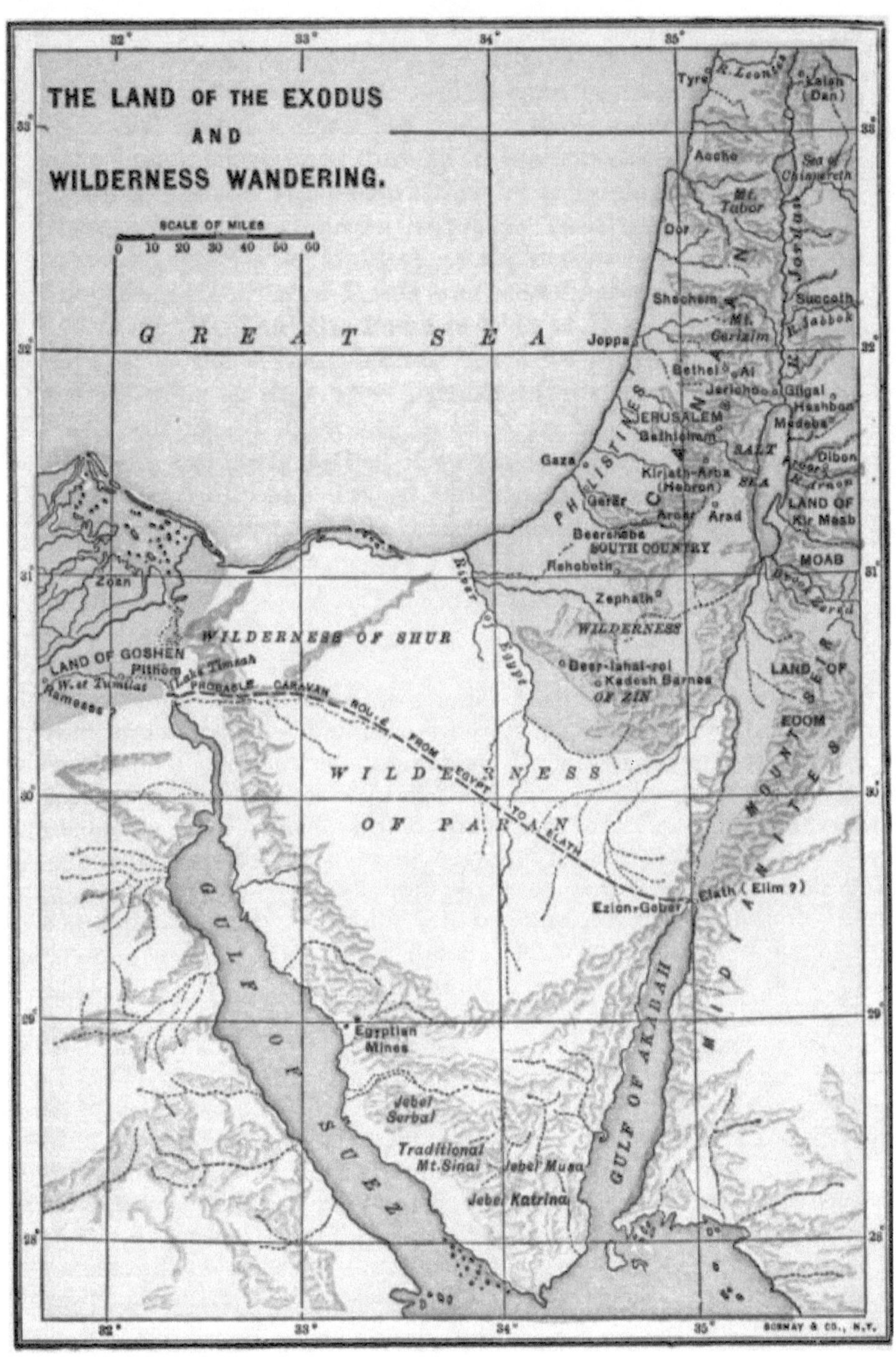

The Land of the Exodus and Wilderness Wandering

Borway & Co., N.Y.

XIII

THE HEBREWS IN THE WILDERNESS AND EAST OF THE JORDAN

Identification of Mount Sinai.—Lateness of the Traditional Identification.—Probable Route of the Hebrews.—Kadesh-barnea.—Effect of the Wilderness upon the Life of the Hebrews.—Evidence that the Hebrews Aimed to Enter Canaan from the South.—Reasons Why They Did Not Succeed.—Tribes that Probably Entered Canaan from the South.—The Journey to the East of the Jordan.—Stations on the Way.—Conquests East of the Dead Sea.—Situation of Heshbon.—Sojourn of the Hebrews East of the Jordan.—Its Significance.

Identification of Mount Sinai. Desert sites are so readily forgotten, and the records of this period in Israel's history were committed to writing so many years after the events transpired, that it is now impossible to follow the Israelites with certainty in their desert wanderings. Their first aim after leaving Egypt was to find a safe asylum. In this quest the experiences of their leader, Moses, would influence them to find at least a temporary refuge with his kinsmen, the Midianites. Their second aim was to worship at the sacred mountain the God who had so signally revealed himself to them. According to the Northern Israelitish traditions (Ex. 3:1) the mountain of God was near the wilderness, where Moses was pasturing the flock of Jethro, his father-in-law. In all the biblical narratives it is implied that Sinai was not far from the land of Midian and that the home of the Midianites was to the south or east of Mount Seir. All the earliest references in the Old Testament, as for example, Judges 5:4, 5 and Deut. 33:2, indicate definitely that Mount Sinai was at least near the Mount Seir range, if not identical with one of its peaks.[66] Furthermore, recent excavations have shown that the road which led along the western arm of the Red Sea to the Mount Sinai of later tradition passed important Egyptian garrisons, stationed there to guard the extensive quarries and mines which for centuries had been worked under the direction of the Pharaohs. This route would also have taken the Israelites far away from their kinsmen and their ultimate goal, into a barren country, incapable of supporting a large body of men and filled with hostile Arab tribes.

Lateness of the Traditional Identification. The tradition which identifies the mountain of God with Jebel Mûsa, in the southern part of the Sinaitic peninsula,[67] cannot be traced earlier than the fourth or fifth centuries of the Christian era. The detailed itinerary of Numbers 33 is generally recognized to be one of the latest sections in the Old Testament and embodies the late Jewish conception of the wilderness period. All attempts to identify the sites here mentioned have proved uniformly unsatisfactory.

Probable Route of the Hebrews. Of the two or three sites mentioned in the biblical narrative, Elim, with its twelve springs of water and seventy palm-trees, is probably the fertile spot at the end of the northeastern arm of the Red Sea known in later biblical times as the port of Elath. A journey of two hundred miles along the main caravan route from Egypt would bring the Hebrews to this point after three weeks comfortable travel. From there the highways branch northward toward Canaan. If Sinai was their first objective point, the earliest biblical references to this mountain indicate that from Elim they probably turned to the northeast and followed the way of the Arabah until they reached that one of the many peaks in the southwestern part of the Mount Seir range which was regarded by their Midianite kinsmen as the special abode of Jehovah. Here Moses' Midianite father-in-law visited the Israelites. Here, in keeping with an ancient custom of the desert, a sacred covenant was made with their God, which became the basis of their later social and religious life.

Kadesh-barnea. Late Jewish (*cf.* Jos. *Ant.* IV, 4:7) and modern Moslem traditions make the picturesque Wady Mûsa, in the heart of which was the marvellous Edomite capital, Petra, the scene of their desert sojourn; but the older biblical narratives indicate that from Sinai the Hebrews turned to the northwest. A desert journey of sixty or seventy-five miles would bring them into the midst of the series of bold, rugged mountains, cut in every direction by dry wadies, known to-day as the Jebel el-Magrah, in the southwestern part of the South Country. In one of these wadies was the famous spring of Kadesh-barnea, still known as Ain Kdês, the Holy Spring. The water gushes out through several openings from the side of a steep limestone cliff and is caught in a series of artificially constructed basins. The stream which arises from this spring, as it runs down the valley, converts it into what seems in contrast to its barren surroundings a little oasis. As in the case of most desert streams, the waters soon disappear, however, beneath the desert sand. Here, in the heart of the wilderness, and yet only a few miles east of the point where the highway that ran from Elath to Beersheba was joined by another which came across the desert from Egypt, the Israelites apparently established their central camp.

Effect of the Wilderness Life Upon the Hebrews. The spring of Kadesh is still a favorite resort of Arab tribes, but its waters are not sufficient to support permanently even a small Bedouin clan. It is only as the tribes wander from place to place, ever seeking new pastures for their flocks, that the inhabitants of this southern wilderness are able to subsist. If the Israelites remained in this region for a generation, as the later traditions state, they must have reverted to that nomadic life which still survives in the desert.[68-71] This experience was not without value to a race which must work out its destiny in the face of great obstacles. It taught them to endure want and hardship. The presence of constant danger not only developed courage and skill in warfare, but also bound them closely together. At any moment they were subject to attack from hostile tribes. Their life and that of their families and flocks depended upon their finding from time to time springs of water and pasture lands among the rocky wastes that would supply the necessities for their strenuous existence. The constant deep sense of dependence developed those religious impulses which are very strong in the heart of the Semites. The long marches through the sombre wilderness by day and by night fostered habits of meditation and kept ever before their vision the God who revealed himself through the striking phenomena of nature. The sense of racial unity which bound together the Hebrew clans tended to develop the belief, not in many, but in one tribal God, who had delivered them from the land of Egypt, who was protecting them from ever-present dangers, and who was leading them on to the realization of their destiny. Their nomadic life, with its constant change from place to place, gave little opportunity for the growth of local shrines and institutions. As a result, their worship was freed from those elaborate forms and ceremonies which in more settled communities took the place of true religion. Thus during those desert wanderings, under the leadership of Moses, an ethical religion was born into the world that laid stress not merely on ritual, but on righteousness.

Evidence That the Hebrews Aimed to Enter Canaan From the South. In the scanty and somewhat confused biblical traditions regarding the life of the Hebrews in the wilderness there are clear indications that at first their intention was to enter Canaan from the south. Their camp at Kadesh, in the South Country, was doubtless chosen as a base from which to advance into Palestine, for it was near one of the main highways which led into the land from the south. Their battle with the Amalekites, recorded in Exodus 17:8-16, is further evidence that their ultimate goal was Canaan, for the Amalekites were Bedouin tribes living in the wilderness on the southern borders of Palestine. According to the isolated passage, found in Numbers 21:1 and evidently taken from a very early source, certain Hebrew clans at least were found fighting with the Canaanites, who dwelt in the city of Arad, about nineteen miles south of Hebron. They were defeated, however, some were taken captive, and probably the rest were driven back into the wilderness. The story of the spies in Numbers 13 and 14 is, on the whole, the clearest proof of the ambitions of the Hebrews. From Kadesh a picked group of men were sent along the great highway past Rehoboth and Beersheba to Hebron and southern Canaan to investigate conditions, with a view to conquest.

Reasons Why They Did Not Succeed. The report of the spies makes it clear why the Hebrews, as a whole, did not enter Canaan from the south. Their statements are in perfect accord with the conditions revealed by contemporary Egyptian inscriptions and the results of recent excavations. Already the territory of southern Canaan was fully occupied. The larger cities were surrounded by strong walls and their inhabitants were in possession of the most advanced equipment for military defence known to that age. These defences were practically impregnable against the attack of nomadic tribes. Furthermore, the natural line of approach for the invasion of Canaan was not through the South Country. Its barren wastes did not supply a sufficient base from which to make an attack. The conquest of a land like Canaan by nomads required a comparatively fertile intermediate territory, where the besiegers might settle and derive the supplies necessary for a siege that might last many years. The reasons, therefore, why a majority of the tribes abandoned their original purpose to enter Canaan from the south and chose the more favorable route through the east-Jordan land are obvious and valid.

Tribes That Probably Entered Canaan From the South. There are intimations, however, that certain desert tribes, later absorbed into the Hebrew empire, found their way into Palestine from the south. Caleb, who figures in the story of the spies as an advocate of advance from the south, appears in the narrative of the first chapter of Judges as a tribe established on the southern borders of Judah. It is probable, therefore, that the Calebites gradually advanced through the South Country to the possession of the territory which they ultimately occupied. The same is true of certain Midianite clans, like the Kenizzites, who shared with Israel the worship of Jehovah, the God of Sinai. Possibly even before the exodus, certain of these clans had gained a footing on the borders of Canaan; at any rate they, together with the Jerahmeelites, are later found firmly intrenched to the southeast of Judah.

The Journey to the East of the Jordan. The account of the march of the Hebrews from Kadesh to the east of the Jordan is in perfect harmony with the peculiar topography of this region. The shortest way was across the dry valley of the Arabah, past the southeastern end of the Dead Sea and northward through central Moab; but this involved a journey through a part of the wilderness which can be made by large bodies of men only when they are provided with camels and are able to carry full supplies for the journey. For women and children, such a journey was exceedingly difficult even if they were inured to the life of the wilderness. Still more dangerous was the march of a large tribe through the centre of Moab, for its highways were difficult and strongly guarded. A second way, which, according to biblical narrative, the Hebrews seriously considered, was the narrow, rocky road which led through the heart of Edom to the great eastern desert highway. Without the consent of the Edomites, a passage by this easily defended way was absolutely impossible. Inasmuch as the request of the Hebrews was refused by the Edomite king, the only way that remained was the long détour around the southern end of Mount Seir. Accordingly, they retraced their way southeastward to Elath. Thence they turned abruptly to the northeast and took the broad highway northward along the borders of the desert, where the streams of pilgrims pass to-day on the journey from Damascus to Mecca (*cf.* p. 52). The way was through hot, rocky deserts and it is not strange that the Israelites indulged in bitter complaints.

Stations on the Way. The earliest Old Testament narrative has preserved a list of the stations on the highway by which the Israelites approached Moab. Most of these, as the names indicate, were but stopping-places in the desert, corresponding probably to the stations on the modern pilgrims' road. Thus the name Beeroth Bene-jaakan means Wells of the Sons of Jaakan, and was probably named after the Arab tribe that roamed in this desert region. The second station from this point, Jotbathah, is described as a land of flowing brooks. This is an excellent description of the modern important city of Maan, near the station on the Damascus-Mecca railway, from which the traveller to-day sets out for Petra, that lies about twenty-five miles due west. Maan is a little oasis made by a beautiful flowing brook, which soon loses itself, however, in the sands of the encircling desert. It is almost the only spot along this dry highway from the north to the south where the weary traveller hears the refreshing ripple of flowing waters. Farther north the road passes over the high, parched plateaus where, according to the ancient song in Numbers 21:17, 18, the Hebrew chieftains joined in digging, or more probably in cleaning out the well from which the much-needed water might be secured. The third station farther north bears the name Nahaliel, which means Torrent Valley of God. It was apparently at this point that the Israelites turned westward, following perhaps the ravine which leads from the east to the great valley of the Arnon. Bamoth, the next station, which means high places, was probably some height to the north of the ravine, possibly the Jebel er-Ram (the High Mountain). The fragment of the ancient poem found in Numbers 21:14, 15, reflects the profound impression which the deep valleys of the Arnon made upon the Hebrew invaders. Waheb, in Suphah, was possibly a place in the Wady es-Sufeiy, which opens into the Arnon from the east and thus would lie in the line of Israel's approach. The city of Ar, mentioned in the same connection, possibly represents the shortened form of the well-known city of Aroer, on the heights to the north of the Arnon.

Conquests East of the Dead Sea. From the banks of the Arnon, which marked the northern boundary of Moab, the Hebrews set out for the conquest of the Amorite kingdom of Sihon to the north. The decisive battle was fought in the open, near the city of Jahaz, on the borders of the wilderness. The site of the city has not yet been identified. According to the Moabite stone (lines 18-20) it was the head-quarters of the northern Israelites in their war with King Mesha of Moab. Later it was captured by the Moabite king and joined to the city of Dibon, which lay a little north of the Arnon. Eusebius, in his *Onomasticon* (264-294), places it between Medeba and Dibon. This battle gave the Hebrews possession of the upland pastures and fertile fields lying between the Arnon and the Jabbok.

Situation of Heshbon. Sihon's capital, Heshbon, became the capital of the first Israelite state. It crowned the top of a low rocky hill, which rose gradually from the rolling plains. On the east the plains extend unbroken to the desert with its fringe of purple mountains. It lay, therefore, in the midst of one of the most fruitful regions in the east-Jordan land and commanded the wide plains which extended in every direction. The city itself did not possess great natural strength. Its inhabitants were obliged to depend upon walls for defence. At present its top is strewn for acres with ruins of small ancient houses and what were once an ancient fortress and temple; but there are no traces of a great encircling wall. The water supply apparently came from the large pools in the shallow valley to the east. The city was, therefore, ill-fitted to stand a protracted siege. This fact probably explains why the ancient Amorite king chose to meet his foe farther south. The city is two thousand eight hundred and sixty-six feet above the sea-level and commands a wonderful view of the blue Gilead mountains in the north, the gorge of the Jordan to the southwest, the central plateau of Canaan on the west, and Medeba, set on a slightly elevated hill across the rolling plains, to the south.

Sojourn of the Hebrews East of the Jordan. Heshbon was the key to the east-Jordan land. Through it ran the central highway from Moab northward. Westward the road led rapidly down to the Jordan Valley, past Abu Shittim, the Meadow of the Acacias, to the main fords opposite Jericho. At Heshbon and on these high uplands of the east-Jordan the Hebrews had ever before them the land of Canaan and the open road inviting them to enter. According to the oldest biblical narratives, the tribes of Machir and Manasseh also won for themselves homes in Gilead, in the rich territory between the Jabbok and the Yarmuk. A later narrative states that even at this early period the Israelites crossed the Yarmuk and conquered the kingdom of Og, king of Bashan, whose capital was the strange, rock-cut city of Edrei in the valley of the upper Yarmuk.

Its Significance. This east-Jordan land supplied in fullest measure the training and opportunity for expansion which the Israelites required before they entered upon the larger task of conquering the lands across the river. Here they learned to cultivate the soil as well as to follow the flocks. The survivors of the conquered Amorites began to instruct them in the arts of agriculture and in the secrets of that higher civilization which had been developing for centuries in Palestine. Here, amidst these highly favoring conditions, their numbers rapidly increased, until they began to feel the need of new fields for colonization. At the same time they were constantly subject to the pressure of Arab invasion, which kept sweeping in from the eastern desert. Meantime the armies of Egypt had been withdrawn and the old feuds and wars between the different races of Palestine had sprung up. No strong power had come to the front in northern Syria. By 1150 B.C. Palestine was ready to receive the race for which it had been preparing through the long ages.

XIV

THE SETTLEMENT IN CANAAN

The Approach to the Jordan.—Crossing the Jordan.—Strategic Importance of Jericho.—Results of Recent Excavations.—Capture of Jericho.—Evidence that the Hebrews Were Still Nomads.—Roads Leading Westward from Jericho.—Conquests In the South.—Conquest of Ai and Bethel.—Incompleteness of the Initial Conquest.—Migration of the Danites.—The Moabite Invasion.—The Rally of the Hebrews Against the Canaanites.—The Battle-field.—Effect of a Storm Upon the Plain.—Results of the Victory.—The East-Jordan Tribes.—The Tribes in Southern Canaan.—The Tribes in the North.—Effects of the Settlement Upon the Hebrews.

The Approach to the Jordan. About the middle of the twelfth century B.C. the Hebrew tribes from Egypt crossed the Jordan into Canaan. They probably approached the river by the main highway which to-day skirts the northern side of Mount Nebo,[72] crossing the Wady Heshban, and entering the Jordan Valley where the Wady Kefrein broadens into the meadow on which still stands a group of acacias, the Valley of Shittim (Acacias), of the Hebrew narratives. After the late spring and summer freshets the lower Jordan may be forded at two points. One is at the shallow place where the Wady Kelt pours its waters and mud into the Jordan. The other is six or seven miles farther north, just below the point where the Wady Nimrin comes down from the highlands of Gilead. Probably the Hebrews crossed by this northern ford.

Crossing the Jordan. The older biblical account of the crossing states that it took place in the time of harvest, when the Jordan was overflowing its banks. The statement which follows is unintelligible except as it is explained by the unique characteristics of this strange river: "Its waters rose up in a heap, a great way off at Adam, the city that is beside Zarethan, and those that went down toward the Sea of the Arabah, the Salt Sea, were wholly cut off" (Josh. 3:16b). Like the Missouri River in America, the Jordan frequently changes its course. At certain points higher up the river, especially where the Samaritan hills come down close to its shores and the Jabbok pours in its waters from the east, the river sometimes undermines the clay banks, with the result that it is temporarily dammed up, leaving the bed below comparatively dry. The name of the town Adam, where its waters "rose up in a heap," means *red earth*. It is probably represented by the Tell ed-Damieh which stands near the famous Damieh ford, just below the point where the Jabbok enters the Jordan. A reliable Moslem historian records that in the year 1257 A.D. the Sultan Bibers found it necessary to send workmen to repair the foundation of the bridge (Jisr Damieh) at this point, in order to save the retreating Moslem army. The task seemed impossible because of the spring floods, which were then on; but to their amazement, when they arrived at the bridge the men found the river-bed empty. By working rapidly they were able to complete the repairs before the waters again rushed down. Naturally they regarded this remarkable phenomenon as a special divine interposition, although the historian does not fail to state that the immediate cause was a huge landslide a little farther up the river. This later analogy certainly throws much light upon the great event, which like the exodus, made a profound impression upon the faith of the Hebrews.

Strategic Importance of Jericho. Six miles across the white terraces that rise from the bed of the Jordan close to the foot-hills of the western plateau, which here projects far out into the valley, lay the ancient Canaanite town of Jericho.[72] It stood on an eminence a few feet above the level of the plain. The old city is to-day but a deserted egg-shaped mound about one thousand one hundred feet long and five hundred wide, with three smaller mounds on the top. The total area of the ruin is about twelve acres. The average height of the mound is about forty feet above the plain. Immediately below it to the east is the 'Ain es-Sultan, known in Hebrew times as the fountain of Elisha. To the south the Valley of Achor, through which runs the perennial stream of the Kelt, comes down from the heights of southern Samaria. Immediately back of the ancient city ran the road over the heights past Michmash and Ai to join the central northern highway through Judea and Samaria. Jericho, therefore, not only commanded the two southern fords of the Jordan, but was also the key to the highways, which led to northern and southern Israel. Before it stretched broad, rich fields, which could be easily irrigated by the streams which came down from the western hills.

Results of Recent Excavations. Recent excavations have disclosed the extent and strength of this old Canaanite city. Long stretches of the ancient wall[73] have been laid bare, both in the northern and southern ends of the mound. This wall is remarkably well-preserved and of excellent workmanship.[74] On the native rock was first placed a filling of loam and rock and on this was built a wall of rubble, sixteen feet high and six to eight feet thick, bulging outward. The spaces between the stones, which were very large at the bottom, were carefully filled with smaller stones. On top of this foundation wall was a supplemental wall of burnt brick, six or seven feet in thickness, averaging even now in its ruined condition about eight feet in height. As a result, the city was practically impregnable. At the northern end of the mound was a citadel, made of unburnt bricks, three stories high, with a stone staircase leading to the top. It takes little imagination to picture the imposing character of this old Canaanite city, small in area, but guarded by walls from twenty-five to thirty-five feet in height and of a thickness that surpassed those of many a mediæval fortress.

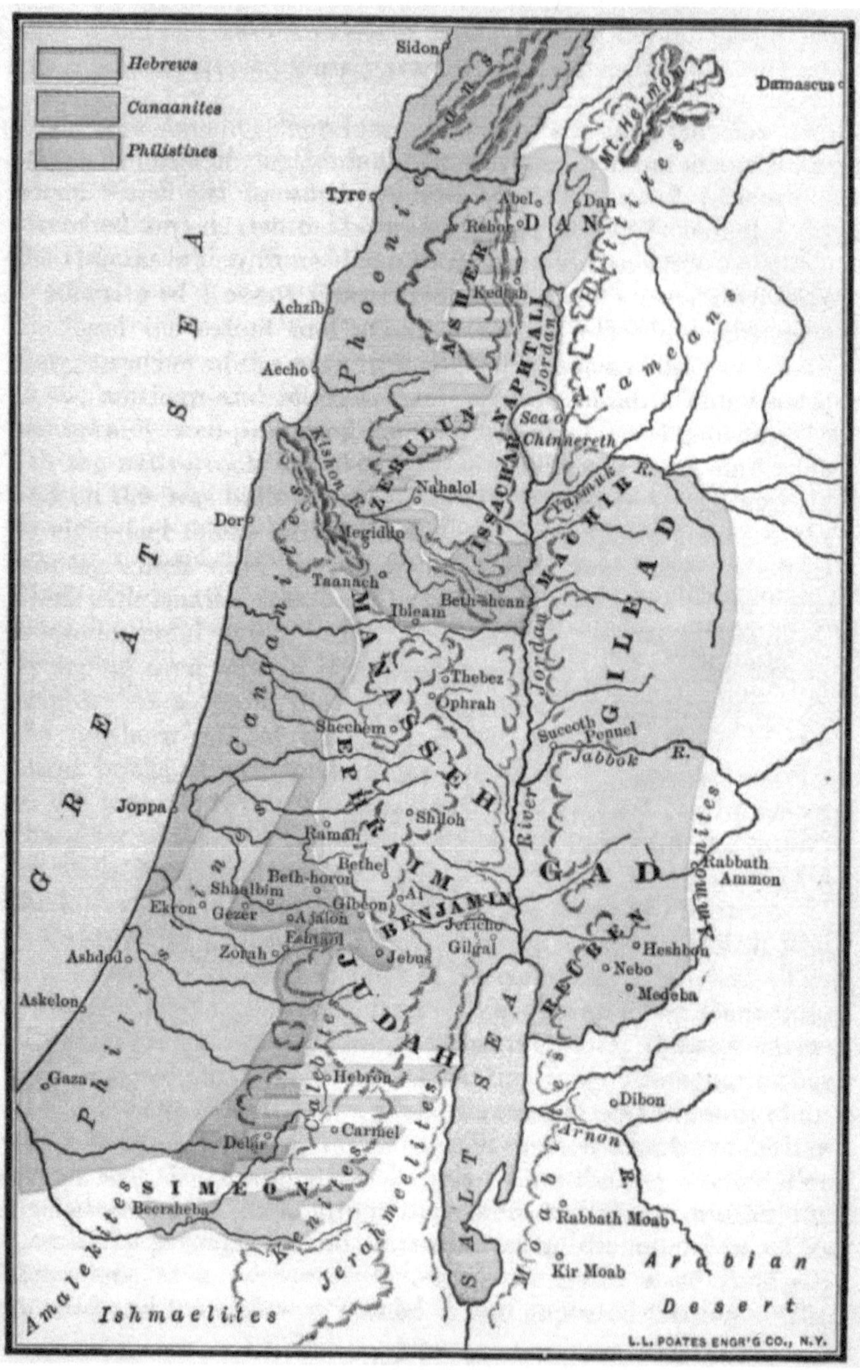

Territorial Division of Canaan After the Final Settlement of the Hebrew Tribes

L.L. Poates Engr'g Co., N.Y.

Capture of Jericho. These excavations both confirm and supplement the biblical account of the conquest of Jericho. The walls are better preserved than those of any other Canaanite city thus far uncovered, indicating, as the oldest Hebrew narrative implies, that the city was captured by stratagem rather than by siege, or as the later tradition suggests as the result of a miracle. The story of the spies in the first chapter of Joshua shows that the Hebrews had friends within the city itself. The probabilities are that, while they were marching around the Canaanite stronghold and thus distracting the attention of its defenders, at a preconcerted signal the gates were suddenly opened and the Hebrews rushed in and captured the city. The character of the ruins suggest that the old Canaanite city was abandoned for several centuries and that the top of the mound was cultivated, thus confirming the statement of the biblical historian that the city was entirely destroyed. Later a small Israelite town, dating from about 700 B.C., was built on the southeastern side of the mound. This may represent the rebuilding of the city in the days of Ahab, as recorded in I Kings 16:34.

Evidence That the Hebrews Were Still Nomads. This complete destruction of Jericho after its capture by the Hebrews is significant. The city was the natural key to the west-Jordan country and therefore its chief defence against invaders from the east. Their abandonment of this outpost indicates that the Hebrews were still nomads, simply intent upon seizing the upland valleys, where they could pasture their flocks, rather than agriculturists, ready to settle down on the plains and able to perfect the conquest of the land.

Roads Leading Westward from Jericho. From Jericho three main roads led up to the central plateau of Palestine. The one followed a ridge directly west from Jericho,[75] running at first a little north of the deep, narrow, rocky channel of the Wady Kelt.[25] The second road led up over the steep, barren, waterless wilderness of Judea, through difficult passes to Jerusalem. It offered many obstacles and no attractions to the invaders. A third road turned to the southwest, leaving the Jordan valley opposite the northern end of the Dead Sea, crossing the deep gorge of the Kidron in the vicinity of the present Greek convent of Mar Saba. Thence it ran directly on through Bethlehem to join the great central highway southward to Hebron.

Conquests in the South. This rocky trail may well have been the route followed by the tribes of Judah and Simeon, when, according to the ancient narrative in the first chapter of Judges, they went up to the conquest of Canaan. Apparently they did not attempt to capture the stronghold of Jerusalem, which remained in the hands of the Jebusites until the days of David. The town of Bezek, which they first conquered, has not yet been identified. It would naturally be looked for at Bethlehem or at the stronghold of Bethzur farther south. The text is clearly corrupt and possibly the original reading contains the name of one or the other of these southern cities. The most important acquisition of the Judahites was the city of Hebron in the south. This ancient town lay in a shallow valley and was protected by no natural defences.[76] Allying themselves with certain Arab tribes, they extended their conquests far out into the borders of the South Country. The situation of Debir is still in doubt. It is usually identified with Dhaheriyeh, southwest of

Hebron, where the hills of Judah descend to the wild South Country. In its vicinity are certain springs, which correspond to those assigned to one of the clans of the Calebites. To the southeast, with the aid of the Kenites, the Judahites succeeded in conquering the border fortress of Arad, seventeen miles southeast of Hebron. It stood at the head of the Wady Seyal, which runs up in the direction of the Dead Sea past the later fortress of Masada. Here dwelt the semi-nomadic Kenites. The Simeonites, with the aid of the Judahites, also captured the city of Hormah, far out in the South Country, and in this wild region, in closer touch with the tribes of the desert than with the Hebrew tribes of the north, they lived their free, nomadic life.

Conquest of Ai and Bethel. The strong tribes of Ephraim and Manasseh, under the leadership of Joshua, took the more direct western road over the heights above Jericho. While at this period the true home of the Canaanites was still on the plains, certain of them, or else the descendants of later immigrants, had already ascended these heights and built small upland villages. The soil was not sufficiently rich to support a large population. Probably the inhabitants still depended to a great extent upon their flocks for sustenance. At the head of the upland valley, along which the road ran, was the village of Ai, sufficiently strong to repulse the initial attacks of the Hebrews. It was finally captured, however, by means of strategy, in which the wily sons of the desert were adept. In the same way they captured the sacred city of Bethel, which is generally identified with the present Beitin,[77] two or three miles to the northwest of Ai. The ruins on this site are so meagre that its identification is by no means certain. If they represent the ancient city, it was always insignificant—a place of pilgrimage rather than of residence. The present village lies on a gradually sloping hill, strewn with large limestone rocks. It lacks the commanding view characteristic of the other high places of Palestine. Its outcrop of rock furnished abundant sites for ancient altars and for the rocky pillow on which, according to Hebrew tradition, rested the head of the fugitive Jacob. It is important strategically, because near it converge the ancient roads from the east, the north, and the south. It was captured by a sudden attack which caught the inhabitants unprepared.

Incompleteness of the Initial Conquest. It is probable that certain other small villages in the uplands near Ai and Bethel, were captured by the Hebrew tribes that turned northward. The later traditions record an important battle near Gibeon, which swept westward down through the pass of the Upper and Lower Beth-horons. The older narrative, however, found in the first chapter of Judges, states very definitely that the Hebrews did not capture any of the important cities on the plain except Jericho and that all the important towns in central Canaan still remained in the possession of the older inhabitants. One zone of strong cities, beginning with Gezer on the west, including Shaalbim, Ajalon, Gibeon, and Jerusalem, remained in possession of the Canaanites. Farther north, beginning with Dor on the Mediterranean coast, another line of strong Canaanite cities extended across the Plain of Esdraelon to the Jordan, including Megiddo, Taanach, Ibleam, and Bethshean. These cities commanded all the important highways from north to south. Still farther north the chief cities of Galilee were still held by the Canaanites. Thus, in the early stages of the settlement in Canaan, the Hebrews, who at this time came in from the east-Jordan land, succeeded in intrenching themselves only at two points: (1) in the heights of Judah, from whence they gradually extended their conquests, first to the south and then to the north; and (2) in the highlands of southern Samaria, gradually spreading down the western hills and pressing northward through the valleys of Samaria and Galilee. In the north they readily affiliated with their kinsmen who, like the Asherites, had probably remained in the land since the first invasion in the days of Amenhotep IV.

Migration of the Danites. The eighteenth and nineteenth chapters of Judges contain an exceedingly old and vivid picture of the way in which the different tribes individually won their homes in this land, where there was no political unity and where each tribe and city fought its own battles single-handed. At first the little tribe of the Danites had settled at a point where the Valley of Sorek penetrated the Judean hills on the west and opened out into a diamond-shaped valley. Here the Danites were pressed by the Judahites on the south, the Ephraimites and Benjamites on the north, and above all by the Philistines, who were able to enter this fertile valley by its western gateway. Acting on the advice of the spies whom they had sent out to find a more favorable place of abode, a large body of the Danites migrated to the north. At the foot of Mount Hermon, amidst the rushing waters which come from the copious sources of the Jordan, they found a Sidonian colony.[78] It had probably been established as a trading outpost, for past it ran the great highway from Damascus through Northern Israel. It was cut off from all connection with its parent city by the heights of upper Galilee. The Danites suddenly attacked the city, put to death its inhabitants, and changed its name from Laish to Dan. Thus was founded a city which became the famous sanctuary of the north.

The Moabite Invasion. All the earlier narratives of the Old Testament indicate that the Hebrews undertook the conquest of Canaan, not as a united nation, but as independent tribes. At first they appear to have contented themselves with the least desirable and therefore unoccupied regions. These were scattered throughout the wide extent of the land and were separated by zones of Canaanite cities. The result was that the local Hebrew tribes soon fell a prey to the older races. Early during the period of settlement the Moabites who were at first confined to the south of the Arnon, swept over this natural barrier and appeared at the fords of the Jordan opposite Jericho. They even exacted tribute of the Hebrew tribes in southern Canaan. The Moabite oppression was overthrown by the Benjamite Ehud, who treacherously slew the Moabite king and rallied the strong clans of Ephraim. By seizing and holding the two lower fords of the Jordan they succeeded, with the aid of this great natural barrier, in keeping back the Moabites; but it is evident that by this time these aggressive foes had largely reconquered the old kingdom of Sihon and subjugated the Hebrews who remained east of the Jordan and south of the Jabbok.

The Rally of the Hebrews Against the Canaanites. The rapid increase of the Hebrews led the Canaanites to revive the old coalition, which in the days of Thotmose III had its natural centre at Megiddo.[63] Again this important city was the rallying place of the Canaanites. On the great plain that extends for miles in front of this ancient fortress was fought the battle which decided the possession of central Canaan. Only the Hebrew tribes of central Israel rallied on the battle-field. The Asherites in the west, the Danites in the north, and the Reubenites across the Jordan remained by their ships or with their flocks. No mention is made in the biblical narratives of the tribes of Judah and Simeon, far in the south. According to the older poetic account of the battle, Deborah, who issued the call that rallied the strong central tribes, belonged to the tribe of Issachar, whose territory lay on the northeastern side of the plain. Here near Deborah's home gathered the Hebrews, ill-organized but patriotic and brave. Down along the highway, which ran through the territory of Napthali from the northwestern end of the Sea of Galilee (*cf.* p. 53), rushed Barak with his sturdy warriors. Evidently the Hebrews had hitherto confined their fighting to the hills, where they had had a great advantage; but now, forty thousand strong, they ventured out on the plain to meet the Canaanites who were equipped with horses and chariots and who were fighting on their own natural battle-field.

The Battle-field. The Hebrews, however, chose their ground wisely. On the eastern side of the great plain the hills from the south almost meet those from the north, so that here the Hebrew warriors from all parts of the land could unite without a long journey across the open plain. On the other hand, they were there reasonably free from the danger of a flank attack, for the only direct and feasible approach to the battle-field from Megiddo was straight across the plain to the northeast. Farther to the west the Kishon is ordinarily not fordable, while east of Megiddo, opposite Taanach, are probably to be found the Waters of Megiddo, mentioned in the ancient song, for here many springs burst from the plain, rendering it muddy and practically impassable far into the summer. The Hebrews evidently took their stand on the northeastern side of the Kishon,[79] where the main highway crosses it about seven miles from Megiddo. The river here ploughs its muddy way through the plain, which rises gently toward the northeast to the position occupied by the Hebrews. Its fords are treacherous at all times and especially so in spring. In crossing this point as late as April, our horses would probably have foundered in its sticky mud had not some camel-drivers waded out into the middle of the stream and guided us over the one narrow place where it was possible to cross without being submerged. As we looked back two hundred yards beyond the river, its low, sluggish stream was completely hidden. Had we not recently crossed, we would not have suspected that it ran across the seemingly unbroken plain. Not even the usual bushes fringed its bank to proclaim its winding course.

Effect of a Storm Upon the Plain. Evidently the Hebrews waited before offering battle until the Canaanites had crossed and were thus cut off from the possibility of quick retreat. The ancient poem of Judges 5 also indicates that they chose for the battle the time of year most advantageous for them. The references to Jehovah coming on the clouds from Sinai and pouring out his waters, to the stars fighting in their course against the Canaanites, and to the swollen Kishon, clearly show that the battle was fought in the spring and that, while it was in progress, one of those drenching thunder-storms that sweep over the plain at this time of the year demonstrated to Hebrew and Canaanite alike the presence of Israel's God. The loamy soil of the plain dries quickly and is then very hard, but when wet becomes at once a hopeless morass. The horses' hoofs sink deep into the muddy soil and are withdrawn with that peculiar sucking sound which the author of the poem in Judges 5 has successfully reproduced. The Canaanites, never famous for bravery, were quickly thrown into confusion. In their mad endeavor to get back to Megiddo, chariots, horses, and horsemen plunged headlong into the treacherous, swollen Kishon, and were swept away.

Results of the Victory. Apparently the Canaanite leader, Sisera, swerved to the northward from the Kishon and escaped over the hills of lower Galilee. Exhausted with his flight he took refuge in the tent of a wandering Kenite and there met the most ignominious of fates—death at the hands of a woman. Thus the Hebrews were left masters of central Canaan and possessors of the opulent cities and the material civilization, which had been developing in Palestine for over a thousand years. In the southern zone, the Canaanite cities remained unconquered until the days of the united Hebrew kingdom, but they ceased to be a menace to Hebrew expansion. Thus at last, after two or three centuries of wandering, of struggle, and of training, the different Hebrew tribes entered into their heritage and continued to occupy it until Assyria and Babylonia destroyed their independence and carried their leaders into exile.

The East-Jordan Tribes. In the east-Jordan territory the Reubenites settled just north of the Arnon. They were the first to occupy their lands and the first to disappear from history. The territory was rich and productive, but exposed to attack from the Moabites on the south, from the Arabs on the east, and from the Ammonites on the northeast. In the days of Mesha, the Moabite king (the ninth century B.C.), they had evidently disappeared, only the Gadites being mentioned. The Gadites were equally exposed to attack from every side, but they were more strongly intrenched among the hills and deep wadies that lie south of the Jabbok. They were also more closely in touch with their kinsmen across the Jordan and protected on the north by the strong east-Jordan tribes of Manasseh and Machir, whose territory extended to, if not beyond, the Yarmuk and eastward to the borders of the desert.

The Tribes in Southern Canaan. West of the Jordan the tribe of Simeon guarded the southern outpost, but in time almost completely disappeared from Hebrew history. The strong tribe of Judah, from its mountain heights spread westward to the borders of the Philistine Plain and at a later period absorbed the territory of the Canaanite cities, which extended from Gezer to Jerusalem. The little tribe of Benjamin was wedged in between the great tribes of the north and the south. The southern boundary of its territory ran close to Jerusalem and on the east it touched the Jordan. Northward to the Plain of Esdraelon and from the Jordan to the Plain of Sharon extended the rich, fruitful territory of Ephraim and Manasseh.

The Tribes in the North. The tribe of Issachar, profiting most by the results of the great battle beside the Kishon, in which it had played a central rôle, entered into possession of the fertile territory lying south of the Sea of Galilee, probably spreading across the Plain of Esdraelon to Mount Gilboa and the boundaries of northern Samaria. Zebulun occupied the territory extending up into the hills of lower Galilee. Upper Galilee was divided between the tribe of Napthali on the east and Asshur, whose territory extended to that of the Phœnicians on the west. In the upper Jordan valley, at the foot of the southern slope of Mount Hermon, the warlike energetic tribe of Dan was strongly intrenched.

Effect of the Settlement Upon the Hebrews. Apparently the Hebrew settlement of Canaan occupied fully a century. With the exception of two or three important engagements, the process was one of peaceful settlement rather than of conquest. It was a process to which there are many analogies, especially in the history of Babylonia and Syria. A stronger, more virile race pressed in from the desert and gradually conquered and absorbed the more highly civilized but less energetic peoples resident in the land. It was only in exceptional cases that the earlier Canaanite population was completely destroyed. Shechem, and later Jerusalem, are familiar examples of the way in which the conquerors and the conquered lived side by side, freely intermarrying and in time completely fusing with each other. This process was especially natural and easy in Palestine, because the older population simply represented earlier waves of invasion from the desert. The conquerors and the conquered shared in common many traditions and institutions. Inevitably the invaders gave up their nomadic habits and adopted the agricultural pursuits, the civil institutions, the sacred places, and many of the religious rites of the Canaanites. The marvel is that during this transitional period of settlement they preserved their loyalty to Jehovah, the God who had guided their fathers in their wilderness wanderings.

XV

THE FORCES THAT LED TO THE ESTABLISHMENT OF THE HEBREW KINGDOM

The Lack of Unity Among the Hebrew Tribes.—The Scenes of Gideon's Exploits.—Gideon's Kingdom.—Reasons for the Superiority
of the Philistines.—Scenes of the Samson Stories.—The Decisive
Battle-field.—Fortunes of the Ark.—The Sanctuary at Shiloh.—
Samuel's Home at Ramah.—The Site of Gibeah.—Situation of
Jabesh-Gilead.—The Sanctuary at Gilgal.—The Philistine Advance.—The Pass of Michmash.—The Great Victory Over the Philistines.—Saul's Wars.

The Lack of Unity Among the Hebrew Tribes. The powerful influence of
the peculiar physical contour of Palestine on its inhabitants was clearly illustrated
during the latter part of the period of settlement. Although masters of Canaan,
there was apparently no political unity between the different Hebrew tribes. Like
the petty Canaanite kingdoms, which they had conquered, they were all intent
upon their own problems and fought their battles independently. The story of
Jephthah reveals the same conditions in the east-Jordan country. The result was
that the Hebrews soon fell an easy prey to the invaders who pressed them on
every side. The Ammonites on the east were ever eager to push their borders to
the Jordan. It was only the energetic leadership of Jephthah, a local champion of
the tribe of Manasseh, that delivered the Hebrews for a time from these invaders.
The land of Tob, where Jephthah took refuge, was probably in northern Gilead.
The name may be represented by that of the village and wady of Taiyibeh, across
the Jordan east of Bethshean. Jephthah's success only aroused the enmity of the
powerful tribe of Ephraim, west of the Jordan, and the story in Judges 12 reveals a
state of inter-tribal warfare rather than of united action against their common foes.

The Scenes of Gideon's Exploits. As the event demonstrated, the only influence sufficient to overcome the physical forces working for disunion was a strong
and prolonged attack from without. The attacks of the Midianites, recorded in the
Gideon stories, were too intermittent to bring about a permanent organization of
all the Hebrew tribes. Gideon's victory, however, possesses a large significance,
for it led to the establishment of the first Hebrew kingdom. Ophrah, Gideon's
home, is not to be confused with the town farther south in the territory of Benjamin. It was designated by the biblical historians as Ophrah of the Abiezrites,
being named from the clan to which Gideon belonged. It has been identified with

Ferata, six miles southwest of Shechem; but this site is more probably the Pirathon of the book of Joshua. The Ophrah of Gideon is best identified with 'Ain el-Farah, about ten miles northeast of Shechem, at the head of the Wady Farah, which flows southeast into the Jordan. Gideon's march, therefore, with his three hundred brave followers, would be directly down this valley and across the Jordan, either at the present Damieh ford or farther north, opposite the point where the Jabbok breaks through the hills of Gilead. The common identification of Succoth with Tell Deir Alla, suggested by the Talmud, would point to the northernmost of these two fords. The present ruin of Deir Alla is a high mound on the eastern side of the Jordan, about a mile northwest of the Jabbok. It commanded the great highway along the east side of the Jordan and also the road inland that followed the course of the River Jabbok. It was therefore an important strategic point. If this identification of Succoth is correct, the site of Penuel must be farther to the east along the valley of the Jabbok. The mounds known as Tulûl ed-Dahab, that rise abruptly to the height of about two hundred and fifty feet in the middle of the valley four or five miles east of Deir Alla, fully satisfy the biblical references to this important stronghold that was later rebuilt by Jeroboam I (I Kings 12:25). Ancient ruins and the remains of a great wall and platform built of massive stones crown the eastern hill. Close to its northern side runs the road from the Jordan to the desert. The mention of Jogbehah, as an index of the route along which Gideon pursued the fleeing Midianites, indicates that the way of retreat lay to the southeast in the direction of Rabbath-Ammon. Jogbehah may without reasonable doubt be identified with the ruins of Jubeihat, which lie north of the present road from the Damieh Ford through Es-Salt on to Amman. This route would have been the more natural line of retreat, for from Jogbehah it was easy for the Midianites to escape directly eastward into the desert. Anywhere east of the Jordan the retreating Arab host would have felt secure from the attack.

Gideon's Kingdom. The significance of Gideon's victory lies not so much in the courage with which he responded to the relentless law of blood revenge, nor the greatness of his victory, but in the fact that when he returned his followers and certain of the cities near Ophrah asked him to rule over them and to transmit his authority to his sons. Thus a local chieftain was transformed into a king. The kingdom thus established would probably have survived had it not been for the cruelty and folly of the son who succeeded him. In its widest bounds, Gideon's kingdom was apparently very small. In addition to Ophrah, Shechem, which was at this time the chief city in central Samaria, Thebez, a town three miles north of 'Ain el-Farah, and doubtless the conquered cities of Succoth and Penuel, across the Jordan to the east, acknowledged his authority. Probably the villages and territory included within these bounds also enjoyed his protection. In its broadest bounds his kingdom probably did not extend more than twenty-five miles from north to south and the same distance from east to west.

Reasons for the Superiority of the Philistines. The foes whose aggressions compelled the Hebrew tribes to unite in common defence and thus gave rise to the Hebrew kingdom were the Philistines. These hardy immigrants from the islands and shores of the northeastern Mediterranean had entered western Palestine during the reign of Ramses III, at about the time when the Hebrews were intrenching themselves in the east-Jordan land, preparatory to their advance upon the uplands of Canaan (*cf.* p. 84). It was inevitable that these strong peoples should ultimately clash. The Hebrews succeeded in capturing the central plateau, but the Philistines soon surpassed them in military strength and organization. This difference was largely due to the characteristics of the territory in which the two peoples settled. In striking contrast to the home of the Hebrews, Philistia was divided by no natural barriers. All its territory was a gently rolling plain. Its people were united by similar occupations and interests. The result was that, while the Hebrew tribes were fighting their battles independently or were even engaged in civil strife, the kings or tyrants who ruled over the four or five leading Philistine cities had already formed a close confederacy and were fighting as a united people. The rich fertility of the land which they occupied also accelerated their development. Their territory lay on the great commercial highways of the eastern Mediterranean, so that they received the culture and the products of Egypt on the one hand and of Phœnicia and Babylonia on the other. Their exposed position and lack of natural defences also hastened the development of their military organization and equipment. Their cities were surrounded by strong walls and in battle they employed chariots and horsemen as well as infantry. It is easy, therefore, to understand why the Hebrews were beaten in the early engagements.

Scenes of the Samson Stories. The Samson stories represent the earlier stages in the protracted struggle between the men of the hills and the men of the plains. The home of this hero of popular story was the Danite town of Zorah, situated on the hill which guards on the north the entrance to the Valley of Sorek. Two or three miles to the northeast, where the valley broadens, lay the other important southern Danite town of Eshtaol. Somewhere between these two points was the Camp of Dan, and here Samson was buried after his stormy, dramatic career. Up the valley which runs eastward from Zorah was probably the cave and cliff of Etam, where the Hebrew champion dwelt for a time. Across the valley from the tree-clad hill on which Zorah stood was the town of Bethshemesh, while to the southwest it looked across the waving grain fields, which figure in the Samson story, to Timnath, only five miles away. With the exception of Gaza, which lay a long day's journey across the plain, the scenes of all Samson's exploits were not more than five or six miles from his boyhood home. Possessed of ungoverned strength and passions, the hero was a typical product of this western borderland and a forerunner of that more serious conflict which soon raged between plain and hill.

The Decisive Battle-field. The scene of the decisive battle in which the Hebrews were overwhelmingly defeated and the ark of Jehovah fell into the hands of the Philistines may have been at a short distance from the Plain of Sorek. It is probable, however, that Aphek must be sought farther north, where broader plains lead up to the heart of central Israel, for the Philistines were intent not merely upon border warfare, but upon the conquest of the land of the Hebrews. In the Greek text of Joshua 12:18 an Aphek in Sharon is mentioned. Thotmose III in his list of conquered cities also speaks of an Aphek north of Lydda and not far from Ono. Later, when the Philistines invaded Israel by the Plain of Esdraelon, they rallied at Aphek, which was evidently near the coast road that ran along the eastern side of the Plain of Sharon. Aphek, therefore, must have been situated on the southeastern side of this plain, commanding the passes that led into Benjamin and southern Ephraim. A little later the Philistine garrisons were at Michmash and Gibeah, indicating that the line of approach was across the more open valley of Ajalon, thence through the Beth-horon pass.

Fortunes of the Ark. From the northern battle-field, the ark was first borne in triumph to the Philistine city of Ashdod near the coast. Thence, to avert a plague, it was carried to Gath, which is probably identical with Tell es-Safi, that guards the entrance to the Valley of Elah. From there it was transferred to Ekron in the north. As the lowing cows drew it back across the plains to the Hebrew territory they must have turned to the southeast, following the Valley of Sorek, until they reached the city of Bethshemesh, beside which runs to-day the railway, as it enters the Judean hills. Kirjath-jearim, where the ark finally rested, was probably about five miles due east of Bethshemesh, farther up the valley which led toward Jerusalem.

The Sanctuary at Shiloh. The history of Samuel, the seer who was able to interpret the meaning of this great crisis in Israel's history and to point out the way of deliverance, opens at Shiloh, in the territory of southern Samaria. This little town was east of the central highway and at the northern end of a fertile plain, from which valleys radiate in all directions. The town itself lay on a rounded, rocky hill, lower than those around it, and was encircled by deep valleys on the east, on the north, and on the west. The hill rises in terraces to a flattened knob now crowned with extensive ruins.[80] The rude mosque and spreading tree, which are supposed to mark the site of the ancient Hebrew sanctuary, stand in front of the hill; but the cuttings in the native rock, in which the semblance of an ancient altar can still be distinguished, the small rock-cut reservoirs, and the level terrace near by all suggest that the site of the rude sanctuary in which the ark was at first deposited lay back of the hill now crowned with the ruins of the town. Here doubtless the maidens of Shiloh once took part in the religious dances. Here the people from all parts of the land resorted at the annual feasts, and here Samuel sat at the feet of the aged Eli. It is a quiet spot,[81] with picturesque views of mountain and plain, central yet apart from the streams of commerce and war—a fitting place for worship. It never recovered, however, from its destruction at the hands of the Philistines after their great victory and from the loss of prestige which came from the capture of the ark. Even during the days of Samuel, its traditions appear to have been transferred to the northern Gilgal, five miles over the hills to the southwest.

Samuel's Home at Ramah. Samuel's home was evidently not far from Shiloh and in the territory of southwestern Ephraim. Of the many towns, which bear the name, Ramah, or high place, the present Beit Rima, twelve miles in a straight line from Shiloh and eight from the northern Gilgal, corresponds perfectly with the biblical references to the home of Samuel. It lies in a straight line about eighteen miles northwest of Saul's home at Gibeah. Saul's quest for his father's asses took him over the high ridges and through the deep, picturesque valleys of western Benjamin and Ephraim. A few trees still grow on the hills, suggesting they were once densely wooded, and rushing, perennial streams dash along the valleys toward the Plain of Sharon. Ramah itself is situated where the hills of Samaria descend to the western plain. Near by the natives still worship a Mohammedan prophet, Neby Saleh, whose tomb is the goal of many pilgrimages. On the hill to the east we found many stones set up by pious pilgrims as they caught the first glimpse of this sacred shrine. It would seem that, in this modified form, the spirit of the great prophet of Ramah still dominates this wild region, which is a little world in itself, apart from the rest of Palestine. Here at Ramah, on the heights, where stood the local altar, Samuel directed the sacrifice, and by public act and later by private counsel on the quiet of the house-top[82] inspired the stalwart Benjamite chieftain to perform those deeds of valor which proclaimed him the one divinely fitted and called to deliver Jehovah's people.

The Site of Gibeah. In returning, Saul apparently took the highway which led southeast to the main road through central Samaria and thence directly to Gibeah. First Samuel 14:1-5 and Isaiah 10:29 indicate that Geba, situated on the heights opposite Michmash, was distinct from Saul's home. The reference in Judges 19:12-14 makes it clear that Gibeah lay close to the main road north from Jerusalem but south of the Benjamite Ramah. Saul's native town is sometimes confused with Geba (opposite Michmash), but is probably to be usually identified with the ruins at Tell el-Ful, four miles directly north of Jerusalem.[83] It was a commanding site, two thousand seven hundred and fifty-four feet above the level of the sea, and therefore over two hundred feet higher than Jerusalem and one hundred feet higher than the Mount of Olives. The identification is confirmed by the statement of Josephus (*B. J.* V. 2:1) that Titus, in advancing from the north against Jerusalem, encamped at Gabbath-Saul, that is, the hill of Saul, between three and four miles north of Jerusalem. The town enjoyed the protection of the inaccessible heights of the central plateau and yet commanded the roads which radiated in every direction throughout the land. Like Jerusalem, it was thus central, well protected, and a fitting site for the first capital of all Israel.

Situation of Jabesh-Gilead. The site of the Israelite city of Jabesh-Gilead, across the Jordan, whose messengers aroused Saul to action, has not as yet been absolutely identified. The name is preserved in the Wady Yabis, which runs from the heights of Gilead into the Jordan a little southwest of Bethshean. Eusebius states (*Onomas.* 268.281) that it was on the eastern table-land, six Roman miles from Pella, on the road to Gerasa, the modern Jerash. It is probably represented by the ruins of Miryamim, north of the Wady Yabis, where the ancient road leads up through the Wady Saleh to the heights seven miles southeast of Pella. About these massive, ancient ruins are open plains where the Ammonite hosts could assemble. Here in the early morning was probably fought the first memorable battle in Israel's war for independence.

The Sanctuary at Gilgal. After the destruction of Shiloh it was natural that the Hebrew tribes should assemble at Gilgal, the sacred shrine a few miles to the southwest, and there make king the man who had proved his fitness to lead and his ability to deliver them from their foes. The town itself was two thousand four hundred and forty-one feet above the sea and was approached by a long climb from almost every side. It stood on the top of a round hill jutting boldly out into the midst of deep valleys. The hill is a gilgal, or circle, connected with the rest of the land by a rocky shoulder running to the south. On this shoulder of land are two fine rock-cut thrashing floors. The southern front of the rocky plateau is occupied by the present village of Jiljilia. The space on the north and west is still unoccupied and bears all the marks of an ancient high place. Near the shrine of a Mohammedan saint are two terebinths, probably survivors of the ancient sacred grove. On the northwest, the cuttings in the rock suggest channels to carry off the sacrificial blood, while one rock-cutting resembles an altar, with a reservoir or underground room. About is a large rocky terrace, where one can in imagination see the assembled Israelites as they gathered to proclaim as king the gigantic Benjamite warrior and thus to lay the foundations of Israel's independence and national glory.

The Philistine Advance. The scene of Israel's history was suddenly transferred farther south. The choice of Saul as king was equivalent to declaring war against the Philistines, and Saul's intrepid son, Jonathan, assumed the offensive by attacking their garrison at Gibeah. These active oppressors of Israel soon came streaming up over the pass of Beth-horon[84] to crush the rebellion. At their approach most of Saul's followers vanished and he was left with only a handful of men. For the moment the Hebrew kingdom seemed but a wild dream. Again it was simply the courage of Jonathan that at this crisis turned the tide of war and gave Saul a secure throne. The Philistines had advanced to the fortress of Michmash and, finding no opposition, had dispersed in search of plunder. One band turned back toward Beth-horon in the west, another went north to the southern Ophrah, otherwise known as Ephraim. The third band had gone eastward, along the road which led across the barren wilderness to the Valley of Achor and the Jordan.

The Pass of Michmash. The only remnant of the Philistine army left to guard the Hebrews under Saul was the garrison at Michmash. In early times one important branch of the main highway apparently led from Gibeah to the northeast, past Geba and the pass below Michmash to Ai and Bethel. The highway which led up from the Jordan valley and Gilead in the east ran directly past Michmash, connecting through the pass of Beth-horon with the main highways of the coast. Michmash was therefore the key to central Canaan. The Wady es-Suweinit is broad and shallow in its upper course below the village of Michmash, but to the southeast of the town there is a terraced crag or plateau overhanging the valley, which here has steep cliffs on both sides[85]. This point was probably the scene of Jonathan's brave exploit. Accompanied only by his armor-bearer, he descended the cliff in front of Geba, crossed the deep valley, and climbed up the almost sheer cliff on the other side. The temerity of his act at first only aroused the curiosity and scorn of the Philistines, so that they allowed him to scale the heights unmolested. Their scorn was turned to terror when, like a divine warrior, he attacked and slew twenty of their number. The biblical narrative implies that an earthquake added to the panic, which quickly spread to the ranks of the plundering Philistines.

The Great Victory Over the Philistines. Saul and his warriors on the heights to the south looked across the ravine and saw the tumult among the Philistines.

With his characteristic impetuosity the king, without even waiting to consult the divine oracle, rushed in pursuit of the Philistines and was soon joined by the Hebrews who had fled for refuge to the rocky hills and valleys of Ephraim. The territory was well adapted to the fierce guerilla warfare in which the Hebrews were skilled, and the Philistines, accustomed to manœuvring upon the open plain, were caught at a disadvantage. The pursuit swept down through the valleys to the west, through the pass of Beth-horon, and thence southward to Ajalon, which was the chief western gateway of the hill country.

Saul's Wars. The victory was so complete that for several years the Philistines appear to have left Saul undisturbed. This opportunity he improved to develop his army and to organize his kingdom, which probably did not extend far beyond the Plain of Esdraelon to the north. His capital, Gibeah, was really a military camp, for he was exposed to constant attack on every side. In the south he made a campaign against the Bedouin Amalekites. From the southeast came the attacks of the Edomites, and from the east the Ammonites were seeking to push their bounds farther westward. In this stern school, under the leadership of a bold, warlike king, the Israelites learned not only to fight bravely, but unitedly and therefore effectively.

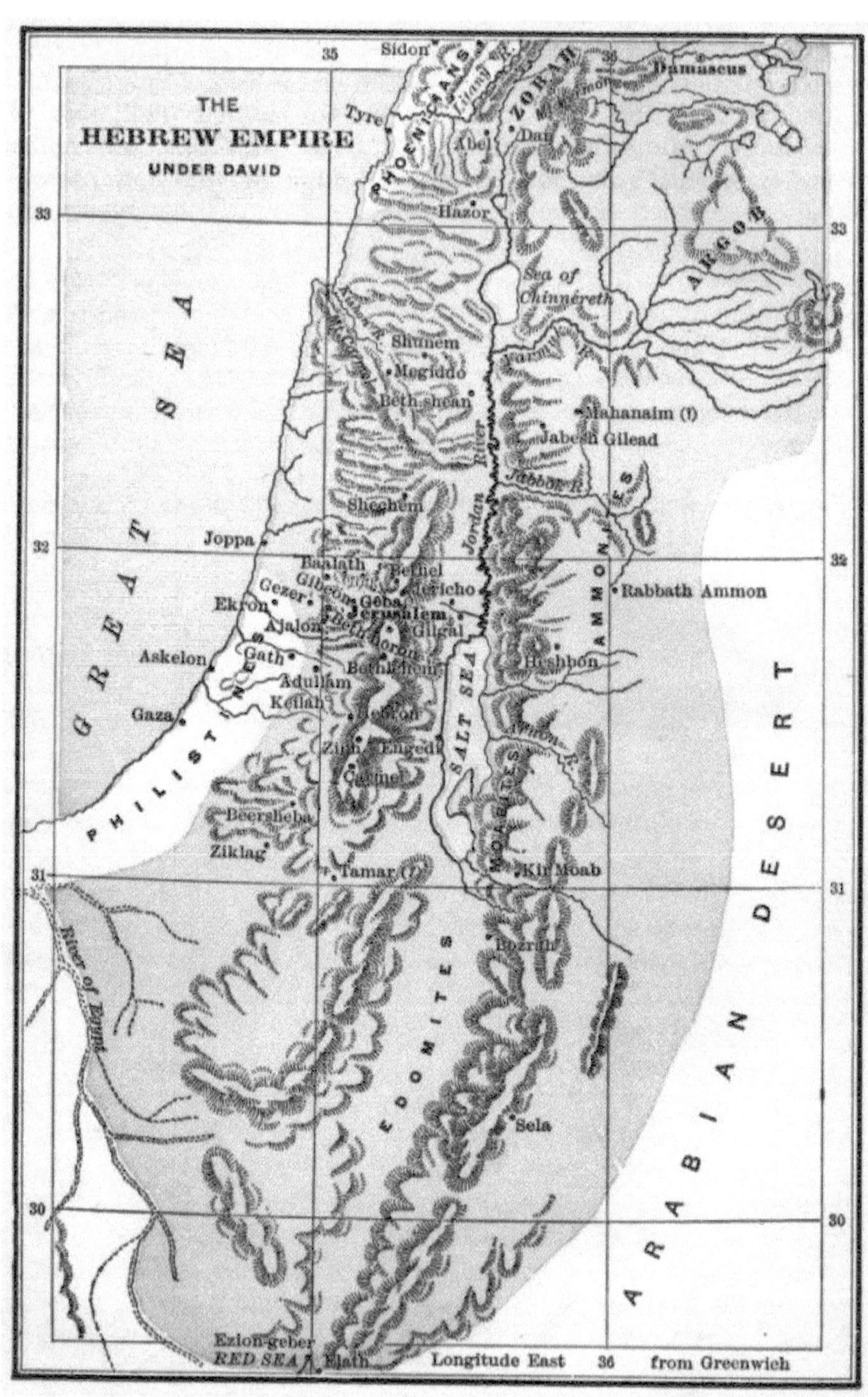

The Hebrew Empire Under David

XVI

THE SCENES OF DAVID'S EXPLOITS

David's Home at Bethlehem.—The Contest in the Valley of Elah.—Situation of Nob.—The Stronghold of Adullam.—Keilah.—Scenes of David's Outlaw Life In Southeastern Judah.—David at Gath.—At Ziklag.—Reasons Why the Philistines Invaded Israel in the North.—Saul's Journey to Endor.—The Battle on Gilboa.—The Remnant of Saul's Kingdom.—Hebron, David's First Capital.—Fortunes of the Two Hebrew Kingdoms.—The Final Struggle with the Philistines.—David's Victories.

David's Home at Bethlehem. The history of the united Hebrew empire gathers about the personality of its founder, David. The life of no other Old Testament character is recorded with greater detail and picturesqueness than that of the shepherd boy from Bethlehem. His native town was beautifully situated on a spur that ran eastward from the watershed of central Judah.[86] It is surrounded on three sides by deep valleys and looks eastward down upon the wilderness of Judea. About it are fields of wheat and barley and on the hillsides are vineyards and groves of olive and almond trees, for it is one of the two most fertile spots in the entire territory of Judah.[23] There are no springs in the village itself, the nearest being about eight hundred yards to the southeast. The inhabitants are dependent upon rock-cut wells or cisterns, of which there are many, or upon the water conducted by an aqueduct from the Pools of Solomon to the southwest. The territory about Bethlehem is pre-eminently the land of the shepherd.[87] The traveller to-day sees almost no cattle or large animals. Their absence is probably due to the limited supply of water and to the frequent outcrops of gray limestone, which make travelling dangerous for cattle and horses. The landscape is dotted with flocks of sheep and goats. The rocky pastures run up to the outskirts of Bethlehem, which appears to have been in ancient times simply a shepherd's village.

The Contest in the Valley of Elah. Bethlehem lies only ten miles south in a straight line from Saul's capital at Gibeah. Hence the journey of the messenger who summoned David to the service of his king was not long. The event which brought the youthful shepherd to the attention of the nation took place in the Valley of Elah,[88] but twelve miles in a straight line west of Bethlehem. Its geographical setting throws much light upon this dramatic event in Israel's early history. The Philistine army was drawn up between Socoh and Azekah in Ephes-dammim, the Valley of Dark-red Lands, doubtless so named from the patches of dark-red ploughed land which in the spring still impart a rich glow to the landscape. Socoh was on the south side of the Valley of Elah and Azekah was across the wady to the northwest. The Philistine position was, therefore, on the southwestern side of the valley, which is here about one-quarter of a mile wide and well adapted to the manœuvring of their chariots. The Hebrew position was evidently across the valley on the steep bluff to the northeast, with its left flank at the entrance of the wady and highway which led to Bethlehem and Gibeah. Through the middle of the fertile valley the mountain torrent has cut a deep ravine, with steep banks on either side and a bed strewn with white stones. The strength of the strategic position occupied by each of the two armies and the danger involved in advancing through the deep ravine, clearly explain their delay in making an attack. The situation also reveals the courage of the youth who dared cross the deep ravine and advance single-handed across the plain against the Philistine champion. It is not strange that the moment David slew Goliath, the Bethlehem shepherd became the idol of the people. It was equally natural that the impulsive Saul should feel a growing jealousy toward the one who seemed to have stolen from him the heart of the people.

Situation of Nob. Nob, where David deposited with the priest the sword of Goliath, thereby consecrating it to Jehovah, was situated somewhere on the heights a short distance north of Jerusalem. Beside the main road, which runs northward, about midway between Jerusalem and Gibeah, is a level plateau, now known as Ras el-Masherif.[89] It is about eight hundred yards from east to west and about three hundred from north to south, and is probably to be identified not only with the Hebrew Nob, but also with the Scopus of Josephus. It commands a clear view of Jerusalem. On one side are ancient rock tombs and cisterns, indicating the presence in earlier times of a small village. While the identification is not certain, the ancient Nob was undoubtedly situated not far from this point. Here David stopped as he fled southward to escape Saul's murderous jealousy. It was here that he committed one of the great sins of his life, in deceiving the priests of Nob, thereby sacrificing them to Saul's fury. From Nob David evidently turned to the southwest to find refuge among the Canaanite cities in the lowland between Judah and Philistia.

The Stronghold of Adullam. Adullam, the stronghold to which he escaped, is without much doubt to be identified with Id-el-ma, in the valley of the Wady es-Sur, two or three miles south of the scene of his victory over Goliath. It is a steep hill, standing out in the valley, with a well at the foot and caves of moderate size near the top. It commands the two roads which lead up from Beit-Jibrin, in the west, and Hebron, to the southeast. From this point it was also possible to watch the paths that came down from the north and the northeast. At the same time it was on the border of the Philistine land, which offered an open asylum to all refugees from the court of Saul. From Adullam a rough, rocky trail, the difficulties of which were no barrier to the clansmen and outlaws who gathered about David, led to Bethlehem, twelve miles away.

Keilah. Between three and four miles south of Adullam, in the Wady es-Sur, lay the important Judean town of Keilah. It is mentioned several times in the Tell el-Amarna letters and was evidently at this time the most important southwestern outpost of Judah. Its terraced slopes are still covered with grain, even as in David's time. These same fields supplied the grain for the threshing-floors which the Philistine marauders came to rob. By delivering Keilah, David was able to proclaim in clearest terms his loyalty to his kinsmen and to win the devotion of the southern clans.

Scenes of David's Outlaw Life in Southeastern Judah. In a walled city David was in great danger of being captured by Saul. He therefore fled to the borders of southern Judah. Here pursuit was more difficult and escape into the rocky wilderness, which extended eastward to the Dead Sea, was easy. David kept close, however, to the settled territory. To the south of Hebron lay the second most fertile spot in all Judah. It was a level plateau, about nine miles long and three wide, covered with fertile though rocky fields and studded with prosperous villages. The town of Ziph, which evidently gave its name to the wilderness to the east where David took refuge, is in the heart of this plateau. The name of the hill, Hachilah, where, according to the oldest tradition, David spared the life of the sleeping Saul, is perhaps still echoed in the name Dhahret el-Kolah, which is given to the range of hills which runs far out into the wilderness east of Ziph.[90] South of Ziph are the towns of Carmel and Maon. They are encircled by fruitful fields and pasture lands. On the borders of these the Bedouin still encamp and exact their toll of the villagers, even as David demanded a gift from Nabal in return for the protection given to his flocks.[26] David's marriage with Abigail, which followed the death of Nabal, strengthened the loyalty of the southern tribes and gave him wealth and a settled place of abode; but, as at Keilah, it exposed him to great danger of capture by Saul.

David at Gath. The necessity of providing occupation for the restless warriors who followed him was probably another reason why David at last sought refuge among Saul's foes, the Philistines. Gath, which is probably to be identified with Tell el-Safi, commanded the point where the Valley of Elah opens into the Philistine Plain. It was the Philistine city nearest to the scene of David's first great victory, as well as to Adullam, whither he had first fled. Throughout the reigns of David and Solomon, Gath figures as the gateway to the land of the Philistines. Its king, or tyrant, received David readily and showed him the hospitality that is eagerly accorded in the East to a fugitive from the court of a rival king. David's rare personal charm also won this Philistine chieftain, even as it did all with whom he came in contact. The region about Gath, however, was thickly settled and presented no field of activity for David's followers. Hence he was assigned a frontier town and thereby made the guardian of the Philistine border.

At Ziklag. The identification of Ziklag is uncertain. That which would place it at Zuheilika, nineteen miles southwest from Beit-Jibrin and eleven southeast from Gaza, is on the whole the most probable. The ruin lies on three low hills, and it appears to have been a characteristic border town. From this town David, with his warriors, was able not only to repel all Bedouin attacks, but also to make forays upon the desert tribes that wandered in the wilderness far to the south. It gave Israel's future king and his followers experience in hard, dangerous warfare and yet allowed him, without arousing the suspicions of the Philistines, to show his loyalty to his race and especially to the Hebrew tribes of the south who were most exposed to these Bedouin robbers.

Reasons Why the Philistines Invaded Israel in the North. The presence of David in their midst, as well as their knowledge of the growing weakness of Saul's rule, impelled the Philistines to gather their united forces in another attempt to crush the Hebrew kingdom. This time they wisely avoided the narrow and easily defended passes that led into the heart of southern Israel. Instead, they followed the coast road up across the Plain of Sharon and then cut across possibly past Megiddo to the eastern side of the Plain of Esdraelon. This method of approach enabled the Philistines to advance over broad plains, where opposition was not easy and where their chariots could pass without difficulty. In this way they separated the Hebrews of the north from those of the south at the point where the connection between the different parts of the land of Israel was naturally weakest. Doubtless their aim was also to keep open to commerce the great highway that led from Philistia across the Plain of Esdraelon to Damascus and Babylonia. They apparently took up their position near Shunem, at the foot of Little Hermon, on the northern side of the Valley of Jezreel,[10] while the Hebrew army occupied a strong position on the northern end of the sloping heights of Mount Gilboa.

Saul's Journey to Endor. Saul's night journey to consult the medium of Endor took him across the Plain of Jezreel and up through the wide valley which leads east of Shunem and Little Hermon to the south of Mount Tabor. The small village of Endor lay on the northern slopes of Little Hermon, facing Mount Tabor across the valley.[9] To-day the crest of the hill is pierced by deep caves, in which the squalid natives reside.[91] These caves with their dark passages were well-adapted to the occult arts which still survived, even though Saul himself had earlier tried to banish them from his kingdom.

The Battle on Gilboa. Saul's courage was well illustrated in the final battle on Gilboa. His position was evidently chosen because the northern end of Gilboa commanded the valley of Esdraelon as well as that of Jezreel.[11] To gain control of the highways which led across these valleys, the Philistines were therefore compelled to dislodge the Hebrew army and in so doing to fight against great odds. To make the attack directly on the north from the direction of Shunem was practically impossible, for at this point the Brook Jalud is so deep that it is impassable for an army. The rocky hills of Gilboa also rise very abruptly.[10] The probabilities are that in making the attack the Philistines marched down the eastern side of the Plain of Esdraelon and then advanced toward the heights of Gilboa from the southwest by the sloping terraces that lead gradually to the top. Here they could also utilize their chariots and preserve their battle array. By this formidable army the scattered and disheartened forces that rallied about Saul were quickly defeated. The disaster was overwhelming; the valiant king and his sons fought desperately, with no thought of retreat. Thus fell on the heights of Gilboa the man who laid the foundations of the Hebrew empire, leaving the Philistines in possession of Northern Israel. The half-Canaanite town of Bethshean[12] on the Plain of Jezreel appears to have surrendered at once to the Philistines, for the body of Saul was hung in derision on its walls soon after the battle. From the heights of Gilead in a midnight march across the Jordan came the men of Jabesh-Gilead to capture the body of the fallen king and to bury it within their own territory, that they might thus repay the large debt which they owed to their deliverer.

The Remnant of Saul's Kingdom. Throughout this earlier period the east-Jordan tribes were especially loyal to the house of Saul, probably because of his early act of deliverance as well as his later wars against their foes in the east. It was natural, therefore, that the capital of the remnant of his kingdom should be established at Mahanaim in Gilead. The exact site of this important city of the east-Jordan has not yet been determined. Probably it was at the ruins of Mahneh, north of the present city of Ajlun. Others would identify it with the important later city of Gerasa, the modern Jerash, on a brook which runs north from the Jabbok. A few biblical references suggest, however, that it was nearer the Jordan, but among the highlands to the north of the Jabbok. In any case it was not far from the modern Mahneh. Here Saul's son, Ishbaal, who succeeded him, was out of the direct line of Philistine attack and beyond the reach of the southern Israelite tribes, that had asserted their independence immediately after the battle of Gilboa.

Hebron, David's First Capital. David, their beloved champion, was naturally the choice of these southern tribes. The way in which he disposed of the spoils captured from the Amalekites indicates that beyond doubt, even before the fall of Saul, he was bidding for their loyalty. Accordingly he was made king at Hebron, then the chief city of Judah and the South Country. The ancient city lay on the hill to the northwest of the present town.[76] Its importance depended not upon its military strength, but upon its central position and the presence of perennial springs. Two of the ancient pools are still in use. The one in the northern part of the town is eighty-five feet long and fifty-five feet wide. The other, lower down the valley, is still larger, being one hundred and thirty feet square and twenty-eight feet deep. It is by this largest pool[92] that tradition pictures the hanging of the murderers of Saul's son, Ishbaal. About a mile north of the town, a little west of the old highway, is a spring and pool, called to-day the 'Ain Sarah, which is to be identified without much doubt with the Well of Sirah, where Joab treacherously slew his rival, Abner. Through Hebron runs the great highway from central Canaan to Egypt. From here many less important roads radiate (*cf.* p. 51), making it the great centre and trading place between Palestine, the desert, and the countries beyond. About the city are rocky, fertile fields, and olive and vineyard clad hills. It was, therefore, well chosen as the capital of the small kingdom of which David was here made king.

Fortunes of the Two Hebrew Kingdoms. David's authority evidently extended to a point about five miles north of Jerusalem. The city of Gibeon[93] was on its northern border. This important town was situated on a height two thousand five hundred and thirty-five feet above the ocean, a little west of the main northern highway and on the southern side of the two main roads that led up from the Valley of Ajalon across the central plateau to the Jordan. Part way down the regularly rounded hill on which the village stood was a spring, forming a large pool. Here, in this border town, the warriors of Joab, David's general and those of Abner fought the fatal duel which was characteristic of the border warfare of this period. The Bithron, the ravine through which Abner and his men retired to Mahanaim, was probably the Wady Ajlun east of the Jordan. The result of the battle was indicative of the waning power of the house of Saul and of the growing strength of David. It is also probable that during this period he was still a vassal of the Philistines and so enjoyed immunity from their attacks. He was thus able to develop and organize the resources of his kingdom. On the other hand, the divided northern kingdom was constantly exposed to attack from the warlike Philistines on the west and from the Ammonites on the east.

The Final Struggle with the Philistines. The assassination of Ishbaal by his own followers left the northern tribes no deliverer but David. All his previous training had prepared him for this great task. His acceptance of the fealty of the northern tribes was equivalent to a declaration of war against the Philistines. Regarding this important period, the biblical records are unfortunately incomplete; but from incidental references it is clear that the Philistines did not yield their claim to central Palestine without a severe and prolonged struggle. At one time they were in possession of David's own city, Bethlehem, and he was obliged again to take refuge in the border fortress of Adullam. As at the beginning of the war, they appear to have seized the series of strong fortresses on the northern border of Judah and thus to have cut off the Hebrews of the north from those of the south. The Canaanite cities from Gezer to Jebus, which doubtless acknowledged the Philistine suzerainty, completed the wall of separation.

David's Victories. Strong in the possession of these central cities, the Philistines evidently invaded Judah directly through its two main western portals, the valleys of Sorek and of Elah. David was thus forced to depend for support chiefly upon the tribes of Judah and of the South Country. The territory in which this guerilla warfare was fought, and David's experience and skill, gave him in the end a great advantage. The Philistines were obliged to retire each year to plant and to reap their fields, and in so doing necessarily lost many of the advantages which they had gained. Repeated battles were fought and each time David gained in strength. The two decisive battles were waged in the Valley of Rephaim,[94] a broad, shallow valley to the southwest of Jerusalem, from which connecting valleys ran down to Bethlehem and the south, while the main valley runs westward into the great Valley of Sorek. On this plain, with its broad, cultivated fields, the Philistines were able to mass their forces and at the same time to maintain on the west their connection with the home land. Here also David was able to rally his followers from the south and in case of defeat to have a way of escape into the neighboring wilderness of Judah. On this battle-field the final decisive engagement in Israel's war of independence was fought, and the Hebrews won a sweeping victory. As the biblical narrative states, the Philistines were compelled to abandon their northern garrisons "from Gibeon as far as Gezer." David at last was free to develop and organize that larger kingdom which was destined soon to grow into a small empire.

XVII

PALESTINE UNDER THE RULE
OF DAVID AND SOLOMON

Establishment of Jerusalem as Israel's Capital.—Israel's Natural
Boundaries.—Campaigns Against the Moabites and Ammo-
nites.—Situation of Rabbath-Ammon.—The Water City.—Extent
of David's Empire.—Absalom's Rebellion.—David East of the
Jordan.—Rebellion of the Northern Tribes.—Scenes of Adonijah's
Conspiracy and Solomon's Accession.—Capture of Gezer.—Sol-
omon's Fortresses.—Solomon's Strategic and Commercial Pol-
icy.—Site of Solomon's Temple.—Significance of the Reigns of
David and Solomon.—Influences of the United Kingdom Upon
Israel's Faith.—Solomon's Fatal Mistakes.—Forces that Made for
Disunion.—Situation of Shechem.—Significance of the Division.

Establishment of Jerusalem as Israel's Capital. David's first act as king of
all Israel was to break down the barrier of Canaanite cities which separated the
north from the south, and then to establish a capital that would be free from local
associations and more central than his former capital at Hebron. The Jebusite city
of Jerusalem fully satisfied these conditions and was at the same time by nature
much stronger and better fortified than Hebron. The original city of David apparently included the old Jebusite city on the hill of Ophel[55] with certain additions,
known as Millo, probably running down into one of the adjacent valleys.[95] Possibly, during the reigns of David and Solomon, the dwelling-places of the Hebrews
began to climb across the Tyropœon Valley (*cf.* p. 42) and up the western hill, but
there is no evidence that at this early date the western town was surrounded by a
wall and thus incorporated in the City of David.

Israel's Natural Boundaries. With the establishment of the new capital at Jerusalem and the transference thither of the ark from Kirjath-jearim, the various
Hebrew tribes were brought into a close political and religious union. The prestige
and tactful, conciliatory policy of David were important factors in bringing about
this union. The process was also hastened by the pressure of outside foes and by
the aggressive policy toward them which David at once initiated. On the west
and north the territory of Israel had reached its natural bounds. Never again did
the Philistines make a determined endeavor to override the barrier of the western
hills and conquer the land of the Hebrews. The Phœnicians were, by virtue of their
position, a commercial people with no ambitions for military conquest. On the east

and south, however, Israel's natural bounds were the desert. As long as there were strong nations like the Ammonites and Moabites on the east, separated from the Hebrews only by artificial bounds, there was no guarantee of permanent peace. The past history of Palestine had fully demonstrated this truth and David was not slow in acting in accordance with it.

Campaigns Against the Moabites and Ammonites. The Moabites, who, during the period of settlement, had pushed forward to the fords of the Jordan, were apparently the first to be attacked and to become subject to David. The Ammonites, recognizing the significance of the new west-Jordan power, assumed the initiative and insulted David's messengers. To aid them in the conflict they called in certain of the Aramean princes in the north. After the downfall of the old Hittite kingdom these Aramean peoples had pressed in from the northeast and taken possession of the greater part of central and eastern Syria. The desert highway that ran through the Ammonite capital led northward through these Aramean states and thus established a close commercial and political bond between the two peoples. The Arameans, living on the plains and in close touch with the most advanced civilization of the Semitic world, were possessed of chariots and all the equipment of ancient warfare. In these allied forces, therefore, the armies of David met no mean foes; but in the school of constant and strenuous warfare he had developed a strong fighting force, and in Joab he possessed one of the best generals of the age.

Situation of Rabbath-Ammon. The decisive battles of this campaign were fought near or in Rabbath-Ammon. The city was surrounded by rolling plains, especially on the west, which offered ample opportunity for the manœuvring of armies. The strength of the city itself consisted in its huge acropolis, surrounded, like Jerusalem, by deep valleys. On the north it was connected with the surrounding hills by a low, narrow neck of rock. At this point were built great protecting walls and towers. The hill itself consisted of three terraces rising from east to west, with a main gateway on the south side. Each of the succeeding terraces was defended by a wall. The highest area, which included several acres, rose nearly three hundred feet above the surrounding valleys, and it was, therefore, the largest and in many ways the strongest natural fortress in all Palestine.

The Water City. The Water City,[96] which was first captured by Joab, was probably in the valley of the Jabbok, which runs along the southern side of the acropolis. This valley, and that which comes in from the north along the western side of the acropolis, is the site of the modern city of Amman. The great Roman city was also built for the most part in the Valley of the Jabbok, or, as it is now called, the Wady Amman. Here the waters of the brook, which were carried by aqueducts along different levels and which were supplemented by gushing springs, fully justify the name of Water City. Situated in the valley, it was most exposed to the attack of the Hebrews. When it was captured, the supply of water and food would be cut off from the citadel above, so that, as indicated by the biblical narrative, the fall of the entire city would be the inevitable result of a long siege.

Extent of David's Empire. The conquest of the Ammonites and the Moabites and the defeat of the Arameans enabled David to extend the bounds of his empire to the desert. In the northeast it probably never extended beyond Mount Hermon, which was its natural boundary in that direction. In the south he fought a decisive battle with the Edomites in the Valley of Salt, which was probably at the southwestern end of the Dead Sea near the border line between southern Judah and Edom. This Arab race, in its difficult mountain fastnesses, was held in control by means of Hebrew garrisons established throughout the land. By this means David's southern boundary was extended to the eastern arm of the Red Sea and the Sinaitic Peninsula, thus attaining in every direction its natural barriers. In less than one generation, as a result of the energy, tact, and broad statesmanship of David, the physical limitations of Palestine were overcome and a strong empire was established along the southeastern Mediterranean.

Absalom's Rebellion. As later events quickly proved, however, the unity of the Hebrew Empire was chiefly dependent upon the personal charm and ability of the man who built it up. The discordant elements were still present and only required an opportunity to break forth into a flame of civil war. Absalom, inspired by a treasonable ambition, succeeded in winning away the affections of the southern tribes and in stirring up the rivalry between the north and the south. This rivalry was traceable not only to racial differences, but to the fundamental variations between the physical environment and contour of Northern and Southern Israel. It was natural that Absalom's rebellion should be launched in Hebron, the old capital of David's kingdom. In fleeing from the rebels David aimed to put between himself and them that great natural barrier, the Jordan valley, which separates Palestine into its two great divisions. Among the hills and deep wadies of the land of Gilead he felt most secure. Here he was in the midst of a prosperous people, intensely loyal to a ruler whose wars and victories had at last given them immunity from the attack of their strong foes. This part of Palestine was least swayed by the passions of the hour and most loyal to its deliverer. Here also David could rally his followers, without identifying himself with the tribes of the north, as opposed to those of the south.

David East of the Jordan. In fleeing from Jerusalem, David did not follow the line of the modern carriage-road down to the Jordan, but went farther north, over the Mount of Olives, avoiding the barren wilderness of Judea, which lay immediately to the east. According to the Targums, Bahurim, the home of the Benjamite Shimei, is to be identified with Almon, the present Almit, one mile beyond Anathoth. By continuing a little farther north it was possible to reach the direct highway from Michmash to the Jordan by way of Jericho. David probably crossed the Jordan at the upper of the two southern fords. From this point many roads led northeastward into Gilead (*cf.* p. 54). At Ishbaal's capital, Mahanaim, somewhere north of the Jabbok, he made his head-quarters. The forest of Ephraim was doubtless either immediately north or south of the Jabbok, not far from the Jordan, among the wild hills and deep ravines still clad with great groves of oaks,[97] whose spreading branches often reach down to only a few feet from the ground. The traveller through that region to-day has little difficulty in picking out in imagination the great oak whose extended branches he can picture catching and holding the head of the fleeing Absalom.

Rebellion of the Northern Tribes. The wild and sudden rebellion which sprang up among the northern tribes because David in his hour of triumph had shown favor to the tribes of the south spread far up the Jordan valley. Its leader was a certain Sheba, of the hill country of Ephraim. The rebellion was quickly put down in central Israel, but the rebels took their final stand far in the north, in the city of Abel-beth-maacah, at the northwestern end of the Jordan valley. It is to-day an imposing mound, standing out in the midst of the valley, overlooking miles of verdant meadow land, with a lofty and easily defended acropolis. Ruins on the southeast are indicative of its strength and importance. Through the intercession of a brave woman, the people of the city turned over the rebel to Joab, and thus the rebellion was put down. The contrast, however, between the level, unbroken fields about Abel-beth-maacah and the gray limestone hills that encircled Hebron is significant of the wide breach between the north and the south, which the tact of a David could only temporarily heal.

Scene of Adonijah's Conspiracy and Solomon's Accession. The closing scene in the tragedy of David's family life was in Jerusalem. Overwhelmed by the crimes of his sons and the burden of his own great sin, the king in his later days retired more and more from public life. The question of who should succeed him was still open. The conspiracy of his oldest son, Adonijah, by which this ambitious prince sought to make his succession sure, culminated in a great feast "by the Serpent's Stone, which is beside En-rogel or the Fuller's Spring." By many the Fuller's Spring is identified with the Virgin's Fount in the Kidron valley[54] southeast of Jerusalem. But this identification is impossible, for it was at Gihon, which is clearly the ancient name of the Virgin's Fount, that Solomon a little later was proclaimed king at the command of David. Thus in II Chronicles 32:30 it is stated that "Hezekiah stopped the upper spring of the waters of Gihon and brought them straight down on the west side of the city of David," that is, to the present Pool of Siloam on the western side of Ophel (*cf.* also II Chron. 33:14). This accords perfectly with the statement in I Kings, that when Solomon was proclaimed king at Gihon, he and his followers went up again to the city which lay on the heights. The scene of Adonijah's feast,[98] therefore, must have been below the royal gardens to the south of the city where the Valley of Hinnom joins the Kidron. It was also probably a little north of the Well of Job, which is apparently here called the Fuller's Spring (*cf.* Josh. 15:7). Either it received water from the Virgin's Fount, or else from a more direct source, so that it was called a spring. In the days of Isaiah the open space about was known as the Fuller's Field, which according to Isaiah 7:3, was near the end of the conduit of the upper pool, by the highway which probably ran past the southeastern end of the city. From this point it was not difficult to hear the sound of the trumpets at the Gihon Spring, higher up but obscured by a ridge of Ophel.

Capture of Gezer. The policy of David's successor, Solomon, was one of organization rather than of expansion. Through alliances, sealed in the usual oriental fashion by marriages, he sought to insure the peace of his empire. His alliance with Egypt brought for a brief moment an Egyptian army to the border of Palestine. The aim of this expedition was to aid Solomon in capturing Gezer, the last stronghold left in the hands of the Canaanites. This important strategic point Solomon further fortified, making it one of the seven great fortresses upon which he depended for the defence of his land.

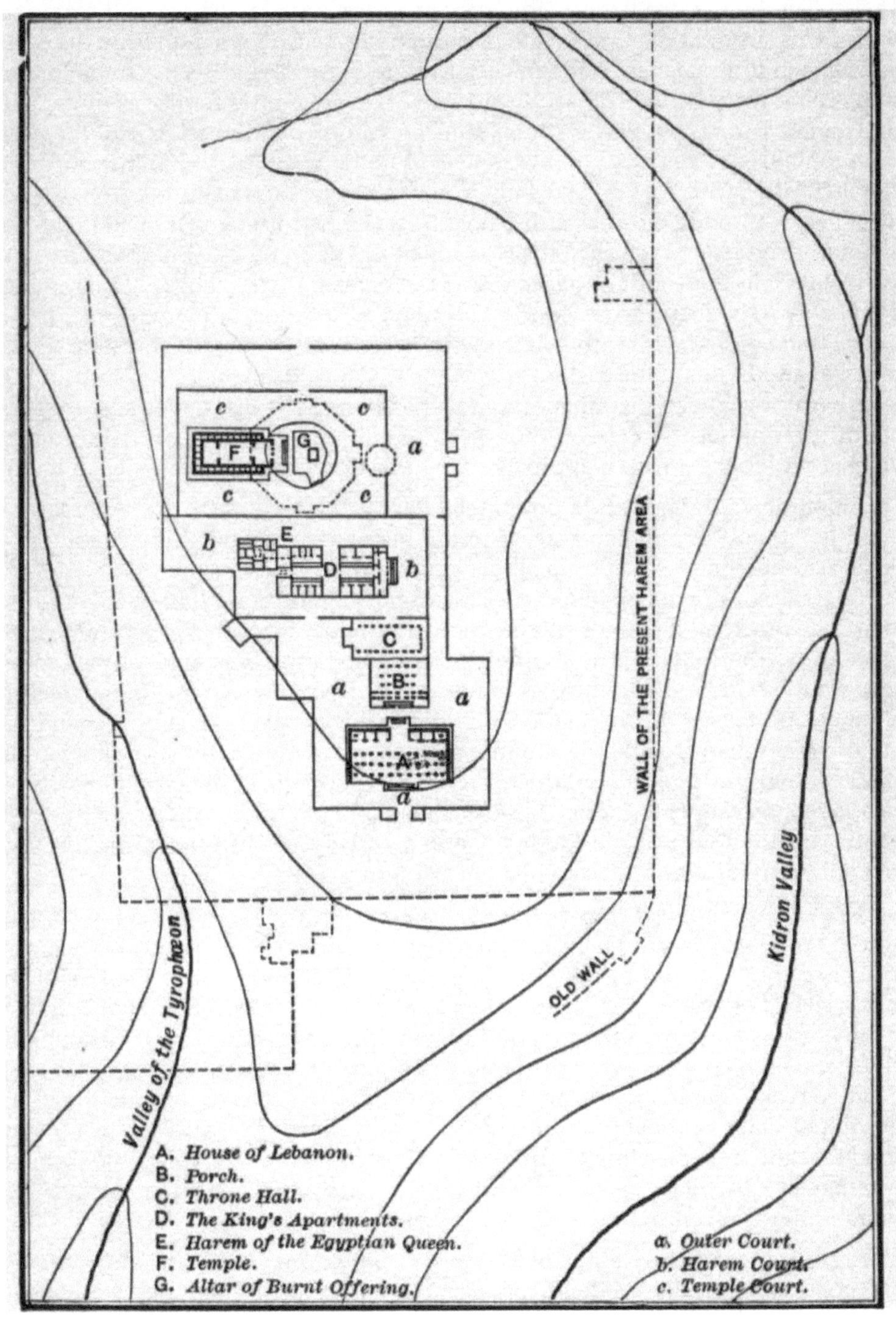

Plan of Solomon's Palace (According to Stade)

Solomon's Fortresses. Solomon also fortified Lower Beth-horon, which was situated on the flat, fertile hill which commanded a wide view over the western plains. This stronghold guarded the important highway that led up from the coast, past Gibeon to Jerusalem, with an eastern branch running directly to the Jordan. In the same way the old Canaanite city of Megiddo, on the southwestern side of the Plain of Esdraelon, was fortified, thus enabling Solomon to control the great trade route from Damascus and Phœnicia to Philistia and Egypt. In the north the city of Hazor, a little east of Lake Huleh, on the road which ran north from the Sea of Galilee, was made the chief stronghold. It was a city often mentioned in the Tell el-Amarna letters, as well as in the story of an Egyptian traveller of the fourteenth century B.C. In the south, Jerusalem was the great military centre. Tamar, which is probably to be identified with the Thamara of Eusebius and Jerome, southwest of the Dead Sea, a day's journey from Hebron, guarded the road which ran to Ezi-on-geber and Elath on the eastern arm of the Red Sea. Baalath, the seventh stronghold, has not yet been identified. From its position in the list, it would seem to be one of the southern fortresses, though it may be identical with Kirjath-jearaim, which guarded the western approaches to Jerusalem through the Valley of Sorek.

Solomon's Strategic and Commercial Policy. It is significant that Solomon apparently did not deem it necessary to guard his eastern frontiers. The conquests of David had delivered Israel from all danger of attack from this quarter. Solomon's chief defences were massed on the west and north, indicating that the foes whom he feared were the Philistines and the more distant invaders that might come from Egypt or northern Syria. The southern fortress of Tamar was evidently intended to guard the trade route to the port of Ezion-geber, from which the united fleets of Solomon and Hiram of Tyre made their long journeys past the coast of Arabia and out into the Indian Ocean. The situation of the land of Ophir is not certain, but the character and names of the products brought back by the Phœnician and Hebrew traders point strongly to India. The so-called "Land of Ophir" was probably either Abhira at the mouth of the Indus, or else a seaport of eastern Arabia, through which the products of India reached the Western world.

Site of Solomon's Temple. The culminating act of Solomon's reign was the building of his palace and temple. His public buildings were reared on the northern continuation of the hill of Ophel, as it rises gradually above the site of the ancient Jebusite city.[99] The jagged limestone rock, rising still higher and farther to the north was without much doubt the ancient threshing-floor of Arunah, the Jebusite, on which was reared the famous temple of Solomon. The irregular mass of native rock, with its peculiar cuttings,[100] which now stands in the centre of the Mosque of Omar, probably represents the great altar for burnt offerings, which stood east and therefore immediately in front of the Hebrew temple. This shrine of Solomon took the place of the older royal high place at Gibeon, where still a rock-cut altar may be seen.[93]

Significance of the Reigns of David and Solomon. The reigns of David and Solomon gave Palestine what it had never had before and what it rarely had again in its troubled history—a period of comparative peace and prosperity, in which the rich resources of the land could be fully developed. The progress of the Hebrews during this glorious half-century was most marvellous. From a struggling, oppressed, disintegrated group of nomads they suddenly developed into a strong, opulent, and united kingdom, becoming masters not only of their own territory, but of that of their hereditary foes. The earlier Canaanite population of Palestine was also completely absorbed and its agricultural civilization assimilated by the conquerors.

Influence of the United Kingdom Upon Israel's Faith. The great and supremely vital contest that was waged during this period of prosperity was that between the worship of Jehovah, which the Hebrews brought with them from the desert, and the different Canaanite cults which they found strongly intrenched in the land. If the Hebrews had been defeated beside the Kishon, or if David had not overcome the Philistines in the Valley of Rephaim, it is doubtful whether or not the religion of Jehovah would have emerged victorious in this great contest. The topography of the land of Palestine strongly favored the development of many different sanctuaries, each devoted to the worship of some local god. It was only a strong race, under a powerful central government, that could overcome the influence of physical environment and hold to its faith in one God. The establishment of the united Hebrew kingdom early in their history was therefore a mighty factor in the development of Israel's faith in one supreme Divine King.

Solomon's Fatal Mistakes. Solomon's selfish ambition to imitate the splendor of the oriental courts about him blinded him completely to the best interests of his family and nation. The one important force that held together his people after the danger of foreign invasion had been averted was their loyalty to their Divine King. In tolerating and patronizing the gods of his allies under the very shadow of Jehovah's temple, though it was demanded by Semitic usage, he committed a fatal error, for he thereby weakened the unity of the Hebrew nation as well as his own hold on the people's loyalty. He also failed to appreciate the spirit and traditions which his subjects had inherited from their free life in the desert and from the days of tribal independence when they had been struggling for their homes in Palestine. The Hebrews, still in close contact with the life of the desert, were suspicious of all centralized authority. They were restive under a rule which imperiously commanded them to toil under royal task-masters and to bring to the king the best fruits of the soil. From their nomadic ancestors they had inherited a thoroughly democratic ideal of the kingship, in which the first duty of the king was to act as the leader of his subjects rather than to treat them as his slaves. Solomon's policy, therefore, threatened to take away the two most treasured possessions of the Hebrews—their democratic ideals and their loyalty to one God, ruling supreme over his people.

Forces That Made for Disunion. The men prominent in the history of the united kingdom had come from the southern tribes of Judah and Benjamin. Many of the northern tribes had for the first time been brought into real touch with the rest of their race in the days of David and Solomon. The large population and by far the greater resources were found in the north. Solomon devoted most of his building energy to developing the south; but it was inevitable that before long the superior strength of the north would assert itself. While the secluded and barren hills of Benjamin and Judah restricted their inhabitants to a relatively slow development, the broad valleys and the fruitful fields of Northern Israel, cut by great highways of commerce, offered to its people every opportunity to acquire wealth and culture. During the period of stress and struggle David was able with rare tact and organizing ability to bind together these diverse elements in the kingdom and to overcome the fundamental differences of physical environment; but even during his reign the wide breach between the north and the south was revealed. It is doubtful whether or not, in the new stage of Israel's development, even David could have overcome these wide differences. Unfortunately, Solomon's foolish policy only tended to emphasize them, and his son, Rehoboam, by his tyrannical reply to the reasonable demands of the northern tribes, made harmonious union forever impossible.

Situation of Shechem. The scene of the final breach between the north and south was the old Canaanite city of Shechem,[101] in the heart of the territory of Ephraim, the most powerful northern tribe. The town was one of the most beautifully situated cities in Palestine and at the same time the least easily defended. It lay in a valley between one-half to a mile in width, between the two highest mountains in Samaria—Ebal Ebal and Gerizim. The mountain slopes on either side were clothed with vineyards and olive groves. From Gerizim on the south twenty-two springs burst from the rock, irrigating the gardens of the ancient town, which, like the present city of Nablus, clung close to the southern mountain. Because of its peculiar position, the city was long and narrow, extending from east to west. The open valley at each end offered no natural defence and the overhanging heights rendered it especially open to hostile attack. Its importance was due to the rich territory which encircled it and to the important highways which connected it with Jerusalem and Hebron in the south, with central Israel, Damascus, and Phœnicia in the north, with the coast plains on the west, and with the Jordan valley on the east. At Shechem all these great roads focused, making the city throughout all its history an influential commercial metropolis.

Significance of the Division. The result of the fateful conference at Shechem was a division of the territory of Israel along the natural line marked out during the period of settlement and during the early Philistine wars. The boundary line followed the Wady Kelt up from the Jordan to the vicinity of Michmash and thence turned a little south of the Benjamite Ramah, running through Gibeon and westward to Gezer. To Northern Israel fell fully two-thirds of Palestine and at least three-fourths of its arable land. The division left Judah a complete geographical and political unit, and, thus dissevered from the more heterogeneous elements of the nation, free to develop its own life and faith. The division and the civil wars which followed inevitably weakened the strength of both kingdoms and prepared the way for that fate which overtook each in turn. In losing their strength and unity, they preserved, however, their two most distinctive and precious possessions—their democratic traditions and their undivided loyalty to Jehovah.

XVIII

THE NORTHERN KINGDOM

The Varied Elements in the North.—Capitals of Northern Israel.—The
Aramean Kingdom.—The Philistine Stronghold of Gibbethon.—
Omri's Strong Rule.—Ahab's Aramean Wars.—Strength and
Fatal Weakness of Ahab's Policy.—Elijah's Home.—The Scene
on Mount Carmel.—Ancient Jezreel.—Situation of Ramoth-Gilead.—Elisha's Home.—Jehu's Revolution.—Rule of the House of
Jehu.—The Advance of Assyria.—Amos's Home at Tekoa.—Influence of His Environment Upon the Prophet.—Evidence Regarding Hosea's Home.—View from Jebel Ôsha.—Conquest of Galilee
and Gilead.—The Exiled Northern Israelites.—The Fate of Northern Israel.

The Varied Elements in the North. The northern kingdom was rich in resources but lacked unity. Within its limited territory were found almost every kind
of climate, flora, and fauna. Its population was as varied as its physical contour.
In the east-Jordan land the shepherd and the Bedouin still held sway. Its valleys
in the west-Jordan were the home of the agriculturist. The cities on its western
borders and beside the great highways were already beginning to engage in commerce. Around the Sea of Galilee were thriving fishing villages. Every type of civilization, therefore, the nomadic, the agricultural, and the commercial, was to be
found within its bounds. In view of its mixed population, its varied interests, and
its exposed situation, the only force that could hold together Northern Israel was
a strongly centralized military régime. When a dynasty became weak, a stronger
man mounted the throne. Hence Northern Israel's history is a series of bloody
rebellions in which assassins, rising from the ranks of the army, seized the throne
and founded short-lived dynasties.

Israel and Judah After the Division of the Hebrew Empire

Capitals of Northern Israel. Jeroboam, who was called to the throne of Northern Israel after the division, came from the ranks of the common people. His home was in the small, as yet unidentified town of Zeredah in Mount Ephraim. At first he established his capital at Shechem, but this city was incapable of defence and so the centre of authority was transferred across the Jordan to Penuel near Succoth. The occasion of this transfer was probably the invasion of Palestine by Shishak, king of Egypt, who overran and plundered the west-Jordan territory. Later the capital was transferred again to the city of Tirzah, somewhere west of the Jordan. The identification of this city is uncertain. It may have been at the modern town of Telluza, situated on a hill one thousand nine hundred and forty feet above the level of the sea, immediately north of Mount Ebal. The town has many ancient cisterns but no spring. This identification would correspond to the statement of an early traveller (Borocardus) that Tirzah was on a height three leagues east of Samaria. The other more probable site is at Teiasir, about twelve miles northeast from Shechem, on the main highway that leads from this ancient capital through the Ophrah of Gideon to Bethshean and the upper Jordan valley (*cf.* p. 54). Teiasir is a central and commanding site, with extensive ruins to the north which indicate that it was once an important city. In II Kings 15:14 it is stated that "Menahem went up from Tirzah to Samaria," which applies excellently to Teiasir down near the Jordan but not to Telluza, which is one thousand feet higher and five hundred feet above Samaria. There is little doubt, therefore, that Teiasir represents the ancient northern capital.

The Aramean Kingdom. Northern Israel suffered from its exposed position. At first there was war between Judah and its northern rival, which resulted disastrously for the southern kingdom. To aid them in the conflict, the southern Israelites made the fatal mistake of calling in the Arameans to attack their foes on the north. By this time the Arameans had taken possession of northern Syria and established themselves at the ancient city of Damascus, which lay on a fertile oasis out in the desert, on the border line between Syria and northern Arabia.[42] By virtue of its central position it commanded the land trade of Egypt, Palestine, and Phœnicia on the west, and of Arabia, Mesopotamia, and Babylon on the east. It was "the harbor of the desert." The Aramean kingdom, with its capital at this favorable point, rapidly developed great wealth and military resources, and soon became a menace to the independence of both Hebrew kingdoms, for the natural line of expansion of this Aramean kingdom was toward the south. The exposed position of Damascus alone saved the Hebrews from complete subjugation.

The Philistine Stronghold of Gibbethon. From the southwest the Philistines, availing themselves of the weakness of the two Hebrew kingdoms, fortified Gibbethon. This border fortress was the scene of repeated sieges. It is probably to be identified with Kibbiah, which lies in the foot-hills, seven miles northeast of Lydda. Kibbiah is eight hundred and forty feet above the ocean level and in the heart of the debatable territory between hill and plain. The possession of Gibbethon by the Philistines was a constant menace to the cities of southern Ephraim, but its strength seems to have baffled the Israelite armies for several decades.

Omri's Strong Rule. It was while besieging this Philistine stronghold that

Omri, after the death of the adventurer, Zimri, was elected king by his soldiers. He proved to be in many ways the strongest king who ever sat on the throne of Northern Israel. The transference of his capital from Tirzah to the strong central city of Samaria[59] demonstrated his military skill and organizing ability. He also reconquered the territory of the Moabites as far as the Arnon, and, as is recorded on the Moabite stone, established strong garrisons throughout this territory.[46] He was not able, however, to repel the Aramean armies that at this time came marching down through the open highways from the north.

Ahab's Aramean Wars. Omri's son, Ahab, proved an even more able general than his father. In a series of engagements, in which he fought against great odds and against armies equipped far better than his own, he repelled the Arameans, who overran his territory. In the first engagement, which was fought near Samaria, the Hebrews, profiting by the blind overconfidence of the enemy, won through a sudden attack. The decisive battle was fought a year later near Aphek. This city is not the Aphek on the southeastern side of the Plain of Sharon, but is probably to be identified with the modern town of Fîk, beside the important highway which runs from the southern end of the Sea of Galilee northeastward toward Damascus. Ahab's courage was shown in thus going out to meet his foe on the northeastern border of his territory. The town lay on the top of the plateau at the end of a valley that looked down upon the Sea of Galilee on the west. The battle was probably fought on the level plain of the Jaulan, which ran east of the town, and resulted in the complete defeat of the Aramean army and the capture of its king.

Strength and Fatal Weakness of Ahab's Policy. Ahab was contented to make a favorable treaty with his fallen foe. The captured Israelite cities were restored and a trading quarter was set aside in Damascus for the Hebrew merchants. Ahab evidently sought in every way to develop the commercial resources of his kingdom. His marriage with Jezebel, the daughter of the Tyrian king, was intended to cement more closely the relations with this great commercial people on the west. Viewed from the point of view of world politics, Ahab's policy in maintaining the natural boundaries and in developing the commercial resources of his nation was sound. By his contemporaries he was doubtless regarded as a most successful king. His fatal mistake, however, was that of Solomon: in his pursuit of material splendor he disregarded the inherited beliefs and rights of his subjects. The official recognition of the Canaanite worship of his Phœnician queen was even more of a menace to the pure worship of Jehovah in Northern Israel in the days of Ahab than in Jerusalem in the days of Solomon. Northern Israel was pre-eminently Baal's land. Here the Canaanites had been most strongly intrenched and their religious traditions still pervaded the land. Communication with the Canaanites on the Mediterranean coast was exceedingly close and there was much in these ancient Baal cults to attract the prosperous, pleasure-loving, cosmopolitan people of Northern Israel. Ahab's policy did not contemplate a substitution of the worship of the Tyrian god, Baal Melkart, for that of Jehovah, but it did mean obscuring the fundamental characteristics and demands of Israel's God.

Elijah's Home. It was natural that the prophet who was able to analyze the situation and to point out its dangers, should come from the borderland of the desert where Moses had first impressed upon his people the unique character of Jehovah. Tishbe, the town from which Elijah came, will probably never be identified with absolute certainty, but it was somewhere in the land of Gilead. Modern tradition fixes it at Mar Elyas, a village a little north of the modern town of Ajlun in northern Gilead. Amidst this land of deep, rushing river-beds and steep, tree-clad hills, which gradually merge into the desert, was reared this stern champion of Jehovah and foe of the degenerate cults of agricultural Canaan. In one of these wadies, which cut down through the Gileadite hills toward the Jordan, Elijah found a refuge when the drought parched the fields west of the Jordan. His other home was Mount Carmel, whose fertile top and noble vistas resembled his native land across the Jordan.

The Scene on Mount Carmel. Excepting when he found refuge in the Phœnician city of Zarephath, which lay on a promontory about eight miles south of Sidon, and again at Horeb far in the south, Elijah performed his life work almost entirely in the narrow strip of land which lay between Gilead and Carmel. It was somewhere on the eastern end of Mount Carmel,[102] where it jutted out far into the Plain of Esdraelon, that he summoned king and people to the great conference which revealed to them the vital issue between the religion of Jehovah and that of Baal. Modern tradition identifies it with a site called El-Mahrakah, Place of the Burning. A spring a little below favors the conclusion that this was an ancient sanctuary. This retired spot, far away from the distractions of the city life below, was eminently fitted for the delivery of the prophet's brief but searching message. It looked along the western side of the plain to the old stronghold of Megiddo, the centre of the ancient Canaanite kingdoms. Due east lay the battle-field beside the Kishon where Jehovah fought for his people and demonstrated in a language that a child nation could understand, his superiority to the local baals. To the south were the fertile, undulating hills and valleys of Samaria, to the north those of lower and upper Galilee, while eastward across the plain were the hills where lay the prophet's home, and far away in the northeast rose the snowy height of Mount Hermon. It was a scene that spoke clearly and impressively of Jehovah's might and of his tender love and care for his people. When at last, after the great convocation was over, the lightning flashed and the thunder rolled across the plain, none could doubt that Jehovah was still in the midst of his people demanding their undivided loyalty.

Ancient Jezreel. Jezreel, Ahab's northern capital, is ordinarily identified with the present town of Zerin,[11] although the absence of ancient ruins at this point renders the identification exceedingly doubtful. The village lies on a broad elevation rising three hundred feet above the plain and is encircled by fertile fields which extend for miles in almost every direction. The statement in I Samuel 29:1 that "the Israelites encamped by the fountain in Jezreel" implies that the ancient site was either further east near the copious spring now known as 'Ain el-Meiyiteh, or else to the southeast under the northwestern end of Mount Gilboa beside 'Ain Jalûd which is probably the famous Spring of Harod of Judges 7:1. Jezreel was on the central highway from Northern to Southern Israel and guarded the entrance to the Valley of Jezreel. Under royal patronage this fertile land would quickly be transformed into a paradise of gardens and vineyards. Ancient Jezreel, however, was a paradise in which a man listened to the tempting voice of his wife to his undoing. In reaching out and taking with his ruthless hand the vineyard of Naboth, Ahab condemned his family to exile and death. The voice of the dauntless prophet of Gilead pronounced his doom. Near this same vineyard the dogs licked the blood of Ahab, as his body was borne back across the Plain of Jezreel from the scene of his last battle with the Arameans.

Situation of Ramoth-Gilead. Like many of the east-Jordan sites, the identification of the famous city of Ramoth-Gilead, which was the scene of so many battles between the Hebrews and their northern foes, is uncertain. By some it has been identified with Reimun, a few miles west of Jerash, on one of the northern branches of the Jabbok, but this is on no important highway and has neither water nor the ruins of an ancient city. Eusebius apparently identifies Ramoth in Gilead with Es-Salt, fifteen miles west of Rabbath-Ammon, but this is too far south to satisfy fully the biblical references and has no large plain near by where chariots could manœuvre. Possibly the modern Jerash, which lies on a northern confluent of the Jabbok, was the site of the famous stronghold.[44] The name Ramoth implies that it was on a broad height and its prominence as a frontier town in the Aramean wars indicates that it was in northern Gilead. It may have been situated on the site of the modern Remtheh in northeastern Gilead. The modern town is to-day occupied by a Turkish garrison and stands near the point where the main road from Bethshean and the upper Jordan valley joined the great pilgrim highway on the edge of the desert. This identification would be in accord with the statement in I Kings 4:13, that Solomon's prefect, who resided in Ramoth-Gilead, collected taxes not only from the Manassite towns of Jair in Gilead, but also in the region of Argob, which is in Bashan. The latter region probably lay to the north and east of the upper waters of the Yarmuk. The implication in Josephus's Antiquities VIII, 15:4, that Ramoth in Gilead was a three-days' march from the city of Samaria, also favors the conclusion that it was the extreme outpost of the east-Jordan land. The other possible and, on the whole, most probable site is that suggested by Principal Smith, of Aberdeen University. He identifies it with the present city of Gadara. This town lies one thousand one hundred and ninety-four feet above the sea-level, on a bold plateau which runs out from the hills of Gilead. This height, two miles wide and at least four miles in length from east to west, is bounded on the north by the deep valley of the Yarmuk, on the west by the Jordan, four and one-half miles away and over one thousand eight hundred feet below, and on the south by the Wady el-Arab, which cuts a deep gorge into the Gileadite hills. It is due south of Aphek, where was fought the great battle between the Hebrews and the Arameans under Ahab, and is on one of the chief highways which leads up from the Jordan through Arbela to join the pilgrim highway, to Damascus and Arabia. It is, therefore, the chief gateway and at the same time the natural fortress which guards northern Gilead. On the wide level plateaus about there is ample room for the manœuvring of chariots and an important road leads directly from it across the Jordan to Ahab's northern capital.

Elisha's Home. According to Jerome, Abel Meholah, the home of Elisha, was about nine miles south of Bethshean. The name, Meadow of the Dance, or of the Circle, implies that it was a low-lying valley. All these indications point to 'Ain Hel-weh, a ruined mound beside a gushing spring on the western side of the Jordan valley. It was surrounded by fertile fields. Throughout all his work Elisha, in contrast to Elijah, revealed his familiarity and close touch with the agricultural civilization of Northern Israel. The scenes of a greater part of his activity were the Jordan valley and the plains of Jezreel and Esdraelon, which lead into it from the west.

Jehu's Revolution. The culminating act of Elisha's work was to call Jehu to the kingship. The call came to him as he was directing the siege of Ramoth-Gilead. It is easy in imagination to follow his furious ride down the heights from Ramoth-Gilead across the Jordan and along its western side, past Bethshean and up the Valley of Jezreel to the northern capital of Ahab. On the open plain near the city of Jezreel he slew his master and thence rode into the city to complete the slaughter of the house of Ahab. By the sword he not only mounted the throne, but rooted out the Baalism against which Elijah and Elisha had both contended.

Rule of the House of Jehu. The history of Northern Israel for the next two generations is a record of humiliation and disaster. Jehu secured his position on the throne by paying a heavy tribute to the king of Assyria, whose armies were hovering on his northern borders. The active and ruthless Aramean king, Hazael, overran Northern Israel, destroying most of its warriors and extracting heavy tribute. In this hour of Israel's weakness the Philistines made forays into the south, carrying off Hebrews as slaves to foreign markets. It was not until Jehoash, the grandson of Jehu, came to the throne of Israel that the tide turned. Damascus, attacked in the rear by a northern Aramean people, was unable to cope with the Israelite armies. The east-Jordan territory was reconquered by Jehoash's son, Jeroboam II, and the Moabites again laid under tribute. For the first time in Israel's history a prophet arose in the land of Galilee. In the small town of Gath-Hepher, situated on a hill a little west of the highway which runs north from Nazareth, lived Jonah, the son of Amittai. He predicted that Jereboam's kingdom would extend, as it did later, from the southern end of the Dead Sea to the gateway between the Lebanons in the north, that marked the southern boundary of the strong northern Aramean kingdom of which the capital was Hamath. Again Northern Israel touched its widest bounds. Pride and self-confidence took possession of the nation. The military nobles who rallied about the king, enriched by the spoils of war, enslaved their fellow-countrymen whose fortunes had been depleted by the disastrous Aramean wars. Outwardly Northern Israel seemed strong and prosperous, but within were social wrongs which were eating the very vitals of the nation.

The Advance of Assyria. It was at this time that Assyria became the dominating factor in Northern Israel's history. This enterprising and ambitious nation was apparently an offshoot of the old Babylonian empire. It occupied the fertile plains east of the upper Tigris. As early as the eighteenth century B.C. it began to break away from the authority of Babylon. About 1100 B.C. Tiglath-pileser I laid the foundations of the Assyrian empire by campaigns in Babylonia, Elam, Mesopotamia, and Syria; but it was not until 854 B.C. that Assyria touched Israel. Then, according to the annals of the Assyrian king, Shalmanezer II defeated Ahab, together with the other princes of Syria, at the battle of Karkar. By 842 he had conquered practically all of Syria and received tribute from Jehu of Israel. During the reigns of the next two Assyrian kings the advance of this great world power was stayed. But when Tiglath-pileser IV founded a new dynasty he injected fresh energy into the empire, recovered its lost territory, and advanced to the conquest of Palestine.

Amos's Home at Tekoa. It was probably about the time when Tiglath-pileser IV began to institute his aggressive policy that Amos delivered his epoch-making sermon at the royal sanctuary in Bethel.[77] His home was at Tekoa, twelve miles south of Jerusalem, and but twenty-two from Bethel. Tekoa was the eastern outpost of Judah. Broad, rich fields lay on the north and west, but to the east it looked down upon the barren rounded hills that descended to the Dead Sea and toward the bold uplands of Moab in the distance. The town was situated on an elevated plateau which commanded a view of nearly all the places mentioned in the prophet's sermons: Kirioth in Moab, the region about Bethel and Gilgal, and the roads that led to Philistia, Egypt, and Edom. The dominant feature in the landscape was the Dead Sea, with its blue waters, its rising mists, and its gray, purple, and yellow cliffs. It was a grim, rugged, awe-inspiring outlook and clearly made a deep impression upon the thought and life of the prophet. Among the dry, rock-covered pasture lands, that run up to the eastern side of the town of Tekoa, the prophet received his training.[103] To-day, as in the past, it is the land of sheep and goats. The wildness of the region and the proximity to the desert demanded strong, stalwart shepherds, inured to hardship, keen to detect the presence of a foe, quick to repulse the attack of wild beast or lurking Arab robbers, and tender in their care of the young and the injured. Among these silent, treeless hills or beside the occasional spring, the traveller to-day meets this type of shepherd, silent and resourceful, armed with his short, heavy, wooden staff.

Influence of His Environment Upon the Prophet. Here Amos learned to champion the cause of the oppressed, to scent danger from afar, and faithfully to sound the alarm. His occupation doubtless took him to the annual festivals and market days at Jerusalem and Bethel, where his shepherd training asserted itself. He could not shut his eyes to the cruel oppression of the poor and dependent classes by the rich, greedy nobles. From afar he also noted the approach of the Assyrian lion. Being a faithful shepherd he could not remain silent. As he meditated on the situation in the quiet of his shepherd life among the hills about Tekoa, the conviction deepened into certainty that Jehovah in these varied ways was speaking to him, calling him to sound the note of alarm that the rulers of Israel might see the peril, right the wrongs, and thus save their nation. The influence of his shepherd's life and point of view is present in all his utterances. His message is a clear blast of desert air, sweeping through the corrupt atmosphere of the city, tainted as it was by that degenerate Canaanite civilization which still polluted the centres of Northern Israel's life.

Evidence Regarding Hosea's Home. A few years after Amos appeared at Bethel a prophet arose in Northern Israel itself, who reiterated the message of the shepherd from Tekoa in equally impressive terms. The superscription of Hosea's prophecy is unfortunately silent regarding his home. Local oriental tradition, however, has supplied this lack. One of the most commanding heights of southern Gilead bears the name of Jebel Ôsha, which is the Arabic for "Mountain of Hosea." Here, according to a tradition at least three hundred years old and perhaps based upon an older Jewish original, the prophet was buried. Here the Bedouin still sacrifice sheep in his honor. Possibly local tradition has preserved a fact unrecorded in the biblical narrative. It is indeed significant that Hosea alone of all the prophets makes frequent mention of the land of Gilead and reveals an intimate knowledge of its history. Thus, for example, he refers in 10:14 to the time when Shalmen, probably the Assyrian king Shalmanezer III, laid in ruins Beth-arbel in the day of battle. The city referred to is clearly one of the two east-Jordan towns bearing this name, and in all probability the Arbel east of Pella in the heart of northern Gilead. In 12:11 he declares: "In Gilead is iniquity, yea, they have wrought vanity." Again in 6:8, probably referring to the unidentified city east of the Jordan mentioned in Judges 10:17, he declares:

> Gilead is a city of evil-doers,
> Tracked with bloody footprints,
> And as bandits lay in wait for a man,
> So a band of priests murder on the way to Shechem,
> Verily they commit deliberate crime.

View From Jebel Ôsha. The bold heights of Jebel Ôsha commanded a view of most of the places mentioned in Hosea's prophecies. Across the valley lay the territory of the great tribe of Ephraim whose name is constantly used by him as a synonym for Northern Israel. A little to the northwest were the heights of Ebal and Gerizim, which guarded Shechem and the highway which led directly to the city of Samaria. From the same mountain height could be seen to the northwest the rounded top of Mount Tabor, which is the northernmost point mentioned by Hosea. Directly across the Jordan was the northern Gilgal, and a little to the southwest was the table-land of Bethel. Farther south was the height of Ramah. Hosea's prophecies also contain a surprising number of references to the lower Jordan valley, which lay stretched out immediately below the mountain peak which to-day bears his name. Just opposite were probably to be found the ancient cities of Admah and Zeboim. The former may be identified with the city of Adam, mentioned in the second chapter of Joshua (*cf.* p. 86), which probably stood near the Damieh ford, just below the point where the Jabbok enters the Jordan. Farther north the Plain of Jezreel comes down to the Jordan, while to the southwest one may see the Valley of Achor, the present Wady Kelt, cutting its way through the western hills toward Ai and Bethel. Hosea also refers to Baal-peor in southern Gilead and to Shittim in the valley below, near the lower fords of the Jordan. Thus there are many indications in the ancient prophecy that Hosea lived among the hills of Gilead, and that, like Amos, he was a man who moved among the heights with a broad outlook ever before him. The message which these two prophets proclaimed was as different as the vistas which opened before them. Amos used the figures of the shepherd; Hosea those of agricultural life. Amos looked upon the evidence of Jehovah's might and justice; Hosea upon fertile fields and tree-clad hills, which spoke of Jehovah's love and his gracious provision for his people's needs. Thus the messages of these two contemporary prophets supplemented each other, the one proclaiming Jehovah's justice, the other Jehovah's love.

Conquest of Galilee and Gilead. The rulers of Northern Israel, however, were as irresponsive to Hosea's pleadings as they were to Amos's stern warnings. The result was that when in 734 B.C. Tiglath-pileser IV invaded Northern Israel, an assassin sat on the throne and the rank and file of the people were crushed by the cruelty and oppression of those who should have defended them. Northern Israel was swept by the armies of the conqueror. Ijon, which was a city on the rich plain in northern Galilee between the Litany and the Nahr el-Hasbany, that still bears the name Merj Ayun (Ijon); Janoah, a city in the heights six miles east of Tyre; Abel-beth-maacah, at the upper end of the Jordan valley; Kadesh, Hazor, east of Lake Huleh and Ijon, were among the important cities captured in northern Galilee. Lower Galilee and Gilead were also overrun, their leading citizens transported to Assyria, and their territory annexed to that of the Assyrian empire.

The Exiled Northern Israelites. Tiglath-pileser IV left to Hoshea, the last king of Northern Israel, simply the territory west of the Jordan and south of the Plain of Esdraelon. After ruling for a decade as the vassal of Assyria, this king rebelled. For nearly three years his capital, Samaria, held out against the Assyrian armies, but at last, late in 722 B.C., Samaria fell before the conqueror and twenty-seven thousand two hundred and ninety of its citizens were deported to different parts of the Assyrian empire. Some were settled in the province of Gozan on the upper waters of the Habor River, which flows southward into the Euphrates. They found a home, therefore, near the centre of Mesopotamia. References in the Assyrian inscriptions suggest that Halah was a city in western Mesopotamia. The third colony of exiles were settled in the Median cities to the east of Assyria.

The Fate of Northern Israel. The great majority of the people of Northern Israel were left behind in their cities and villages. To destroy their racial unity colonists were imported by the Assyrians from three cities—Babylon, Kutha, which is probably the Assyrian Kutu, a city a little northeast of Babylon, and Sippar, north of Babylon. Other colonists were brought from Hamath, the capital of the conquered northern Aramean kingdom. These colonists were in time absorbed by the native population. In later history this mixed race is known as the Samaritans. [104,105] For the next century Northern Israel largely lost its political and religious significance and became simply a part of the great Assyrian empire. In its brief history it demonstrated the great truth that prosperity, opportunity, and culture do not necessarily develop strong national character. At the same time through its prophets it gave to the world certain truths regarding Jehovah's justice and love which are the corner-stones of the faith of humanity.

XIX

THE SOUTHERN KINGDOM

Effect of Environment Upon Judah's History.—Shishak's Invasion.—
War Between the Two Kingdoms.—Amaziah's Wars.—Uzziah's
Strong Reign.—Isaiah of Jerusalem.—His Advice to Ahaz in the
Crisis of 734 B.C.—The Great Rebellion of 703 B.C.—Home of the
Prophet Micah.—Judah's Fate in 701 B.C.—Isaiah's Counsel in a
Later Crisis.—The Reactionary Reign of Manasseh.—Two Pro-
phetic Reformers.—Situation of Anathoth.—Josiah's Reign.—The
Brief Rule of Egypt.—Jehoiakim's Reign.—The First Captivity.—
The Second Captivity.—The End of the Southern Kingdom.

Effect of Environment Upon Judah's History. Compared with the history of
the northern kingdom, that of the southern, for the first two centuries following
the division of the empire, was petty and insignificant. Judah was shut in by its
natural barriers from contact with the larger life that surged up and down the
coast plains and through the broad valleys of Northern Israel. While it survived,
the northern kingdom protected it largely from Aramean and Assyrian invasions,
so that during this period there were few great crises to call forth statesmen and
prophets. Jerusalem, because of its size and prestige, completely overshadowed
the other cities of Judah, so that most of the important events in the history of the
southern kingdom took place in or near the capital. The natural unity of this little
kingdom also freed it from the diverse and disintegrating influences that made
Northern Israel's history one of civil war and bloodshed. The result was that until
Jerusalem's destruction in 586 B.C. the family of David, practically without inter-
ruption, continued to sit on the throne of Judah.

Shishak's Invasion. In 945 B.C. the throne of Egypt was seized by a Libyan
mercenary by the name of Sheshonk, known to the biblical writers as Shishak.
He set to work at once to restore the ancient glories of the empire. To this end he
invaded Palestine and Syria and, according to the records which he has inscribed
on the great temple at Thebes,[106] he succeeded in capturing one hundred and
fifty-six cities and districts. The cities lying along the Philistine Plain, including
Socho, Ajalon, and Beth-horon, Gibeon in the north and Sharuhen and Arad in
the south were among those captured. According to the biblical record Rehoboam
stripped the temple of its wealth in order to pay tribute to this foreign conqueror.

War Between the Two Kingdoms. As soon as the Egyptian forces were
withdrawn, Northern Israel, by virtue of its greater resources, first recovered its

strength and fortified the town of Ramah, five miles north of Jerusalem. Ramah stood on a prominent hill two thousand six hundred feet high, near the intersection of the main highways running north, south, east, and west. From this fortress it was possible to cut off all commercial relations between Judah and the north. The king of Judah retaliated by hiring the aid of the Arameans. When the Northern Israelite army was withdrawn the fortress at Ramah was razed to the ground. With materials taken from this ruin the king of Judah fortified the old stronghold of Geba, two miles to the northeast, thus gaining control of the main highway from the Jordan to the Philistine Plain. In the same way Mizpah, an imposing, massive hill to the northwest of Jerusalem, was fortified. Mizpah[20] lies about two miles south of Gibeon,[93] through which ran the old division line between the north and the south, so it is evident that in this border warfare the boundary between the two kingdoms remained practically the same as before. Soon both were forced to unite against their common foe, the Arameans, so that, with one disastrous exception, neither attempted again to encroach upon the territory of the other.

Amaziah's Wars. In the division of the two kingdoms, Edom and the South Country fell to Judah. Shishak so completely weakened Judah that it appears to have early lost control of the Edomites. Amaziah, the father of Uzziah, was the first who succeeded in winning a decisive victory over these southern foes of the Hebrews. The battle was fought, as in the days of David, in the Valley of Salt, southwest of the Dead Sea. The narrative adds that he took Sela (the Rock) by storm. It is not clear whether this was a border fortress or, as many hold, Petra, the marvellous capital city of the Edomites, which lies in a narrow gorge, cut out of the heart of the many-colored limestone mountains that rise between the Ghôr and the Arabian desert.[50] Elated by this victory, Amaziah foolishly challenged the king of Northern Israel to battle. The decisive engagement was fought at Beth-shemesh, the prosperous town that lay on the southern side of the Valley of Sorek. It was almost due west of Jerusalem and in the heart of the lowlands along which the northern army probably approached. Following up the victory, the Northern Israelites tore down two hundred yards of the northwestern wall of Jerusalem at the point where the city mounted the northern plateau and was, therefore, most exposed. They also looted the temple and royal palace, thus completing the humiliation of the southern kingdom. The conspiracy which resulted in the flight and execution of Amaziah at Lachish, the southwestern outpost of Judah, was probably the fruit of his folly.

Uzziah's Strong Reign. Uzziah, who succeeded his father, rebuilt the walls of Jerusalem and strengthened them by towers that guarded the northwestern and southwestern gates of the city. He also extended the influence of Judah in the south, building the important port of Elath. In a campaign against the Philistines he captured Gath, whose power had already been broken by the Arameans, Jabneh, west of Gezer, and Ashdod farther south. The death of this strong king, therefore, marked a crisis in the life of Judah, for his successors were inefficient and at this time Assyrian armies began to invade Palestine.

Isaiah of Jerusalem. It was in the year that Uzziah died that Judah's great prophet, Isaiah, entered upon his work. His intense loyalty to his nation and his conception of the transcendent majesty of the Divine King who ruled over Israel, reveal his southern birth and training. His familiarity with king, court, and the problems of the nation leave little doubt that he was a citizen of Jerusalem and possibly a scion of one of its noble families. At first, like Amos, he devoted himself to denouncing the crimes of the ruling class and the inevitable result of their cruelty, greed, and disregard of public responsibility.

His Advice to Ahaz in the Crisis of 734 B.C. When, in 735, Northern Israel and Damascus united and endeavored to force Judah to combine with them in a coalition against the invader, Tiglath-pileser IV, Isaiah entered upon his work as a statesman. In person he went to advise Ahaz, as the king was probably investigating the defences of Jerusalem, in view of the possibilities of an impending siege. The place of meeting was evidently south of the city, where the valley of the Tyropœon joined that of the Hinnom near the pool where, in earlier days, Adonijah had rallied his followers.[107] Isaiah's advice, however, to make no alliances, but to simply trust Jehovah for deliverance, was rejected by king and people. Ahaz became a vassal of Assyria, and not only turned over the silver and gold of the temple and palace to the invader, but went in person to Damascus to pay homage to Tiglath-pileser.

The Great Rebellion of 703 B.C. The great crisis that called forth the majority of Isaiah's recorded sermons came thirty years later, when Judah was again tempted to enter into an alliance with the other states of Palestine in an endeavor to break free from the rule of Assyria. In common with the other little states of Palestine, it was a victim of its intermediate position between the great world-powers, Assyria and Egypt. Under a new Ethiopian dynasty, Egypt's ambitions were again beginning to stir and Assyria was the chief barrier to their realization. Therefore, Egypt by promises of help encouraged the states of Palestine to revolt against Assyria. In 711 B.C. the Philistine towns of Ashdod and Gath did actually rebel. It was only by going about in the garb of the captive, proclaiming in this objective way what would be the consequence if Judah rebelled against Assyria, that Isaiah was able to arrest the attention of the nation and save it from fatally compromising itself. When the great Assyrian king, Sargon, died in 705 B.C. the temptations to rebel were too strong to be resisted. Merodach-baladan, of the ancient Babylonian royal line, at once instigated a successful revolt in the lower Tigris-Euphrates valley and sent emissaries to Palestine to stir up the vassal states in a general uprising against Assyria. Tyre, Edom, Moab, Ammon the Philistine cities, and certain of the neighboring Bedouin tribes united in raising the standard of revolt against their common foe. Egypt again promised assistance, and, although Isaiah protested with all his powers, Judah was drawn into the coalition. Hezekiah was made the southern leader of the rebellion.

Home of the Prophet Micah. Sennacherib, the successor of Sargon, after putting down the rebellion in southern Babylonia, advanced with a large army to the reconquest of the eastern Mediterranean states. It was probably while the Assyrian king was advancing from the north that Isaiah's contemporary, Micah, uttered his warning against the venal and greedy nobles of Judah. The home of the prophet was Moresheth-gath. Eusebius and Jerome describe it as a small village a little east of the modern Beit-Jibrin, which commands the entrance to the Valley of Zephathah, through which ran the highway from Jerusalem to Gaza. Another important road ran from Hebron past the mound which represents without reasonable doubt the ancient Gath, and thence along the coast plains to the north. It was the centre of a prosperous agricultural life and at the same time shared the peculiar characteristics of these frontier towns. From his home among the foot-hills[108] Micah was able to watch the movement of Assyrian armies and to keep in close touch with the world-politics of his day. Like Amos, he was inspired by the sense of approaching danger to turn his attention to conditions within the nation and to endeavor with all his prophetic power to prepare it for the coming crisis. The note of alarm sounds through all his early utterances. In imagination he pictures the effects of the coming invasions and in the sound of the names of the villages about his home he finds suggestions of the calamity about to overtake them. His eyes fall first on Gath, which lay to the northwest on the highway along which the Assyrian army would naturally approach. His vision sweeps southward, including Shaphir, the modern Suafir, five miles southeast of Ashdod on the Philistine Plain, Zaanan and Lachish to the southwest, and other small villages on the western borders of Judah. His eye rests last of all upon Mareshah, which has recently been identified beyond doubt with the large Tell es-Sandahannah, one mile south of Beit-Jibrin. The latter was the most important city near Micah's home, for it guarded the pass and stood near the junction of the great highways that radiate from this point.

Judah's Fate in 701 B.C. Judah experienced in 701 B.C. the calamities that Isaiah and Micah had predicted. The annals of Sennacherib state that the Assyrian king conquered forty-six of the cities of Judah, together with innumerable fortresses and small towns in their neighborhood; over two hundred thousand captives, and horses, mules, asses, camels, oxen, and sheep without number were carried away as spoils. In the picturesque language of the conqueror, "Hezekiah was shut up like a bird in a cage in the midst of Jerusalem" until he was forced to surrender and to pay a huge tribute of gold and silver.

Isaiah's Counsel in a Later Crisis. In this great crisis the wisdom of Isaiah's counsel was vindicated beyond question and his authority became so strong with king and people that an attempt was made to remove certain of the surviving heathen symbols from the popular worship. In the later crisis of 690 B.C., when Sennacherib advanced to the conquest of Egypt, the prophet by his advice was able to save Jerusalem. While engaged in the siege of Lachish, the imposing fortress on the Philistine Plain on the southern side of the Wady el-Hesy, Sennacherib sent messengers demanding the unconditional surrender of Judah's capital. From the point of view of the Assyrian king it was dangerous to leave in his rear a strong fortress like Jerusalem, which had already proved a centre of rebellion. His demand, however, was unreasonable, for there is no evidence that Jerusalem, at this later time, was guilty of sedition. In the light of these changed conditions, instead of predicting calamity as a penalty for rebellion, Isaiah advised Hezekiah to refuse to surrender his city to destruction. The calm, unflinching faith of the prophet overcame the fears of the king and thus preserved Jerusalem for another century. Without waiting to carry out his threats against Jerusalem, Sennacherib advanced against Egypt. From the variant traditions it appears that in the marshy land on the eastern side of the Nile delta his army was overtaken by a plague and he was forced ignominiously to retreat.

The Reactionary Reign of Manasseh. Assyria continued, during the reign of Hezekiah's successor, Manasseh, to maintain its control of Palestine. Assyrian and Babylonian customs and religious institutions pervaded the land as never before. Two legal contracts, drawn up in the usual Assyrian form and dating from the years 651 and 648 B.C. in the reign of Manasseh, have been discovered in the mound of Gezer. The one records the sale of a field and the other of an estate with the house and land. The owner of the land was a Hebrew (Nethaniah) but the joint owners of the estate and the twelve witnesses were nearly all Assyrians, indicating how strong was this foreign influence at the time. The weak Manasseh was a leader in a wide-spread reaction against the exalted religious and ethical teachings of the prophets. The old Canaanite cults were largely revived and the worship of Babylonian and Assyrian deities was introduced even into the temple at Jerusalem. Silenced by persecution, the faithful prophets and priests devoted themselves to putting the principles proclaimed by Amos, Hosea, and Isaiah into definite laws that would shape the daily life of the people. The results of their work are preserved in the book of Deuteronomy, which became the basis of the later reformation of Josiah.

Two Prophetic Reformers. The two leaders in the great reform movement were Jeremiah of Anathoth and Zephaniah, who seems to have had great influence over his kinsman, the young Josiah. Zephaniah was apparently a native of Jerusalem. Most of his prophecy is devoted to denouncing the different forms of apostasy and the crimes of oppression then prevalent in the capital. While Jeremiah was not a citizen of Jerusalem, he came from a neighboring village and was also in close touch with the political, social, and religious life of the capital.

Situation of Anathoth. The little town of Anathoth,[109] his home, lay to the northeast of Jerusalem, just over the Mount of Olives, at the point where the hills began to descend to the barren wilderness to the east. It stood on a low, rounded hill. The limestone rocks crop out at many points, imparting a rugged appearance to the landscape. A thriving fig orchard on the western side of the modern town recalls the forceful figure by which Jeremiah contrasted the Jews left in Palestine with the exiles in Babylonia. The low stone and mud buildings of the present town are crowded close together and the dirty streets and people remind the traveller of the men of ancient Anathoth who persecuted their illustrious townsman. On the south the view is shut off by the rising hills, but toward the northeast lies Gibeon and Ramah and to the north Michmash, with its inspiring memories. The chief view from Anathoth, like that from Tekoa, is toward the Jordan valley and the Dead Sea. The gray, barren hills let themselves down in gradual terraces to the depths below. To the northeast are the tree-clad hills of Gilead, while across the Dead Sea rise the rounded, rocky cliffs of the Moabite plateau. Like the homes of most of the great Hebrew prophets, it is a place of broad outlook. The general impression of Anathoth is grim, stern, and sombre, although here the harsh, barren landscape of the south merges into the more fertile and pleasing hill country of the north. Even so in the character of Jeremiah were blended the sternest, most exalted sense of justice and a love for his nation and his countrymen so tender and strong that he was ready to give his life, if need be, to save them from the evils which he saw impending. Through all his sermons these two motives struggle, sometimes the one and sometimes the other breaking forth into expression.

Josiah's Reign. In Josiah the reformers found an energetic leader. It was during his reign that the Scythian hordes poured down from southeastern Europe. Some of these wild barbarians swept down the eastern coast of the Mediterranean, giving Zephaniah and Jeremiah the texts of their earlier sermons. Others, turning to the east, flung themselves against the Assyrian empire and ultimately, in union with the Babylonians, succeeded in conquering Nineveh itself. The impending fall of Assyria favored the work of the reformers, so that in 621 B.C. the prophetic law-book was brought from the temple and publicly adopted by Josiah in behalf of the people. The record of the institution of this new law indicates that Josiah's authority extended beyond the old bounds of Judah. After the withdrawal of the Assyrian governors it was natural that the surviving tribes of the north should again look to Jerusalem for political and religious leadership. This fact explains why Josiah's last fatal battle was fought against the Egyptian king, Necho, in the vicinity of the old Canaanite fortress of Megiddo.

The Brief Rule of Egypt. Necho, the son of Psamtik I, a Libyan who had succeeded in conquering Egypt, was inspired by the oft-recurring ambition to recover the Asiatic possessions once held by the empire. The approaching fall of Assyria gave him a favorable opportunity. With the aid of the Greek mercenaries in his service, he succeeded in conquering the Philistine cities. The defeat of Josiah at Megiddo in 608 B.C. gave him practical possession of Palestine. In the same way the different states of Syria fell before him, so that between 608 and 605 B.C. he was master of the eastern Mediterranean. This brief Egyptian rule, however, was overthrown by the new Chaldean kingdom, which arose in lower Babylonia and, after the fall of Nineveh, quickly fell heir to the southern and western part of the Assyrian empire. The decisive battle between the Egyptians and Chaldeans was fought at Carchemish, by the Euphrates, in 605 B.C. and resulted in the complete defeat of Necho's army. The Egyptians were speedily driven from Syria and Palestine and the Chaldean authority established in their stead.

Jehoiakim's Reign. By the death of Josiah the cause of the patriotic prophetic party in Judah suffered severely. The younger son of the dead king, who was first put on the throne, was soon deposed by Necho and the selfish Jehoiakim was established as a vassal of Egypt. His sympathies were with the party of reaction and he proved another Manasseh. When the Chaldeans appeared in Palestine their rule was readily accepted, but after a reign of ten years Jehoiakim listened to the seductive promises of Egypt and rebelled against his Chaldean master. It was during the reign of Jehoiakim that Jeremiah delivered the greater part of his sermons. By direct address and object-lesson he denounced the follies and crimes of the king and people and tried to save them from the calamity which he saw impending. When the spirit of rebellion was rife he used all his influence to keep his countrymen loyal to the Chaldeans, but in vain. While Judah was being overrun by the Chaldean armies, Jehoiakim died and was succeeded by his young son, Jehoiachin.

The First Captivity. In 597 B.C. Jerusalem itself fell before the army of Nebuchadrezzar. The king, his nobles, and between eight and ten thousand of the prominent men and artisans, representing in all between thirty and forty thousand souls, were transported to Babylonia. The object of Nebuchadrezzar was to strip the land of its leaders and all who might assist in carrying through another rebellion. Over the Judeans who were left behind was placed Zedekiah, a son of Josiah. The new king was inclined to listen to the voice of Jeremiah and to rule for the best interests of his subjects, but he was helpless in the hands of his headstrong nobles. For nearly a decade Judah submitted to the strong and, on the whole, benign rule of Nebuchadrezzar; but by 593 B.C. the kings of Edom, Moab, Ammon, Tyre, and Sidon encouraged, as of old, by Egypt were again plotting rebellion. Jeremiah did all in his power to save Judah from these fatal entanglements, but false prophets undermined his influence and encouraged the people to hope that Jehovah would perform a miracle in their behalf.

The Second Captivity. In 588 B.C. Zedekiah rebelled against the Chaldeans. Syria and Palestine proved themselves again, as throughout all their long history, a land incapable of united action. Nebuchadrezzar established his head-quarters at Riblah, on the upper Euphrates, beside the great northern highway. From this strategic point, from which history had already demonstrated that the Hebrew coastlands could best be ruled, he directed the campaign against the rebellious states. Most of them surrendered at once. Tyre and Jerusalem alone held out against a protracted siege. The Egyptian army which came to relieve Jerusalem was defeated on the borders of Palestine. It was only the fear of the judgment that would be visited upon them that inspired the followers of Zedekiah to resist as long as they did. Even at the risk of imprisonment and death at the hands of the unprincipled nobles, Jeremiah asserted that the only hope lay in surrender. At last Zedekiah in desperation, after the northern walls of the city had already been broken down by the besiegers, fled by night through the southeastern gate of the city, down through the gorge of the Kidron to Jericho. Here he was captured by the Chaldeans and carried to Riblah on the Orontes. While his life was spared, the nobles and religious leaders who had been active in the rebellion were put to death. About five thousand of the prominent men of Jerusalem were carried with Zedekiah to Babylon. The city and temple were stripped of their wealth and the walls were thrown down, leaving Judah's capital "a ruin and a heap." Israel's feasts were transformed into fasts and her songs into lamentations.[110]

The End of the Southern Kingdom. Not wishing to leave the territory of Judah in utter desolation, Nebuchadrezzar appointed Gedaliah, a grandson of Josiah's counsellor, Shaphan, governor over the Jews remaining in Jerusalem. The new ruler selected as the centre of his government Mizpah,[20, 21] the most commanding point in northern Judah, four and a half miles northwest of Jerusalem. This was one of the two border cities which had been fortified by Asa, in his war against Northern Israel. The northern position of his capital suggests that his authority, like that of Josiah, extended over a part of southern Samaria. This inference is supported by the fact that Israelites from Shechem, Shiloh, and Samaria came, under the protection of his rule, to present offerings at the ruined temple at Jerusalem. Many Jewish refugees soon returned from Moab, Ammon, and Edom to put themselves under the protection of Gedaliah's just and kindly rule. The bright promise of an early restoration of Judah's fortunes was destroyed by the treachery of a certain Ishmael, of the Judean royal line, who, at the instigation of the king of Ammon, went to Mizpah and treacherously slew Gedaliah. Contrary to Jeremiah's advice, the Judahites who survived fled to Egypt, taking him with them. Thus Judah was overtaken with an even more overwhelming fate than that of the northern kingdom. Yet in the hour of its deepest humiliation two brave souls, Jeremiah in Palestine and Ezekiel in distant Babylon, proclaimed in clearest terms that Judah would again be inhabited and that a noble destiny yet awaited their nation. Above all, Jeremiah declared that inasmuch as the old covenant between Jehovah and the nation had been broken by the crimes of the rulers and people, a new and more spiritual covenant would be established between Jehovah and each individual.

XX

THE BABYLONIAN AND PERSIAN PERIODS

Jewish Refugees in Egypt.—Situation of Tahpanhes.—Memphis.—
The Colony at Elephantine.—Results of the Excavations.—Transformation of the Jews Into Traders.—Home of the Exiles in Babylonia.—Their Life in Babylonia.—Conditions of the Jews in
Palestine.—Extent of the Jewish Territory.—Evidences that There
Was No General Return of the Exiles in 537 B.C.—The Rebuilding
of the Temple.—Discouragement and Hopes of the Jews.—Nehemiah's Response to the Call for Service.—Conditions in the Jewish Community.—Preparations for Rebuilding the Walls.—Character of the Data.—The Walls and Towers on the North.—On the
West.—On the South.—On the East.—Significance of Nehemiah's
Work.—Extension of Jewish Territory to the Northwest.—Development of Judaism During the Latter Part of the Persian Period.

Jewish Refugees in Egypt. After the destruction of Jerusalem in 586 B.C. the
Jews were to be found in three great centres—Egypt, Babylonia, and Palestine.
Egypt, because of its friendly attitude toward the Jews and its nearness to southern
Palestine, was the refuge to which most of the Jewish fugitives fled. Inasmuch as
the approach of the Chaldean armies was from the north, the main highway running south from Hebron through the solitary desert was the most natural line of
escape. The result was that a very large proportion of the Jewish race were to be
found from this time on in the land of the Nile. Even before the final destruction
of Jerusalem, both Jeremiah and Ezekiel addressed the Jewish refugees in Egypt.
They were found in four important towns. The two nearest to Palestine were Migdol and Tahpanhes. Migdol means tower or fortress, and the reference is evidently
to one of the frontier towns that guarded the eastern boundary of Egypt. It was
probably the Migdolos mentioned in the *Itinerarium Antonini*, and was situated
midway between Pelusium on the Mediterranean coast and Sele, a little west of
the Crocodile Lake, the present Lake Timsah. This would identify it with the ruins
known as the Tell es-Semut, twelve miles southwest of Pelusium, beside the ancient caravan route that ran from Palestine to Egypt.

Babylonian, Persian, and Greek Empires

The M.-N. Co.

Situation of Tahpanhes. Tahpanhes, the biblical name of the Græco-Egyptian city, Daphne, is represented by the modern Tell Defenneh. It lay on the right bank of the Pelusiac branch of the Nile and close to the caravan route from Palestine. On the north was the marshy Lake Menzaleh. It was, however, close to the fertile lands of the Nile Delta and from the days of Psamtik I an important military and commercial town. Here were settled Greek and Phœnician colonists, and here the Jews who fled with Jeremiah after the murder of Gedaliah found refuge. Here and at Migdol the refugees were in closest touch with their kinsmen who had remained behind in Palestine and were in a position to return thither whenever conditions were favorable. They were also in the midst of a cosmopolitan life that offered them ample opportunity to engage in trade, which must have been the chief occupation of these semi-desert towns.

Memphis. A third home of Jewish colonists in Egypt was Noph, which was the biblical designation of the sacred city of Memphis. This great city lay ten miles south of Cairo, at the southern end of the Nile Delta. It was a large metropolitan city, with an exceedingly diverse population. Herodotus found in the vicinity of the Egyptian temple of Ptah a Tyrian colony with a temple dedicated to the "foreign Aphrodite." Here were probably settled the Jews who had decided to make permanent homes in Egypt, and who may have reared here a temple to Jehovah.

The Colony at Elephantine. The fourth centre of colonization was at Syene in the land of Pathros, the biblical equivalent of upper Egypt. Syene is apparently represented by the modern Egyptian city of Assuan, just below the first cataract of the Nile. In Ezekiel 29:10 Migdol and Syene mark respectively the northern and southern boundaries of Egypt. Recent excavations on the northern end of the island of Elephantine,[111] which lies in the Nile opposite Assuan, have revealed the presence of a large Jewish colony at this point, which flourished during the earlier part of the Persian period and was probably established soon after the fall of Jerusalem. The island is one of the garden spots of the Nile valley. The ruins of the ancient city cover a low-lying hill on the southern end, which is here fully three-quarters of a mile across from east to west. On the east across the river are the heights of Assuan. The view to the south is toward the rocky cataract of the Nile. On the west, across the river, extends the brown, rocky desert.

Results of the Excavations. The importance of the ancient town lay in its position at the head of uninterrupted navigation. From here the caravans set out for Nubia and the upper Nile and for the oases in the east. The town was built of Nile mud bricks, with little houses and narrow streets, and was evidently once the home of a large and dense population. On the western side have been discovered contracts written on papyri in Aramaic, which indicate that here was a large Jewish colony living on a practical equality with the Egyptians, Phœnicians, Babylonians, and Persians, who constituted the population of this ancient metropolis. Familiar Jewish names appear in these contracts, which record the sale of land and houses. An Aramaic letter bearing the date 408 B.C. has also been discovered directed to Bagohi, the Persian governor of Palestine. From these contracts and this letter it appears that during the earlier part of the Persian period there was within the city of Elephantine a Jewish temple of Jahu (Jehovah), surrounded by strong walls and protecting gates. At this Jewish sanctuary regular offerings were presented to Jehovah and the religious customs of the homeland were thus preserved in the very heart of the old heathen city.

Transformation of the Jews into Traders. It is significant that the Jewish colonists in Egypt were settled in four commercial centres. Trade was the chief occupation open to them. Hence the shepherds and farmers of Judah were soon transformed into traders and merchants. Widely scattered as they were, at each important city there were colonies of Jews. In time these were organized into great mercantile companies which, through their agents and branch houses, controlled more and more of the trade of the ancient East. The Jew of to-day is the product of those centuries of commercial training which began with the Babylonian period.

Home of the Exiles in Babylonia. In deporting the Jewish captives from Palestine to Babylonia, Nebuchadrezzar evidently followed the longer, more northern route, through Riblah and Hamath, across the Euphrates at Carchemish, and thence southward through Mesopotamia. Instead of scattering the Jewish exiles throughout the empire, he settled them in a colony on the Chebar River, which is evidently identical with the Khabaru Canal. According to recently discovered inscriptions, this canal ran eastward from Babylon to the ancient sanctuary of Nippur. This region was in the northern part of the great alluvial plain between the Tigris and the Euphrates and was intersected in every direction by canals, which were used both for irrigation and commerce. To escape the spring floods the villages were built on low mud mounds, in many cases ruins of earlier cities. The prophet Ezekiel, who was the pastor and spiritual adviser of the exiles in Babylon, lived at a village named after the mound on which it was built, Tell Abib. Two other similar village mounds were called Salt Hill and Forest Hill. Ezekiel describes their new home as "a land of traffic, a city of merchants, a fruitful soil, beside many waters."

Their Life in Babylonia. In certain psalms are found the echo of the homesickness and longing for their native hills which filled the hearts of the Jewish exiles. But the fruitful soil of Babylonia was a partial compensation for what they had lost. The active commercial life of Babylon, as that of Egypt, developed within them the latent Semitic genius for trade. At first they were evidently settled as a community by themselves, a little Judah in the heart of the great empire. Here they lived in accordance with their laws, under the rulership of their elders, building houses, planting gardens, and rearing up families, as Jeremiah advised in the letter which he wrote them (Jer. 29). The result was that the majority of the Jews in the east became so attached to their new homes that few were found later who would undertake the arduous journey of fifteen hundred miles to return to the stony hills of Judah. For a great majority of those who were exiled or who fled from Judah in connection with the first and second captivity there was no return, even though opportunities were repeatedly offered.

Condition of the Jews in Palestine. The third centre of the Jewish race was Judah itself. Even though Jerusalem was destroyed and its population scattered, the majority of the shepherds and peasants of Judah never left their homes. The captives who were deported by the Babylonians appear to have been taken almost entirely from the capital city. Those who remained in Palestine were probably placed under the rule of the governor of the so-called "Province beyond the River." The title evidently originated in Babylon, for it was the designation of the territory which lay west of the Euphrates and included Syria as well as Palestine. Without organization and the protection of a native ruler the fortunes of the Jewish peasants must have been indeed pitiable. The book of Lamentations contains references to the pitiless persecutions and the frequent forays to which they were subject. Whenever the local government was weakened, Judah was the object of attack from every quarter. On the north were the Samaritans, who could never completely forget their hereditary rivalry with the southern tribes. At this time the Samaritan territory apparently extended southward so as to include the cities of Gibeon and Mizpah. On the east the Ammonites had at last succeeded in pushing their boundaries westward to the Jordan, and in occupying the fruitful hills and valleys of southern Gilead. East of the Dead Sea the Moabite territory evidently extended northward to that recently occupied by the Ammonites. In southern Judah the Edomites, pushed northward by the advance of a strong Arab race, known as the Nabateans, had seized not only the South Country but the old capital, Hebron, and the territory to the east and west. On the southwest they occupied the important city of Mareshah and the adjacent Philistine lowlands.[108]

Extent of the Jewish Territory. The Jews were therefore almost entirely confined to the Judean highlands. Their outposts on the southwest were Keilah and Bethzur, on the west Zanoah, which guarded the entrance to the Valley of Sorek, and Netophah, the modern Beit Nettif, which guarded the entrance to the Valley of Elah. The northern boundary ran within five or six miles of Jerusalem. To the northeast the Jews appear to have held the city of Jericho and the neighboring Plain of the Jordan. Thus the cultivated Jewish territory was little more than twenty-five miles in length and breadth and included the least desirable land of all Palestine.

Evidence That There Was No General Return of Exiles in 536 B.C. The overthrow of the Chaldean Empire by Cyrus in 538 B.C. gave the Jews of Babylon an opportunity to return, for the Persian king reversed the policy of the Assyrians and the Babylonians and aimed to develop the resources and loyalty of each of the many peoples in his great empire. There is no evidence, however, that more than a handful of the Jews in the east improved this opportunity. Cyrus also adopted the policy of appointing native princes as local governors. A scion of the royal house of David was placed over the little sub-province of Judah. This appointment gave the Jews a local government that undoubtedly attracted to the homeland many refugees from Ammon and Moab and especially from the land of Egypt. But the sermons of the contemporary prophets, Haggai and Zechariah, indicate clearly that those who constituted the rank and file of the Judean community and rebuilt the temple were the people of the land and that a general return of the exiles was an event, still in the future, for which they ardently longed.

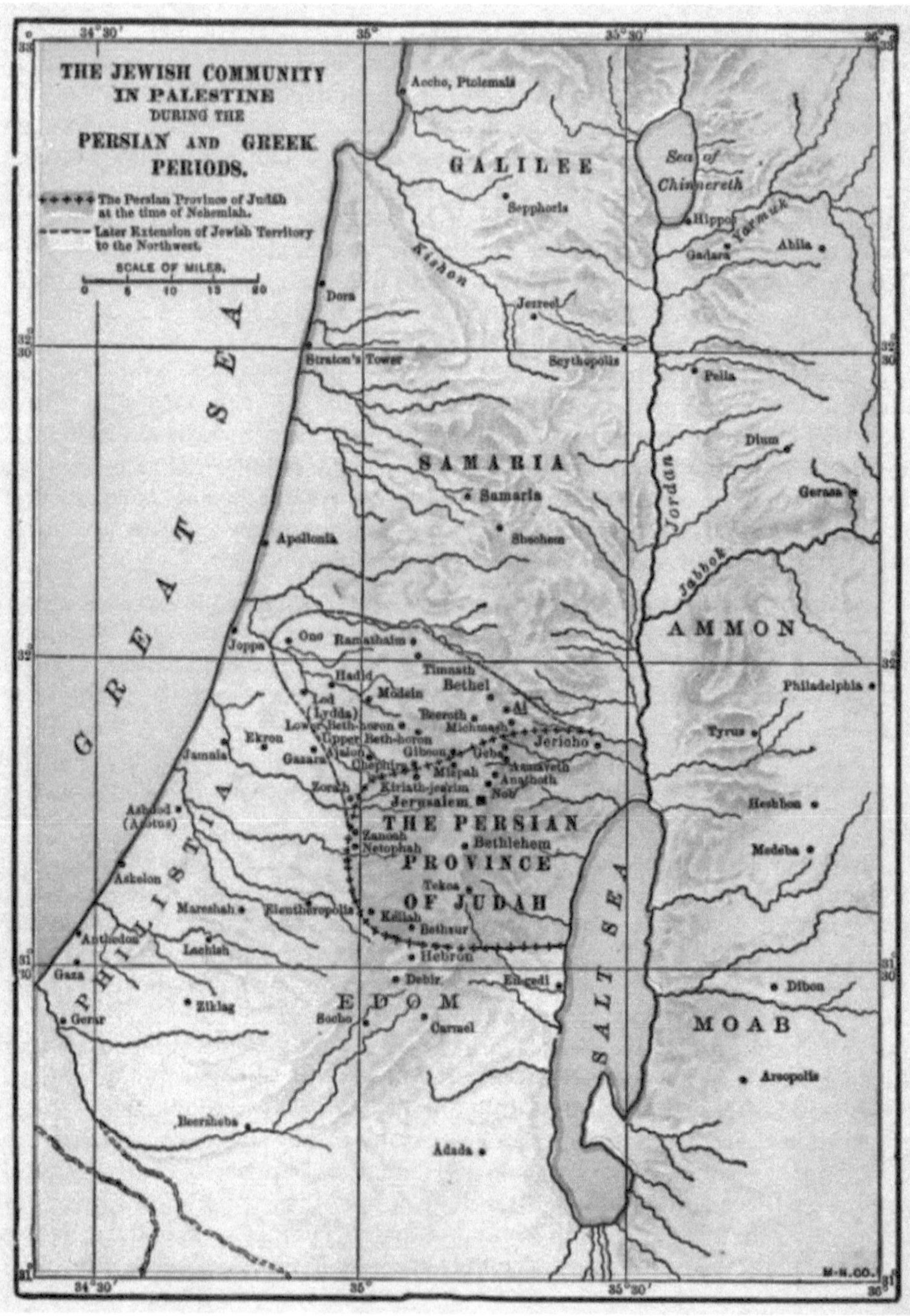

The Jewish Community in Palestine During The Persian and Greek Periods

M-N Co.

The Rebuilding of the Temple. Even during the Babylonian period sacrifices were offered at the great altar of native rock that had stood in front of Solomon's temple. Perhaps even before Cyrus gave full permission to the native peoples to rebuild their cities and temples a few had come back to find homes among the desolate ruins of Jerusalem. It was a small, struggling, and discouraged community to whom Haggai in 520 B.C. addressed his stirring message. His call to rise and rebuild the temple met with an immediate response. He was also seconded by the encouraging words of his contemporary, Zechariah. The rebellions that were then shaking the great Persian Empire to its foundations encouraged the Jews to hope that the opportune moment had arrived to reinstate Zerubbabel. Inspired by these hopes, the temple-building progressed rapidly. The stones for the repair of the walls were apparently found on the temple hill. The timbers for the gates were cut from the hills about Jerusalem, which at this time were, at least in part, covered with trees. By 516 B.C. the work was completed and the Jewish race again had a common religious sanctuary at which to worship.

Discouragement and Hopes of the Jews. The hopes of re-establishing the Hebrew kingdom under a Davidic ruler were, however, completely dashed to the ground. Darius succeeded in putting down the many rebellions and in thoroughly reorganizing the Persian Empire. At this time the descendants of David disappear from Israel's history. For a generation or two the Judean community was overwhelmed with discouragement, for it was the victim of foes from without and of its corrupt and greedy rulers within, who enslaved the people and seized their land. It is not clear what aroused the spirit of the discouraged Judean community. Possibly it was the divinely inspired vision of the great prophet, whose immortal songs are preserved in the fortieth and following chapters of the book of Isaiah. He appears to have been a citizen of Jerusalem, and to the ancient capital city his message is primarily addressed. It was a call, however, to all the scattered remnants of the race to return and do their part in realizing Israel's noble destiny. It was a summons to voluntary, self-sacrificing service. It interprets the discouragements, the calamities, and the ignominies which were then the lot of his race, not as the result of Jehovah's disfavor, but as a supreme opportunity, if nobly improved, to demonstrate to the world the character of the God whom they worshipped and the saving power of the faith which they cherished.

Nehemiah's Response to the Call to Service. Before there could be a general return of the exiles it was necessary that the walls of Jerusalem be rebuilt, and this required resources, influence at the Persian court, and, above all, an energetic, able leader. In sending a deputation to Nehemiah, the royal cupbearer of Artaxerxes, the Palestinian Jews showed great wisdom. At the head of this deputation was Hanani, a kinsman of Nehemiah. The scene of this memorable interview was in the royal palace at Susa, the capital of the Persian Empire. The huge ruins of the ancient city, fully eight miles in circumference, have revealed to the modern excavator its magnificence and beauty. It is possible that the unknown author of the immortal chapters in the latter part of the book of Isaiah was a member of the deputation from Jerusalem. Nehemiah records how profoundly he was moved by the recital of the misfortunes that had overtaken the city of his forefathers. The spirit and message of Isaiah 40-55 pervade the prayer of Nehemiah, recorded in the first chapter of his memoirs. One Jew, at least, was found responsive to the divine call to service. Improving a favorable opportunity, he secured permission to go back and rebuild the walls of Jerusalem. A royal escort and letters to the governor of the province beyond the river prepared the way. His journey from Susa lay along the southern side of the Elamite mountains and thence beside the Tigris, through Mesopotamia by one of the great highways which led from northern Syria to Palestine.

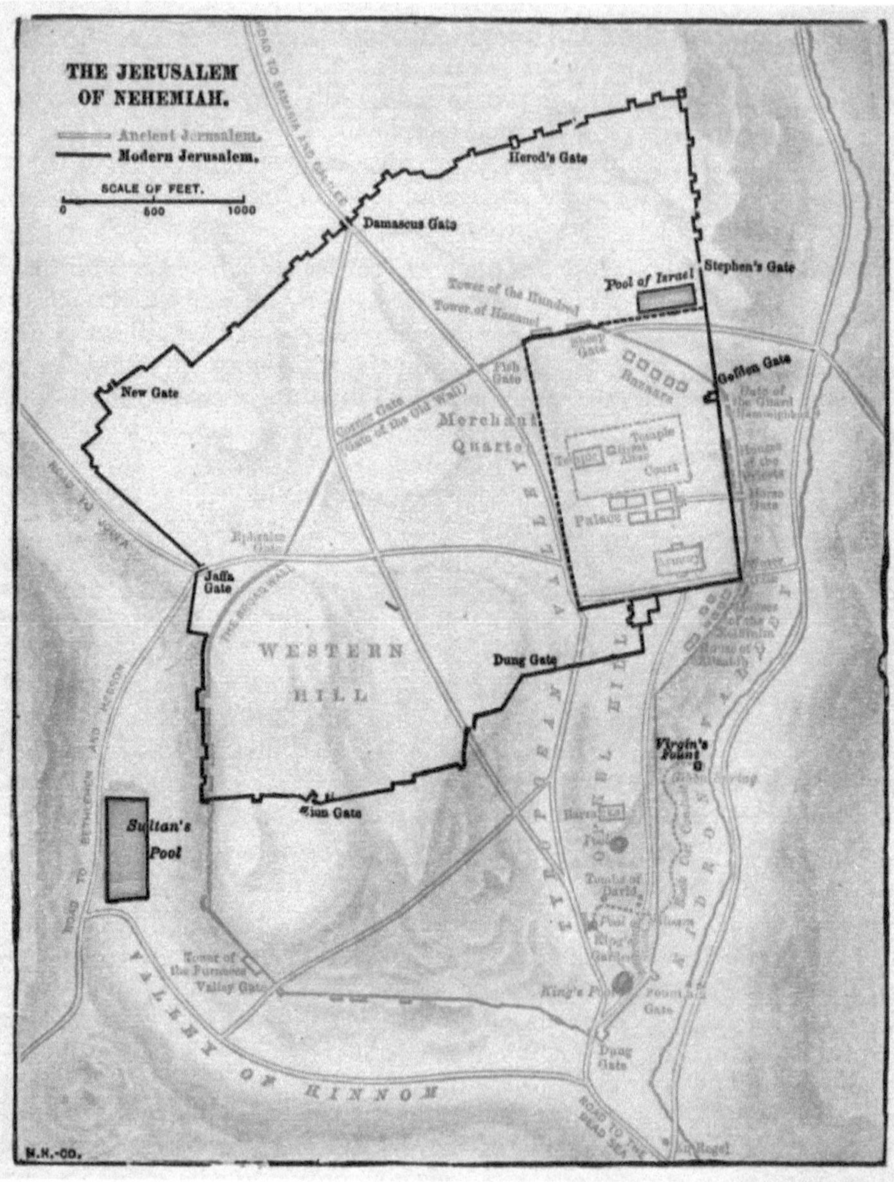

The Jerusalem of Nehemiah

Conditions in the Jewish Community. Nehemiah has given a vivid description of conditions as he found them in Judah. The active foes of the community were Sanballat, the Horonite, whose native town was apparently either Upper or Lower Beth-horon, a certain Tobiah, who had intermarried with the high-priestly family of Jerusalem, and Geshem, an Arabian. Sanballat appears to have been at the head of the Samaritans, Tobiah of the Ammonites, and Geshem of certain Arabian tribes, that probably had already gained a foothold in Palestine. The Judean community had been so long preyed upon by its greedy rulers, led by the high priest and his followers, that Nehemiah found it necessary, as a preliminary, to institute certain drastic social reforms. Like an ancient prophet he preached to the rulers and, by his own example and authority, succeeded in influencing them to set free their countrymen whom they had enslaved, to restore to them their ancestral fields and vineyards, and to promise never again to seize them unjustly.

Preparations for Rebuilding the Walls. Nehemiah's chief work, however, was the rebuilding of the walls of Jerusalem. In accordance with the royal grant, he was allowed to cut timber for the gates in the king's park, which was probably the so-called Gardens of Solomon, south of Jerusalem, near Etam. Under Nehemiah's direction the working forces were carefully organized. Work was begun on all parts of the wall at once and different groups of workmen were assigned to definite sections of the wall. While half of the people worked, the other half stood by with their weapons, ready to repulse an attack. Inspired by Nehemiah's energetic personality and by the constant danger of attack, the work progressed so rapidly that at the end of fifty-two days the walls were restored.

Character of the Data. The detailed account of the building of the walls and of their solemn rededication furnishes the clearest picture extant of ancient Jerusalem. This account is supplemented at almost every point by the thorough excavations carried on along the line of the western, southern, and eastern walls, chiefly under the direction of the Palestine Exploration Fund. The reconstruction thus rendered possible is especially valuable, for Nehemiah simply restored the walls of the pre-exilic city. With the exception of the northern wall, which is covered by the buildings of the modern city, the reconstruction is reasonably certain at every point.

The Walls and Towers on the North. The account begins with the rebuilding of the Sheep Gate, which apparently stood immediately north of the temple (see map opposite p. 143) and was the way by which the sacrificial animals were brought to the sanctuary. Immediately to the west of this gate the native rock extends northward almost on a level.[56] Hence at this point were built two strong guarding towers, standing apparently on the site occupied in Roman times by the famous Tower of Antonia. In the days of the divided Hebrew kingdoms, the upper end of the Tyropœon Valley, immediately west of the temple area, had been enclosed within the city walls. In Zephaniah 1:11 it was called, because of its peculiar shape, The Mortar. Elsewhere it bears the name of The Second Quarter (II Kings, 22:14, Zeph. 1:10). Through this low depression of the Tyropœon Valley ran the main street of the city. It passed through the Fish Gate which opens in the north to the great highway leading to Samaria. The Fish Gate was probably so named because in the adjoining market quarter the fishmongers sold their fish, which were doubtless brought in early times, as in the Roman period, from the Sea of Galilee. The exact course of the northern wall from this point is not entirely clear, for the ground over which it runs is nearly level and is to-day covered with buildings. The importance of this wall and the difficulty of completely restoring it is shown by the proportionately large number of workmen detailed by Nehemiah to repair it. It probably ran in a southwesterly direction to the Corner Gate, which was also called the Gate of the Old Wall. From this point it would seem that Nehemiah constructed a straight wall to the Ephraim Gate, which corresponds to the western Jaffa Gate of modern Jerusalem.

On the West. Immediately south of the Ephraim Gate the city was especially liable to assault. Here a broad, or double wall was constructed. The remainder of the western wall[57] has been traced by excavations. It ran due south along the brow of the western hill to a corner tower which measured forty-five feet each way and rose twenty feet from an outer ledge of rock. At this point the wall turned obliquely to the southeast, running to the Valley Gate, where it turned due east. The ancient Valley Gate was only eight feet ten inches wide on the outside. Its lower sockets are still in position. The wall on the east was nine feet thick. To the west of the Valley Gate was a tower the base of which measured about forty-five feet in each direction. This was probably the Tower of the Furnaces, so named because near by the potters baked their jars (*cf.* Jer. 18:2-4, 19:1-6).

On the South. From the Valley Gate to the Tyropœon Valley the wall is built along the rapidly descending slope.[55] The comparatively few men assigned to this section indicated that it was practically intact. Where it crossed the lower Tyropœon Valley it was flanked on the outside with six buttresses, resting on a foundation wall about twenty feet thick. The main street, leading down the Tyropœon Valley, has been traced from the southern end of the city to a point opposite the temple area. It varied from twenty-five to fifty feet in width and was paved and provided with a curb. Where it ascended the hill there were broad, low, rock-cut steps, adapted to use by beasts of burden as well as by foot-passengers. Opposite the southern end of the present temple area the main street branched eastward toward the Ephraim Gate. On the east side of the Pool of Siloam were rock-cut steps, probably the stairs referred to in Nehemiah 3:15 and 12:37, which led up to Ophel. The King's Pool was in the extreme southeastern part of the city, south of the Pool of Siloam, from which it received its waters, but enclosed within the ancient city wall. To the north of this was apparently the King's Garden.

On the East. Along the eastern side of Ophel the wall runs on the brow of the steeply descending hill above the Virgin's Fount in the Kidron Valley. There is no gate in this long section of the wall until the tower is reached which is described in Nehemiah as the "Tower that Stands Out." Just above this was the Water Gate, the most important western exit from the city. From this the road led down into the Kidron Valley and on to the Virgin's Fount, whose waters probably gave the gate its name. This gate and the Horse Gate, a little farther to the north, led into the official part of the city. Here on the upper part of Ophel, to the south of the original temple area, were the palace and armory. At the northeastern corner of the city was the Gate of the Guard, where one of the companies that took part in the dedication of the walls, in the days of Nehemiah, stopped before entering the sanctuary. Here excavations have disclosed massive masonry and the course of the original wall, which at this point turns to the northwest. It follows the slope of the native rock, which descends suddenly on the north to the ravine leading up from the Kidron Valley. Inside the walls, between the Gate of the Guard and the Sheep Gate, were the bazaars where the people could purchase those things which were needful for their offerings.[112]

Significance of Nehemiah's Work. In rebuilding the walls, Nehemiah prepared the way for that general return of the Jews, which is implied in the seventh chapter of Nehemiah and confirmed by the later facts of history. The story of Ezra is a late tradition regarding one of these return movements. Nehemiah, in reorganizing the method of distributing the temple dues to the priests and Levites, in discountenancing foreign marriages, in enforcing the Sabbath law, and in providing for the support of the temple, laid the foundations for the institution of the new priestly law and the reorganization of the ceremonial service, which is associated with his name. Nehemiah was thus the restorer of that new Jewish state which rose on the ruins of the old.

Extension of Jewish Territory to the Northwest. Shut in on the south by the Edomites and on the east by the Dead Sea and Jordan valley, the Jewish community naturally expanded toward the northwest. In doing so it followed the great highways, which ran northwestward from Jerusalem out upon the Philistine Plain. By virtue of the new life and strength infused into the Judean community by Nehemiah, it was able to cope with the Samaritan community and to push its boundaries northward. Within two or three centuries the arable Jewish territory was nearly doubled and included such important cities as Ai, Bethel, and Timnath in the north, and Ajalon, the Horons, Modein, as well as Ono and Lod, the later Lydda, far out on the Philistine Plain.

Development of Judaism During the Latter Part of the Persian Period. The Babylonian and Persian age as a whole was for the Jews a period of overwhelming calamity and discouragement, and yet during the latter part of this era scattered remnants of the race began again to restore the temple and capital city. During this era the foundations of Judaism were laid along the lines first outlined by Ezekiel. The priests and scribes succeeded to the earlier authority of the kings and prophets. Loyalty to the law and ritual took the place of the ancient loyalty to the king and state. Judaism, helpless and exposed to the attacks of its powerful foes, stood apart from the rest of the world, finding its joy more and more in worship, in trust in Jehovah, and in the noble ideals and hopes that are voiced in the psalms and wisdom writings of this period.

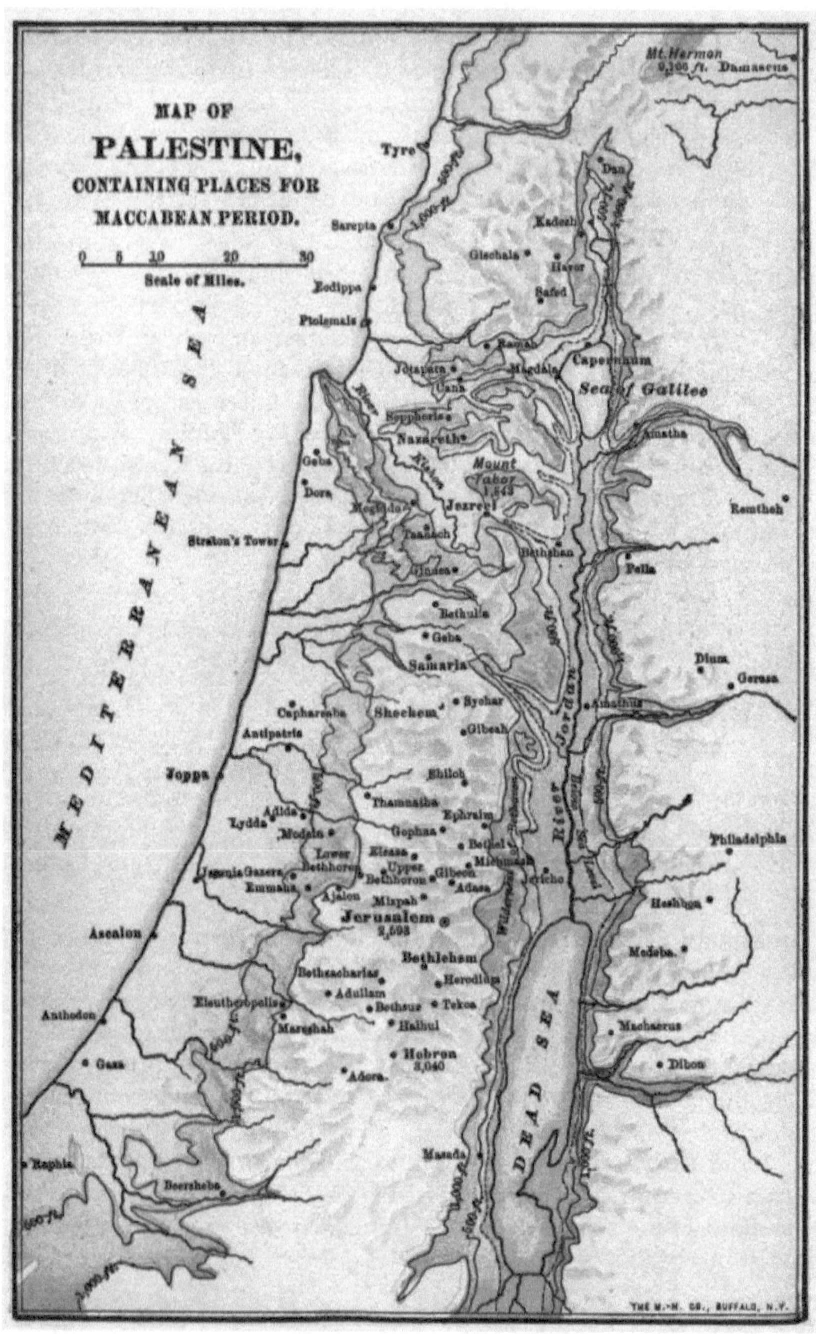

Palestine in the Maccabean Period
(Map of Palestine, containing Places for Maccabean Period)

The M.-N. Co., Buffalo, N. Y.

XXI

THE SCENES OF THE MACCABEAN STRUGGLE

Alexander's Conquests.—The Impression Upon Southwestern Asia.—
The City of Alexandria.—Greek Influence in Palestine.—The Ptol-
emaic Rule.—Situation of Antioch.—Causes of the Maccabean
Struggle.—The Town of Modein.—The First Flame of Revolt.—
Character and Work of Judas.—The Pass of Beth-horon.—Scene
of the Victory Over the Syrian Generals.—Victory at Bethsura.—
Rededication of the Temple.—Campaigns South and East of the
Dead Sea.—Victories in Northeastern Gilead.—Cities Captured
North of the Yarmuk.—The Second Victory Over Timotheus.—
Judas's Return.—Significance of Judas's Victories.—Battle of
Beth-zacharias.—Fortunes of Judas's Party.—Victory over Nica-
nor.—Death of Judas.—Judas's Character and Work.

Alexander's Conquests. The Persian Empire, founded as a result of the conquests of Cyrus and the organizing ability of Darius, after two centuries had become weak, corrupt, and ready for conquest. On the other hand, the Greek civilization, which had been developing for centuries in the little land of Hellas and the
coast lands of the Ægean, demanded an outlet that it might expand naturally (*cf.*
p. 5). At this critical moment in the world's history, Alexander, the Macedonian,
animated by the lust for adventure and by an ambition to make the world more
glorious by disseminating Greek art and culture, set out on his eastern campaigns.
Within less than a decade he carried the standards and culture of Greece across
southwestern Asia beyond the banks of the Indus. After a year of active campaigning in Asia Minor, he completed its conquest in 333 *B.C.* at the great battle of Issus
at the northeastern end of the Mediterranean. With the exception of the cities of
Tyre and Gaza, which were captured only after prolonged sieges, the people of
Palestine readily submitted to the new conqueror. Egypt likewise proved a comparatively easy conquest. By 331 B.C. Alexander was able to turn eastward, and at
the great battle of Arbela, which was fought that year on the plains near the Tigris,
he broke the power of Persia and advanced to seize its eastern possessions.

The Impression Upon Southwestern Asia. Although Alexander the Great
died in 323 B.C., before he was able thoroughly to consolidate and organize his
great empire, his conquests made a permanent impression upon southwestern
Asia. This lasting impression was due in part to the attractiveness and superiority
of Greek art and culture, and to the valor and military skill of the Greek soldiers,

but above all to Alexander's desire to Hellenize the peoples and lands that he conquered. To accomplish this end he rebuilt many of the captured cities on a magnificent scale and established Greek colonies throughout his empire.

The City of Alexandria. The city of Alexandria in northern Egypt was the noblest fruit of Alexander's ambition. Selecting the level strip of land which lay between the Mediterranean and the lagoon of Mareotis, he transformed it into a magnificent city which diverted the trade from Tyre and in time rivalled Rome itself. The site was well chosen, for in front of the city, one mile away, lay the island of Pharos. This he connected with the city by a long causeway, thus providing two large harbors, the eastern, used chiefly in the Greek and Roman periods, and the western, through which the city is approached by modern ships. A canal connected Alexandria with the Canopic or western branch of the Nile and brought to this new metropolis the vast trade of upper Egypt as well as the products of Arabia and India. The city itself was divided into three distinct parts. The Egyptian and native quarter was on the west, while the Greek and official quarter was in the centre opposite the eastern harbor. The Jewish quarter was in the northeastern part of the city. Many Hebrews were attracted here by the privileges which Alexander granted them, especially the opportunity of living under their own laws and local rulers.

Greek Influence in Palestine. Alexander and his successors also transformed the cities of Phœnicia and Philistia and the important towns east of the Jordan into centres of Greek culture and civilization. Large numbers of Greek colonists were settled at Gaza, Ashdod, Askelon, Joppa, and the ancient Accho, which was renamed Ptolemais. In the same way Hippos, Gadara, Pella, Gerasa, and the ancient Rabbath-Ammon, under the name of Philadelphia, became the homes of many of Alexander's veterans and were largely rebuilt after the manner of Greek cities. Thus, from the beginning of the Greek period, the Jewish community in Palestine was encircled by a ring of cities from which emanated the ideas and culture of ancient Hellas. The history of the next few centuries is a record of the great conflict between Semitic and Hellenic ideas and culture and of the ultimate fusion which resulted from this close and protracted contact.

The Ptolemaic Rule. In 320 B.C. Ptolemy Soter, who became the ruler of Egypt after the death of Alexander, conquered the territory of Judea and Samaria. At this time many Jews and Samaritans were transported to Egypt. They were granted special privileges, for the Greek rulers recognized in them valuable allies in the difficult task of ruling the large native population. During the next century Palestine was subject to the Ptolemies. It was the victim of many invasions. By virtue of its position it was the bone of contention between the rulers of Egypt and her rival in the east and north.

Situation of Antioch. About 300 B.C. Seleucus I built the city of Antioch and transferred his capital from the Tigris-Euphrates Valley to this important strategic centre. The city was situated at the point where the Lebanon mountains on the south were separated from the Taurus on the north by the Orontes River. The city lay at the northern end of the great valley between the Lebanons, near the point where the Orontes bends abruptly to the southwest. It was sixteen miles from the sea and not far from the borders of the eastern desert. Here meet the great highways from the Euphrates and from central Syria and Palestine. It was, therefore, an important commercial and political centre. The city itself lay on the broad, fertile plain, which ran northward from the river up the sides of Mount Silpius. Aside from the river and the mountain, it possessed no natural defences, but was dependent upon the huge wall which surrounded it.

Causes of the Maccabean Struggle. In 198 B.C. Antiochus the Great, in a battle near Paneion, the modern Banias, at the foot of Mount Hennon, defeated the Egyptian army and annexed Palestine to the Seleucid kingdom. The Jews gained little by this change of rulers. In 175 B.C. Antiochus Epiphanes mounted the Syrian throne. He had been brought up in the midst of the profligate and imperious young nobles of Rome, and soon proved an unprincipled tyrant. He was a great admirer of Greek art and culture and his two chief ambitions were to adorn his capital and kingdom with magnificent buildings and thoroughly to Hellenize his subjects. Many of the Jews, including certain degenerate high priests at Jerusalem, readily gave up the institutions and traditions of their race and adopted Greek costumes and customs. Through their representatives they led Antiochus to believe that the other Jews would renounce the religion of their fathers. The rank and file of the Jewish nation, however, bitterly opposed Antiochus's policy. Returning from an expedition to Egypt, he found Jerusalem in the hands of a rebel and made this an excuse to turn over the citizens of the city to his bloodthirsty soldiers and to rob the temple of its treasures. Soon after, he set about systematically to root out the worship of Jehovah and completely to Hellenize the Jews. In this endeavor he was aided by the renegade Jews, who constituted a strong Greek party in Jerusalem. In 168 B.C. he sent Apollonius, one of his generals, to put to death all who refused to worship the Olympian Zeus or who preserved copies of the Scriptures. All Jewish religious rites were prohibited, the temple was desecrated, and on its great altar sacrifices were offered to Zeus. The houses and walls of Jerusalem were torn down. The citadel of Acra, which stood either on the hill of Ophel to the south of the temple (*cf.* p. 43), or else immediately to the north on the site of the later Tower of Antonia, was garrisoned with Syrian soldiers and apostate Jews.

The Town of Modein. In the face of this cruel persecution the true character of Judaism asserted itself. Rather than submit to the tyrant's demands, the thousands preferred to die or else succeeded in finding refuge in the caves and deserted places on the borders of Judah. Antiochus's agents, however, met with little opposition until they reached the town of Modein,[113] northeast of the Beth-horons on the borders of the coast plain. Its deserted ruins are to-day one of the most picturesque and impressive mounds in all Palestine. Over it all is flung a luxuriant growth of grain and olive trees. It is surrounded by deep valleys; on the south and west the Wady Malakeh swings in a broad semicircle about the mound, which is nearly a complete circle, one-third of a mile in diameter. To the northwest, connected by a shoulder of land, was the lower town, which was a little larger in area than the acropolis. On the north lay a deep encircling valley which made its defence easy. The sides of the main acropolis rose rapidly in three or four large terraces. It stood apart from the surrounding foot-hills like an emerald set in the midst of black and gray limestone.

The First Flame of Revolt. Modein was a fitting altar of Jewish freedom and patriotism. Here the Syrian official set up a heathen altar. By promises of royal favor he sought to induce an aged priest by the name of Mattathias to sacrifice upon it in accordance with the king's command. To this demand the priest replied that if they alone of all their race remained faithful, he and his family would never forsake the law and ordinances. At the sight of an apostate Jew advancing to sacrifice at the heathen altar the indignation of the stern old priest was kindled. He slew both the offender and the royal official and tore down the altar. He then fled to the mountains with his five stalwart sons. Recognizing in him a leader, the Jews who were faithful to their law soon rallied about him. At first they devoted themselves to tearing down the heathen altars, to enforcing the law of circumcision wherever it had been neglected, and to putting to death all apostates whom they captured. At this critical moment in the life of Judaism they strengthened the courage of those who were wavering and raised a standard about which the faithful rallied in ever-increasing numbers.

Character and Work of Judas. In a few months the aged Mattathias died and was succeeded by his son, Judas, who was known by the distinctive title of Maccabeus. He soon proved himself an unselfish patriot, a devoted champion of the law, and a military leader of rare enthusiasm, energy, and strategic skill. The odds against which he had to contend were seemingly overwhelming. With a few unarmed peasants he was called to meet large armies of well-equipped and well-trained Greek mercenaries. But again, as in the days of David, the rugged physical contour of Palestine was the chief advantage possessed by the Israelites. Selecting a favorable point along the road which led from Samaria to Jerusalem, Judas made a sudden attack upon the Syrian general, Apollonius, and succeeded not only in putting to flight the Syrian soldiers, but also in slaying the leader of the persecution. Henceforth Judas wielded effectively the sword of Apollonius, and his followers armed themselves likewise with the weapons of the slain.

The Pass of Beth-horon. Judas's first open engagement was fought near his home at Modein. Seron was sent with a Syrian army to put down the rebellion. He advanced against Jerusalem by the main northern highway, which led up through the pass of the Beth-horons. At this point the road ascends very rapidly. On the Plain of Ajalon it is but eight hundred and forty feet above the ocean level. At the lower Beth-horon it is one thousand two hundred and forty feet. Thence a steep, rocky road leads to the upper Beth-boron,[84] less than two miles away at the height of two thousand and twenty-two feet above the sea. Four miles farther on it reaches the top of the ascent, which is about two thousand three hundred feet above the level of the sea. The difficult pass, often ascending by rock-cut steps, was the scene of this memorable battle. Here it was impossible for an army to deploy or maintain a regular formation. A few determined men on the heights above were able to turn back a large force. The defeat of the Syrian army was complete. Eight hundred of them were slain during the hot pursuit down the Beth-horon slope. The rest fled to the land of the Philistines, out on the plain. At last, after four centuries of defeat and humiliation, the Israelites found that by courage and united action they could put to flight their heathen foes.

Scene of the Victory Over the Syrian Generals. Fortunately for the Jews, at this crisis Antiochus Epiphanes found his treasury depleted as a result of his luxurious habits and extensive building enterprises. Accordingly he turned over the government of his kingdom to Lysias, one of his nobles, while he gathered a large army and set out on a campaign into Persia, where he ultimately lost his life. The departure of Antiochus reduced by fully one-half the soldiers available for the campaigns against Judas and his followers. But Lysias, appreciating the importance of suppressing the Jewish rebellion at once, sent out an army of forty thousand infantry and seven thousand cavalry under the leadership of three generals, Ptolemy, Nicanor, and Gorgias. They encamped near Emmaus on the southern side of the Valley of Ajalon, not far from the border of the Philistine Plain. This time they avoided the steep and dangerous pass of Beth-horon and aimed to penetrate the highlands of Judah through the narrow and yet direct highway which led up by the Wady Ali, through which runs the modern carriage road from Joppa to Jerusalem. Meantime Judas had rallied his followers near Mizpah.[20] This imposing height was in close touch with Jerusalem and at the same time commanded a view of all the roads leading from the north and west, rendering it practically impossible for the Syrians to overtake him unawares.[93] Apparently the Syrian generals had pitched their camp at Emmaus in the vain hope that by a quick night-march they might surprise Judas and his followers at Mizpah. Anticipating this design, Judas by night transferred his army to a point a little south of Emmaus, probably following one of the wild, deserted valleys which lead from Mizpah to the plain. The result was that when a detachment of Syrian soldiers were sent under Gorgias to capture Judas, they found Mizpah deserted. Meantime Judas boldly attacked the remnant of the Syrian army on the plain near Emmaus and quickly put them to flight. Many were slain; some escaped to the stronghold of Gezer, or Gazara, as it was called at that time, a little northwest of Emmaus; some turned southward into the Philistine lowlands, which were held by the Idumeans; others fled as far as Ashdod and Jamnia on the western side of the Philistine Plain. When Gorgias and his soldiers returned and found their camp in flames they were seized by a panic and retreated into the land of the Philistines, leaving the Jews in possession of rich spoil.

Victory at Bethsura. During the following year the regent Lysias himself gathered together a picked army of sixty thousand infantry and five thousand horsemen and advanced against Judas. This time the Syrians avoided the northern passes and entered western Judah through the Valley of Elah, marched past the old battle-fields of Socoh and Adullam, which were now held by the Idumeans, and thence followed the road which led along a branch of the Wady es-Sur in a southeastern direction. By taking this southern route they reached without opposition Bethsura,[114] on the height which marked the southwestern boundary of Judah, where the road from the west joined the main highway from Hebron to Jerusalem. Rallying ten thousand of his followers, Judas boldly attacked the huge Syrian army in front of Bethsura and again won an overwhelming victory.

Rededication of the Temple. The retreat of their foes left the Jews free at last to enter Jerusalem, to tear down the heathen altar which had been reared by Antiochus, and to restore the temple and its service. Three years after it had been desecrated by Antiochus, the temple was rededicated. The strong fortress of Acra within the city still remained in possession of the Syrian garrison; but Jerusalem was fortified with high walls and strong towers, and joy and confidence again filled the hearts of the Jews.

Campaigns South and East of the Dead Sea. Judas also employed this brief respite from Syrian attack to carry on campaigns against the foes who, doubtless at the instigation of the Syrians, were attacking the Jews on every side. The first battle was with the Idumeans and was fought at Akrabattine, which was probably the steep Scorpion Pass at the southeastern end of the Dead Sea, along which ran the road from Hebron to Petra. On the east-Jordan at this time the Ammonites, under their leader, Timotheus, apparently controlled the entire territory from the Arnon to the Yarmuk. Judas's first east-Jordan campaign was in the territory immediately north of the Arnon, where he conquered the ancient city of Jazer and its villages.

Victories in Northeastern Gilead. Learning that the Jews and descendants of the ancient Israelites settled in northern Gilead were being besieged by Timotheus, that many others had been massacred, and that those in Galilee were also the object of bitter persecution, he gathered eleven thousand of his followers. Simon, his brother, was sent with three thousand soldiers into Galilee, where he succeeded in rescuing the Israelites and in driving the heathen out of the uplands down to Ptolemis. With the remaining eight thousand picked soldiers Judas and his brother Jonathan made a rapid and brilliant campaign through southern Gilead. A march of three days from the east-Jordan to the northeast brought them to the borders of the desert, where they met certain of the Nabateans, an Arabian people who at this time were crystallizing into a strong nation, with their centre southeast of the Dead Sea. Like Judas they were apparently hostile to the Syrians and therefore they met him on friendly terms. Learning through them of conditions in Gilead, he turned suddenly northward and captured the important trading city of Bozrah, far out in the wilderness to the south of the Hauran. The spoils of this city provided his followers with immediate supplies. Thence by a night march he reached the stronghold where the Israelites were being besieged by the Ammonites under Timotheus. In the Greek version of I Maccabees, this stronghold is called Dathema, but in the Syriac version Rametha, which is clearly the modern Remtheh, an important station on the great pilgrim road to the north, about twenty-five miles east of Bozrah. As has already been noted, it is one of the most probable sites of the ancient Ramoth-Gilead. Timotheus and his followers, caught unprepared, were defeated with great slaughter. From this point Judas made a détour to the Gileadite city of Mizpah, mentioned in the Jephthah stories. Its exact site is doubtful. It may be identified with Sûf, the height northwest of Jerash, where are to be found many great dolmens, or possibly it occupied the site of Jerash itself.

Cities Captured North of the Yarmuk. From here Judas evidently marched northward across the Yarmuk to the town of Casphor. In II Maccabees this name appears as Caspin, and in all probability is to be identified with Castle Chisfin in the southeastern Jaulan, a little west of the Nahr er-Rukkad. The next town captured by Judas was Maked, which may be represented by Tell Mikdad, about twenty miles northeast of Chisfin and a little west of the railway from Damascus to Haifa. Bosor without much doubt occupied the site of the modern town of Busr el-Hariri, fifteen miles southeast of Tell Mikdad and on the southern side of the great lava-bed, El Lejah.

The Second Victory Over Timotheus. Meantime Timotheus had gathered another army and awaited Judas near the "brook of water opposite the town of Raphon." An echo of the name of this ancient town is possibly to be found in the modern El-Mezerib. The ancient village at this point, which lay on an island in the midst of a large clear pool, from which flows one of the chief sources of the Yarmuk, well satisfies the situation implied by the vivid description of the battle in I Maccabees. It was on the main highway along which Timotheus would naturally advance from the territory of Ammon and was about ten miles north of Remtheh, the scene of the first battle. Timotheus's hesitation in crossing the brook was rightly interpreted by Judas as a sign of fear. Rushing into the water the Jews again won a complete victory. Their foes, casting aside their weapons, fled for refuge to the ancient sanctuary of Carnaim, which is without reasonable doubt to be identified with the ancient shrine of Ashteroth-Karnaim, eight miles to the north. Following the fugitives, Judas captured this city and burned the temple.

Judas's Return. Then gathering the Jews in the land of Gilead, which in the first book of Maccabees included the east-Jordan territory, both north and south of the Yarmuk, Judas set out for Jerusalem. His road naturally led due southward past the scene of his last great battle with Timotheus. Thence, turning to the southwest, his way was through a narrow pass where probably lay the town of Ephron. Inasmuch as this town opposed his passage, he captured and destroyed it. Thence passing through the ancient Arbela, he followed the main highway that led to the Jordan opposite Bethshean. From there he naturally followed the road along the Jordan valley to Jericho and up to Jerusalem.

Significance of Judas's Victories. Meantime, contrary to his orders, two of Judas's generals had attacked the Philistine town of Jamnia and met with a disastrous repulse. Rallying his forces he advanced against the Idumeans to the south and west of Judah. Hebron was taken and its citadel destroyed. After capturing the surrounding towns he turned westward to Marissa, the ancient Mareshah, which guarded the entrance to the Valley of Zephathah.[108] From there he carried his campaign across the Philistine plain to the ancient city of Ashdod, which he captured and looted. With a comparatively few half-trained soldiers Judas within one year fought more successful battles and captured more strong cities than did David throughout all of his illustrious career. His limited resources and the certainty of another and more overwhelming Syrian attack made it impossible, however, for Judas to hold the territory thus conquered, so that, while his victories represent brilliant achievements, the effect was ephemeral. The refugees whom he brought back to Judah increased its comparatively small population and thus laid the foundations for that Maccabean kingdom which ultimately rose as the result of the dauntless and patriotic spirit that Judas infused into his followers.

Battle of Beth-zacharias. Judas's desperate attempt to capture the hostile garrison in Jerusalem led the Syrians to send for help to Antiochus Eupator, who had succeeded to the throne of Syria on the death of his father. A vast army was gathered, consisting of a hundred thousand infantry and twenty thousand horsemen. Thirty-two elephants also accompanied the army and played an important part in the final battle. Again the approach to the Judean heights was made through the Valley of Elah and up along the Wady es-Sur to Bethsura. Instead of meeting the Syrians at this point Judas retired along the northern road to Beth-zacharias, which lay on the right of the highway a few miles southwest of Bethlehem. Here Judas gave battle to the huge Syrian army, which was drawn up on two wings, one on the heights and the other on the low ground. The elephants, with towers of wood on their backs, were placed in the front of the line of battle. Each elephant was supported by a thousand men armed with coat of mail, and five hundred horsemen. Judas and his followers made a courageous attack upon this huge and imposing host, but they were overwhelmed by sheer numbers. The elephants also were effective in turning the tide of battle. Eleazer, one of Judas's brothers, with the spirit that characterized the family, broke through one of the phalanxes and, creeping under what he supposed to be the royal elephant, pierced it with his spear from beneath and perished under the beast as it fell to the earth. None others were found, however, in the Jewish ranks to follow his courageous example. Judas retired to Jerusalem, where he was besieged by Lysias, the leader of the Syrian forces. Fortunately for the Jewish cause, conditions in the Syrian capital made it necessary for Lysias to retire. He accordingly made a treaty with the Jews in which their religious freedom was fully assured on condition that they would recognize the authority of the Syrian kingdom.

Fortunes of Judas's Party. After securing religious freedom a strong party of the Jews, known as the Hasideans, the forerunners of the later party of the Pharisees, were inclined to accept peace at any cost. The result was that from this time on Judas lost many of his followers. Even the apostate Alcimus, appointed high priest by the Syrian king, was at first accepted by the Hasideans. His deceptions and persecution of the faithful, however, soon drove many back into the ranks of those who, like Judas, were struggling to gain not merely religious freedom, but also complete political independence. In response to the demands of the Syrian party in Judea, a certain Nicanor, formerly master of the elephants in the Syrian army, was sent to check the growing power of Judas and his followers. An engagement was fought at Caphersalama, evidently somewhere near Jerusalem. Many of the Syrian soldiers were slain and the rest fled to the City of David, which had been, from the days of the great Hebrew king, the designation of the hill of Ophel, in the southeastern part of the city. It is exceedingly probable, therefore, that Caphersalama is to be identified with the modern Kefr Silwan,[98] the little village on the eastern side of the Kidron, just across the valley from the City of David.

Victory Over Nicanor. Alarmed by this victory, Nicanor sent for another Syrian army, which he met at Beth-horon. Thence he took the main road that leads over the pass toward Jerusalem. Judas, with his followers, had taken his position near the village of Adasa, at the point where the Beth-horon road joins the central highway southward to Jerusalem. Nicanor fell in the first charge, and his army was so demoralized by the loss of its leader that they threw away their weapons and fled back along the highway toward Gazara, the ancient Gezer. The Jews in the villages along the way attacked the fleeing Syrians with the result that none of them escaped. Profiting by this signal victory, Judas sent an embassy to Rome. His aim was to secure in his unequal contest with the Syrian kingdom the aid of this power, which already was beginning to dominate the politics of the eastern Mediterranean; but before he could receive a reply from Rome, the Jewish champion fought his last fatal battle.

Death of Judas. After the defeat and death of Nicanor, the Syrian king, Demetrius, sent another army into Judah. It entered the land by the way that leads to Gilgal, which was probably either the Gilgal on the Plain of Sharon, north of Antipatris, or else the better-known Gilgal near the ancient Shiloh. In either case the army appears to have reached the central plateau by the road which runs through the valley somewhat north of the Valley of Ajalon and therefore through territory under the control of Syria. Thence the Syrians approached Judea and Jerusalem directly from the north. Meantime, Judas was intrenched not far from his home at Modein. The decisive battle was fought at Elasa, or Eleasa, a half mile north of the steep descent from Upper to Lower Beth-horon.[84] Terrified by the overwhelming numbers of the Syrian army, Judas's small force of three thousand men was soon reduced by desertion to only eight hundred. The courageous Jewish leader made the grave mistake of venturing a battle under these conditions. Even as it was, he was apparently on the eve of victory when he fell slain within the sight of the field on which he had won his first great battle. With his fall the battle was lost and the Syrians were left for a time in almost undisputed possession of Judea. With great lamentation and mourning his followers buried him in the tomb of his fathers at Modein, chanting in modified form the words of David's lamentation over Saul:

> How is the hero fallen,
> The saviour of Israel.

Judas's Character and Work. There are many analogies between the character and work of Saul and of Judas. Both were devoted patriots and courageous warriors. Both laid the foundations for a kingdom, but fell on the battle-field before their task was completed. Both inspired their people with the ambition for independence and taught them how to fight effectively in securing it. Of the two, Judas appears to have been the more balanced and unselfish character. In view of the obstacles with which he contended, he was unquestionably the greatest general that Israel ever produced. The peculiar topography of Judea enabled him to contend successfully with strong armies, but in a prolonged struggle with the Syrian kingdom the advantages were all with the latter. The barren, limited territory of Judea was incapable of supporting a large people or of furnishing the resources for a protracted war. On the other hand, Antioch, which had as its base the great plain between the Lebanons, possessed almost unlimited resources and was the natural centre from which to rule both Syria and Palestine. Judas was able to win his victories not merely because of his dauntless courage and leadership, but because the Syrian kingdom was fatally weakened by the moral corruption and constant dissensions of its rulers. These two elements, courageous and able leadership on the side of the Jews and corruption and inefficiency in the Syrian kingdom, enabled Judas's followers in time to overcome geographical conditions and to build up, as in the days of David, a large and independent kingdom.

XXII

THE MACCABEAN AND HERODIAN AGE

Jonathan's Policy.—Basis of Agreement With the Syrians.—Concessions to Jonathan.—His Conquests.—Simon's Achievements.—His Strong and Prosperous Rule.—Growth of the Two Rival Parties.—Wars and Conquests of John Hyrcanus.—Reign of Aristobulus I.—The Cruel Rule of Alexander Janneus.—The Rivalry of Parties Under Alexandra.—The Influence of Antipater.—Advance of Rome.—The Appeal to Pompey.—His Capture of the Temple.—Palestine Under the Rule of Rome.—Rebellions Led by Aristobulus and His Sons.—Antipater's Services to Rome.—Rewards for His Services.—The Parthian Conquest.—Herod Made King of the Jews.—His Policy.—His Work as a City Builder.—Herod's Temple.—The Tragedies of His Family Life.—The Popular Hopes of the Jews.

Jonathan's Policy. Jonathan, who succeeded his brother, Judas, in the leadership of the Jewish rebellion, combined great skill and energy with a certain craftiness, which enabled him to profit by every turn in the tortuous politics of Syria. It was an exceedingly corrupt age, and Jonathan adopted the standards and methods of his day. The secure hiding-places in Palestine enabled him to elude the Syrians and to recover from the shock which his cause had received as a result of the death of Judas. Jonathan and his followers took refuge first in the wilderness of Judea[24] and the dry, barren wadies that lead down to the Dead Sea, and later in the jungle of the lower Jordan.[36] Into this thicket of reeds and bushes the Syrian general pursued them. On this strange battle-field Jonathan and his followers were defeated, but by swimming across the Jordan succeeded in escaping pursuit. At another time he was shut up in the fortress of Beth-basi, which Josephus identifies with Beth-hoglah, in the midst of the Jordan valley, a little southeast of Jericho. It is more probably to be identified with some one of the many natural strongholds along the Wady el-Bassah, which leads through the eastern part of the wilderness of Tekoa down toward the Dead Sea.

Basis of Agreement With the Syrians. Finding that pursuit was futile, the Syrian general made a treaty with Jonathan, according to which he was allowed to establish his head-quarters at the ancient fortress of Michmash[85] on the northern borders of Judah and to rule in peace as a local chieftain. He in turn was to refrain from attack upon the Syrians, who were intrenched in certain strategic strongholds. Jericho guarded the eastern bounds of Judah. The border fortresses on the north included Beth-horon, the ancient sanctuary of Bethel, Timnath, north of Beth-horon, Pharathon, which is without much doubt to be identified with Farata, southwest of Shechem, and Tephon, which probably represents the ancient Tappuah, a little west of the main highway that leads southward from Shechem. The western border fortresses were Gazara in the northwest and Bethsura, the ancient Bethzur,[114] in the southwest.

Concessions to Jonathan. As a result of the rivalry between the different claimants for the Syrian throne, Jonathan was suddenly raised from his position of comparative unimportance to the virtual rulership of all southern Palestine. A certain Alexander Balas, who claimed to be the son of Antiochus Epiphanes, the arch persecutor of the Jews, finally gave Jonathan the title of high priest and the control not only of Judea, but of the Philistine coast. Jonathan, by the sword, quickly made valid these concessions. Joppa, the natural seaport of Jerusalem, was first seized. Then Azotus, the ancient Ashdod, was captured after a Syrian army had been defeated on the plain before its walls, and the famous temple of Dagon was burned.

Jonathan's Conquests. When Jonathan's patron, Alexander Balas, was overthrown by a Ptolemy of Egypt, the Jewish leader readily transferred his allegiance to the Syrian king, Demetrius II. Ignoring the fact that he himself was struggling for freedom, Jonathan disgraced the Jewish cause by sending troops to aid this tyrant in carrying through a great massacre of his subjects in the streets of Antioch. Already personal ambitions were beginning to obscure the nobler patriotic ideals that had at first actuated the warlike sons of the old priest, Mattathias. In a short time a son of Alexander Balas appeared on the political horizon and won the allegiance of Jonathan by granting him control of the entire coast land from the Ladder of Tyre to the border of Egypt. The Jewish leader improved this opportunity to complete the conquest of the Philistine cities and to capture the stronghold of Bethsura. An army of Demetrius II was also defeated on the Plain of Hazor, west of Lake Huleh. A little later Jonathan led an army into the country of Hamath, between the Lebanons, but met with no serious opposition. Returning to Jerusalem, he tore down a part of the eastern wall opposite the citadel and with the stones built a high rampart in order to cut off the heathen garrison from all contact with the rest of the city. Jonathan, however, soon fell a prey to craft and treachery, which he himself had repeatedly used. Lured into the city of Ptolemais by an ambitious general, who had placed on the Syrian throne the young son of Alexander Balas, Jonathan was captured and later put to death.

Simon's Achievements. By this act Simon, the oldest and most judicious of the five famous brothers, was called to the leadership of the Jewish people. Profiting by the weakness of Syria, he devoted himself to expanding and strengthening his kingdom. The strong western border fortress of Gazara[61] was captured after a short but energetic defence. The heathen population was expelled and Jewish colonies were settled both here and at Joppa. Thus Simon established a direct line of communication between Jerusalem and the Mediterranean trade routes, and opened the way for that foreign commerce which soon brought great wealth to the Jewish kingdom. At last, for the first time in centuries, the citadel at Jerusalem was captured and held by the Jews. The temple mount beside the citadel was made stronger than before and the Jews at last felt that sense of security which came from complete possession of their land and of its fortified outposts.

His Strong and Prosperous Rule. Simon's reign was one of comparative peace and prosperity. A Syrian army invaded the Philistine Plain and took their position at Kidron, which is probably to be identified with Katrah, three and one-half miles southwest of Ekron. Simon sent a strong army against the invaders, under the leadership of his two oldest sons, Judas and John. The battle was fought in the plain between Kidron and Modein. Boldly advancing to the attack the Jewish army put the Syrians to flight, pursuing them to Kidron and the towers near Azotus, which they quickly captured. In gratitude for his patriotic services and beneficient rule, the Jews confirmed Simon in the title of high priest, general, and governor. His rule and that of his son who succeeded him were the fruitage of the earlier struggles and the calm before the storm of foreign invasion that before long again swept Palestine. Like his other brothers, Simon died a violent death. He was the victim of the treachery of one of his sons-in-law, who slew him at the little stronghold of Dôk, in the Jordan valley, on the edge of the western hills about three miles north of Jericho.

Growth of the Two Rival Parties. Simon was followed by his son, John Hyrcanus, who drove his father's assassin from the land. With the military skill of his illustrious father and uncles he combined a strong personal ambition. This is shown not only by his conquests, but also by his employment of foreign mercenaries. His long reign of thirty-one years witnessed the development of the two great parties in Judaism, the Pharisees and the Sadducees. They were the expression of the conflicting ideas and ideals ever present in Jewish life, but now brought into clear relief. The party of the Sadducees comprised the high priestly nobles, whose rank, wealth, and ambitions made them conservatives and led them to support the political ambitions of the Maccabean kings. The Pharisees, on the other hand, were the party of the people. They were the strenuous champions of the law. While the question of freedom of worship was at issue, they had upheld Judas, but they cared little for political glory and preferred to submit to foreign rulers rather than to fight for their independence. They also considered it a sacrilege that warriors like John Hyrcanus should perform the sacred high-priestly functions. Hence from the days of John Hyrcanus the history of the Judean kingdom was that of a house divided against itself.

Wars and Conquests of John Hyrcanus. During the early part of John's reign Judea was again invaded by the Syrians. Jerusalem was besieged and the Jews were again obliged to recognize the old suzerainty. Fortunately for them the Syrian king was intent upon invading Parthia and, therefore, in order to secure the support of John Hyrcanus, left him in possession of his kingdom. After the death of Antiochus Sidetes in this eastern campaign, John was free to complete the conquest of the ancient foes of his race. His first campaign was east of the Dead Sea and resulted in the capture of the old Moabite city of Medeba. He then marched against Shechem and Mount Gerizim, the home of the Samaritans. Their temple was left in ruins and their territory was joined to the Jewish kingdom. The Idumean stronghold, Marissa,[(108)] on the borders of the Philistine Plain, and Dora, or Adora, a few miles southwest of Hebron, were captured and the Idumeans were completely subdued. These close kinsmen and hereditary foes of the Jews were compelled to submit to the right of circumcision and to accept the Hebrew laws. Thus at the point of the sword was brought into the Jewish nation an element which was destined in the end to prove its undoing. Last of all, Hyrcanus conquered, by means of a protracted siege, the then Greek city of Samaria. The Syrian army sent to its relief was vanquished and the city completely demolished.

Reign of Aristobulus I. Notwithstanding its independence and political strength, the Jewish kingdom was at this time largely Hellenized. Aristobulus I, the son of John Hyrcanus, was, as his name indicates, a man strongly influenced by the Greek culture and ideas that were pressing into Palestine from every side. Following the example of the Greek states, he assumed in 104 B.C. the title of king. His brief reign was characterized by great brutality. His mother he allowed to starve to death in prison, and through his insane jealousy he slew his favorite brother. By far the most significant event of his reign was the conquest of Galilee. Its Iturean or half-Arabian population was assimilated to Judaism and the foundations laid for that freer, more virile life which was the background of early Christian history.

The Cruel Rule of Alexander Janneus. Alexander Janneus, the brother who succeeded Aristobulus, was known among the Jews as "the Thracian," and he well deserved the title. His chief interests were war and revelry. By his rash attacks upon the neighboring peoples he repeatedly brought disaster upon his kingdom. He succeeded in alienating his subjects so completely that they called in the king of Damascus to free them from this inhuman monster. In the hour of their success, however, they repented of their action, brought Janneus back from the mountains whither he had fled, and restored him to the throne. Instead of showing gratitude he hung upon crosses eight hundred of the Pharisees who had opposed him, first slaying their wives and children before their eyes. Notwithstanding his rashness and his unmeasured excesses, he succeeded by sheer persistency in extending the bounds of his kingdom, so that at his death his authority was paramount along the Mediterranean coast from Mount Carmel to the borders of Egypt, in central Palestine from upper Galilee to the South Country, and in the east-Jordan land from east of the Sea of Galilee to the Arnon. The outlying Greek cities which he conquered were many of them laid in ruins and the land given up to bands of robbers. At the moment when the Maccabean kingdom reached its widest bounds its decay had already begun and distress was the lot of most of its citizens.

The Rivalry of Parties Under Alexandra. Alexander Janneus was succeeded by his wife Alexandra. The only other woman who had sat on an Israelite throne was Athaliah of Judah, although reigning queens were not uncommon in oriental history. She reversed the policy of her husband and placed the Pharisees, the party of the people, in control. They made the great mistake, however, of using their power to take bloody revenge upon their Sadducean rivals. The result was that the fatal breach between the two parties was broadened rather than healed. The Sadducean and military party rallied about Aristobulus, while the Pharisees upheld the cause of Alexandra's older son, Hyrcanus. Both of her sons were lacking in kingly qualities. Hyrcanus was inefficient and without ambition, more eager to enjoy a quiet life than to assume the responsibilities of government; Aristobulus was imperious and greedy of power.

The Influence of Antipater. At the death of Alexandra, Hyrcanus was made high priest while Aristobulus II assumed the kingship. The division was wise and equable, although in the circumstances a permanent truce between the rival parties was impossible. It was at this crisis that Antipater, the father of Herod the Great, became a power in Jewish politics. Antipas, his father, an Idumean, had been made governor of Idumea by Alexander Janneus. Antipater was suspicious of Aristobulus and eager to secure power at any cost. In the weak Hyrcanus he recognized a tool adapted to his aim. Accordingly he persuaded the high priest to flee from Jerusalem, and enlisting the support of his friend, Aretas, the powerful Nabatean king whose capital was at Petra, he advanced to Jerusalem with a large army, in order to wrest the kingdom from Aristobulus and to make Hyrcanus nominal king. In the first engagement Aretas defeated Aristobulus, who then took refuge with his army in the temple.

Advance of Rome. It was at this juncture that Rome advanced to the conquest of the lands along the eastern Mediterranean. Already this growing world-power had gained possession of Egypt and a foothold in eastern Asia Minor. In 66 B.C. Pompey was sent to crush the allied rival powers of Pontus and Armenia. After accomplishing this mission he advanced southward toward Damascus. Already his lieutenant had ordered the Nabatean army to leave Judea. The contest between the two brothers, Hyrcanus and Aristobulus, gave Rome, which had already acted as a patron toward the Judean kingdom, the desired opportunity to step in and assume control of the much coveted territory. Again Palestine and Syria were the bone of contention between two great world-powers. The political horizon, however, had broadened and now the rivals were Rome in the distant west, and Parthia, the successor of the ancient Persian empire in the east.

The Appeal to Pompey. The Jews had long been aware of the importance of Rome's influence in the territory lying along the eastern Mediterranean. It was natural, therefore, that the claimants for the Jewish throne should refer their case to Pompey. At Damascus representatives of the two factions pleaded their case before him. More indicative still of the spirit of the Jewish race was an embassy representing the people and especially the Pharisaic party, demanding that the claims of both the rivals be set aside, so that the Jews might be allowed in quiet to worship their God in accordance with their sacred laws, under the protecting rule of a foreign power. Pompey reserved his decision until he arrived at Jerusalem. His line of approach was apparently along the Jordan valley past Bethshean, then known as Scythopolis, to Korea, which Josephus describes as the "first entrance into Judea when one passes over the midland countries." This is probably to be identified with the modern Karawa, on the southwestern side of the beautiful plain through which the Wady el-Farah finds its way to the Jordan. Through this wady the highway runs westward to what was at that time the northern boundary of Judea. Aristobulus, anticipating that Pompey's decision would be adverse to him, had shut himself up in the fortress of Alexandrium, built by his father, Alexander Janneus. Apparently this famous fortress stood on the height of Karn Sartabeh, which rises over two thousand two hundred feet above the Jordan valley, just south of Korea and opposite the point where the Wady Farah enters the river. Its top is strewn to-day with large, rough-dressed blocks of stone, which probably belonged to the ancient castle.

Pompey's Capture of the Temple. Aristobulus surrendered when ordered to do so by Pompey, but his followers refused to lay down arms when the Romans approached Jerusalem. Instead, they intrenched themselves on the temple hill. Pompey, aided by Hyrcanus and Antipater, attacked this inner fortress from the north. The deep ravine which led up from the Kidron and the deep cutting across the northern extension of the temple hill made the approach, even at this, the most vulnerable point, exceedingly difficult. By filling in the great rock-cut fosse Pompey was able at last to bring up his battering rams and to surmount the high walls and fortresses that were massed at this point.

Palestine Under the Rule of Rome. In the settlement which followed the capture of Jerusalem, Pompey condemned Aristobulus to follow the chariot as a captive in the great triumphal procession at Rome. Hyrcanus was stripped of all political power, but was allowed to retain his position as high priest. Many of the Greek cities, both along the coast of the Mediterranean and east of the Jordan, were rebuilt. All of them were separated from Judea and placed under the immediate direction of the Roman governor of Syria. Galilee, Judea, and Idumea were annexed to the Roman empire, but governed together as a sub-province. Under Gabinius, who carried out the policy of Pompey, they were divided into five administrative districts, with centres at Jerusalem in the south, Jericho, Amathus, and Gadara along the Jordan valley, and Sepphoris in Galilee.

Rebellions Led by Aristobulus and His Sons. The peace of Palestine was repeatedly disturbed by the attempts of the survivors of the Maccabean house to recover their kingdom. The first rebellion, in 57 B.C., was led by Alexander, son of the deposed king, Aristobulus II, about whom the Sadducean nobility and the military class in Judea quickly rallied. He rebuilt the fortress of Alexandrium, but his followers were defeated by a Roman army before its walls and he was taken prisoner. The next year Aristobulus, with his son Antigonus, escaped from Rome and rallied his followers again at Alexandrium. He soon, however, abandoned this stronghold for the more inaccessible fortress of Machærus, built by his father, Janneus, on a hill in the middle of a deep ravine which led up on the eastern side of the Dead Sea.[38] Being far away from the majority of their followers and without proper equipment for a long siege, the rebels were soon obliged to capitulate. The third rebellion, again led by Alexander, was quickly put down as the result of a decisive battle near Mount Tabor. For years after, bands of robbers and rebels kept central Galilee in a constant state of unrest, until finally the Roman general, Cassius, subdued the country and sold thirty thousand of them into slavery.

Antipater's Services to Rome. During the two decades that followed the Roman conquest of Palestine, Judea was deeply affected by the great convulsions through which Rome passed in its transition from a republican to an imperial form of government. During this turbulent and dramatic era Antipater, the Idumean, remained the ruling power in Judea and profited by each change of ruler. His policy was to retain the friendship of Rome at any cost and to ally himself with the man of the hour. His chief aim was to further his own personal interests. He was influenced by no patriotic zeal or racial prejudices. At the same time he showed great skill in steering his course amidst the storms that swept the Roman world during these tempestuous years. When Pompey was defeated at the battle of Pharsalia in 49 B.C. Antipater actively allied himself with the cause of Julius Cæsar. When an army of the victor marched to the conquest of Egypt he sent Jewish auxiliaries and fought valiantly at their head, both in the siege of Pelusium and that of Memphis. He also at a critical moment influenced the Nabateans and the Jews of Egypt to ally themselves with the cause of Cæsar.

Rewards for His Services. As a reward for his services Antipater was made procurator of Judea. His elder son, Phasael was appointed governor of Jerusalem and his younger son, Herod, of Galilee. Hyrcanus was given the title of ethnarch. Joppa, which opened the trade of the Mediterranean to Judea, was added to the province. The rights of the Jews in foreign countries were also guarded by Cæsar, who always showed himself a patron and friend of the race. His assassination in 44 B.C., and the murder of Antipater by an ambitious Jewish noble one year later, did not undermine the influence of the Idumean house. Mark Antony, who was then Rome's representative in the east, at once appointed Herod and Phasael civil rulers of Judea to succeed their father.

The Parthian Conquest. In 40 B.C., however, the Parthians for a brief time pushed the boundaries of their empire westward to the Mediterranean and placed Antigonus, the son of Aristobulus, on the throne of his fathers. Phasael was treacherously put to death by the Parthians. Hyrcanus's ears were cut off and he was carried captive to Babylon, and the Sadducean nobles who rallied about Antigonus either slew or drove from the land the followers of their former Idumean rulers.

Herod Made King of the Jews. Herod, after many adventures, finally escaped to Rome, where he was given the then empty title of "King of the Jews" at the recommendation of Mark Antony and Octavius. After two years of active campaigning, Herod finally captured Jerusalem, and Antigonus, the last Maccabean king, was promptly put to death by the Romans. In 37 B.C. Herod began his reign as king of the Jews. His dominant policy, like that of his father, was loyalty at all times and at any cost to the ruling Roman faction. Notwithstanding faults, he proved a valuable servant of Rome. The kingdom over which he ruled was the natural eastern boundary of the empire. It contained many elements hostile to each other. The Jews had proved by many rebellions how little their loyalty to Rome could be trusted; and yet it was essential for the integrity of the empire that the peace and strength of this outlying province should be maintained. This task Herod was able to accomplish. Hence, when Augustus, at the battle of Actium in 31 B.C., became master of the Roman empire, he confirmed Herod in the authority which he had hitherto held. Subsequently Augustus added new territory to Herod's kingdom until, with the exception of certain Greek cities on the coast and others east of the Jordan, he ruled over all Palestine from the sea to the desert and from the foot of Mount Hermon to the wilderness in the south.

His Policy. Herod was a tyrant, merciless in putting to death all rivals. He loaded his people with heavy taxes, but he did give them much desired peace. Naturally in this Greek age the son of an Idumean father and an Arabian mother was an ardent advocate of the prevailing Hellenistic culture; yet, with occasional lapses, Herod proved also a defender of the Jewish race and religion.

His Work as a City Builder. As a builder Herod made a deep impression upon the Palestine of his age. After the battle of Actium the city of Samaria had been presented to him by Augustus. Herod transformed it into a Græco-Roman city of the most magnificent type. Its name was changed to Sebaste, the Greek for Augusta, in honor of his patron. On the top of the hill was built the huge Roman temple, the ruins of which have recently been laid bare by American excavators.[59] The city was encircled by a colonnade, twenty yards wide and over a mile long, with pillars sixteen feet in height. A beautiful natural theatre was built on the northern slope of the hill, overlooking the fertile plain. Splendid public buildings made it one of the glories of Herod's kingdom. He also transformed Straton's Tower on the Mediterranean coast into a Græco-Roman metropolis and named it Cæsarea,[115] in honor of the emperor. On a comparatively level plain rose a temple, theatre, amphitheatre, and palaces of marble. Since it was intended to be the seaport of both Samaria and Judea, a great breakwater two hundred feet wide was constructed out of huge stones. The harbor opened to the north, thus protecting ships from the prevailing southwest winds. At strategic points throughout his kingdom he fortified natural strongholds, such as the high conical hill east of Bethlehem known as the Herodium.[86] In Athens and in other cities outside his kingdom Herod reared magnificent public buildings.

Herod's Temple. In many ways the crowning achievement of Herod's zeal for building was the great temple which he reared in Jerusalem. The temple area was first extended to the south so that it was double its former size.[99] A viaduct and four gates connected it with the central and western part of the city. Two large gateways also led up from the ancient City of David on the south. The entire temple area was encircled with a double row of huge marble columns. On the south side of the court were four rows of lofty columns with Corinthian capitals. The sanctuary itself, which stood on its original site in the northern part of the temple area on a platform of native rock, was surrounded by an inner group of elaborate buildings, approached by splendid gateways on the north, east, and south. In front of the comparatively small temple structure was reared a large porch, one hundred cubits high and one hundred cubits broad, which brought it into harmony with Herod's huge constructions. The work on the temple was begun about 20 B.C. Provisions were made so that it continued uninterruptedly after Herod's death. The temple was completed only a few years before the final destruction of Jerusalem in 70 A.D.

The Tragedies of His Family Life. The saddest chapter in Herod's tempestuous career is that of his family life. He was a man of strong and ungoverned passions, in whom intense love, jealousy, and vindictiveness played a prominent rôle. He was also the victim of the intrigues and rivalries characteristic of an oriental harem. The story of the murder of his wife, Mariamne, the Maccabean princess whom he truly loved, and of his two favorite sons, Alexander and Aristobulus, as a result of the plots of his sister, Salome, and of his treacherous son, Antipater, is one of the familiar and most tragic chapters in history. Conscious at last that his wife and sons had been innocent of the base charges which led him to murder them, betrayed by his nearest kinsmen, hated by most of his subjects, and regarded coldly by the royal patron whom he had served so slavishly, Herod the Great was the most pathetic figure in all his wide kingdom.

The Popular Hopes of the Jews. The victories and glories of the Maccabean era, followed by the double tyranny of Rome and Herod, made a profound impression upon the faith and hopes of the Jewish race. Many of them turned with loathing from the bloodshed and the selfish victories of the later Maccabean rulers to the law and the worship at the temple as their chief joy and consolation. In the minds of others these triumphs recalled the glories of the days of David and kindled anew their ambition to see a world-wide kingdom with Jerusalem as its centre and a descendant of David on the throne, who should reign, not as the corrupt, selfish Maccabean kings, but with justice and regard for the welfare of all his subjects. Others, more spiritually minded, like the author of chapters 37 to 70 of the book of Enoch, looked for The Elect One, The Anointed, The Son of Man, who would come to put an end to the reign of the wicked, to purify the earth of all evil, to gather together the faithful, and to establish a universal rule of righteousness. The more bitter the tyranny of Herod and the more galling the yoke of Rome the more ardently they hoped for the speedy realization of these expectations, which were the solace and inspiration of the great body of the Jewish nation. About 4 B.C., while at Jericho the tyrant lay dying who for a third of a century had held the Jewish race powerless in his strong grasp, a few miles away there was born one who was destined to realize, in a manner more glorious than the most enlightened of Israel's prophets had proclaimed, Jehovah's gracious purpose for mankind.

XXIII

THE BACKGROUND OF JESUS' CHILDHOOD AND YOUNG MANHOOD

The Short Reign of Archelaus.—The Roman Province of Judea.—Territory and Character of Herod Antipas.—Philip's Territory.—The Decapolis.—Place of Jesus' Birth.—Situation of Nazareth.—Its Central Position.—View from the Heights above the City.—The Spring at Nazareth.—Roads to Jerusalem.—Jesus' Educational Opportunities.—Scene of John the Baptist's Early Life.—Field of His Activity.—The Baptism of Jesus.—Machærus, Where John the Baptist Was Beheaded.—Effect of John's Death Upon Jesus.—Jesus' Appearance.

The Short Reign of Archelaus. At his death Herod the Great left his kingly title to his son, Archelaus. Archelaus, however, showed himself so tyrannical and tactless in dealing with the Jews that Augustus did not confirm his title to the kingship, but instead made him ethnarch of Samaria, Judea, and Idumea. During his tumultuous reign of ten years he developed the fertile plains about Jericho by means of aqueducts, which brought water for irrigation from the western hills, and also built the city of Archelais on the western side of the Jordan valley, not far from the Maccabean castle of Alexandrium. His rule in the end proved so hateful to the Jews that they sent a deputation of their leading men to Rome to present charges against him. As a result, Archelaus was banished.

The Roman Province of Judea. Inasmuch as Judea was one of the border provinces and had repeatedly proved itself turbulent and rebellious, it was placed under the immediate direction of the emperor and was ruled by a procurator of equestrian rank. The duties of the procurator were primarily to maintain order, to direct the collection of taxes, and decide the more important legal questions. He alone could inflict capital punishment, and to him or his representatives were naturally referred all cases in which Roman citizens were involved. Otherwise, in Judea the administration of the civil as well as of the ceremonial laws was in charge of the Jewish courts, at the head of which stood the Sanhedrin at Jerusalem.

Palestine in the Time of Jesus (4 B.C. – 30 A.D.)

L.L. Poates Engr'g Co., N.Y.

Territory and Character of Herod Antipas. To his son, Herod Antipas, Herod the Great left Galilee and Perea. Galilee at this time extended on the south to the River Kishon on the Plain of Esdraelon. Its western boundaries were the plains of Acre and Tyre. On the north it extended to the River Litany, while its eastern boundary was the Jordan and the Sea of Galilee. Perea was the east-Jordan territory, extending from the territory about the Greek city of Pella in the north to the River Arnon in the south. On the east it was bounded by the territory belonging to the Greek cities of Philadelphia and Gerasa. This region had been formerly occupied by the heathen, but after conquering it the later Maccabean rulers had settled it with Jewish colonists, so that in the Mishna it is reckoned with Judea and Galilee as Jewish territory. Herod Antipas, to whom these fertile provinces were assigned, inherited the lust, the unscrupulous methods, and the building ambitions of his father. In comparison with that of Herod the Great, his long reign was peaceful, and while he taxed his subjects heavily he did not interfere with their personal freedom. Sepphoris, which was situated on a fertile hill on the southern side of the rich plain of Buttauf, in central Galilee, was by Herod surrounded with a wall and raised to the level of an imperial city. Later he built Tiberias on the western side of the Sea of Galilee, transferring thither the seat of government. It was built after the usual plan followed in Greek cities and adorned with splendid public buildings.

Philip's Territory. The northeastern part of Herod the Great's territory, from the foot of Mount Hermon to the upper waters of the Yarmuk, and from the Jordan to the desert, was given to Philip, who ruled under the title of tetrarch. He was by far the best of Herod's sons and he devoted himself to developing the resources of the barren territory over which he ruled. The ancient Paneion, on the southern side of Mount Hermon, was rebuilt and transformed into a Græco-Roman city and made the capital of Philip's possessions. In honor of Augustus he named it Cæsarea, and to distinguish it from the city of the same name, built by his father, it was known as Cæsarea Philippi. He also transformed the fishing town of Bethsaida, on the northern side of the Sea of Galilee, into a city, naming it Julias, in honor of the emperor's daughter.

The Decapolis. One result of the Roman conquest of Palestine was the rebuilding of the Greek cities along the Jordan valley and eastward. Their common origin, civilization, and interests bound them closely together, and they were known as the Decapolis. From the days of Pompey they enjoyed special privileges, but it is not clear that they were brought into political union before the death of Herod in 4 B.C. At this time these cities and the territory which they controlled were set aside from the kingdom of Herod and made responsible simply to the Roman governor of Syria. Scythopolis, commanding the great highway from western Palestine to Gilead and the desert, was the capital of this confederacy, although it was the only city of the Decapolis west of the Jordan. According to Pliny, the other cities were Hippos, Gadara, and Pella on the eastern side of the Jordan valley, Dium, Gerasa,[45] the modern Jerash, Raphana, south of the Yarmuk, and Kanatha on the eastern side of the Hauran. Here the road from Scythopolis joins the great highway from Arabia northward to Damascus, which was the northernmost city of the Decapolis. Later, other cities, such as Arbela, Kanata, and Kapitolias, just south of the Yarmuk, were added to the Decapolis until, according to Ptolemy, there were eighteen cities thus bound together. The influence of these flourishing, enterprising centres of Greek civilization upon the life and thought of Galilee, and even upon Judea, cannot be overestimated.

Place of Jesus' Birth. Up to this period, most of the events of biblical history took place in southern Palestine. Not more than a dozen cities north of the Plain of Esdraelon were mentioned in the preceding thousand years of Hebrew history. Now, however, the background of biblical history is transferred from south to north. Judah, with its narrow, rocky valleys and shut-in views, is left behind, and Galilee, with its lofty hills, its broad open plains, and its far-extending vistas, becomes the scene of the most important chapter in human history. It is true that early Christian tradition points to Bethlehem[86] as the birthplace of Jesus. This tradition is confirmed by Justin Martyr, who describes the scene of the birth as in a cave near Bethlehem. Many such cave-stables are still in use throughout the land of Palestine. For three centuries Bethlehem lay in ruins, so that at last, when Constantine reared the basilica which still marks the traditional site, it is doubtful whether there was any means of determining the actual birthplace. Beneath the church in the eastern part of the present town there are caves, one of which may have been the scene of the familiar story, but the misguided zeal of later generations of Christians has surrounded it with marble and tinsel, destroying the original simple setting.

Situation of Nazareth. For twenty-seven or eight years Nazareth was Jesus' home. Here he received those varied influences which are reflected in his life and teaching. The town of Nazareth[116] lies about one thousand five hundred feet above the level of the sea and fully a thousand above the Plain of Esdraelon to the south. The town itself is one hundred and forty feet below and a mile and a half back of the southern front of the range of hills on which it rests. It stands in the midst of an upland hollow, facing eastward. In the spring the fields in front are green with grain, while olive trees are scattered along the hillside up which the town climbs. The encircling hills, however, are gray and rocky, with only meagre suggestions of verdure, and are at present entirely denuded of trees. Here the shepherd and the tiller of the soil lived and worked side by side.

Its Central Position. Nazareth, in ancient times, was by no means a small, secluded town. It stood in the very heart of lower Galilee. Nearby the great highways radiated in all directions. From Esdraelon came one branch of the great central highway of Palestine. Across the same plain came the main caravan route from the east-Jordan land, from the Desert of Arabia, and beyond. Southward past Nazareth ran two great highways, which connected with the coast roads through Philistia to Egypt. Westward ran a road directly to the southern end of the Plain of Acre, following in part the line of the present carriage road from Nazareth to Haifa. To the northwest ran another well-travelled road, connecting at Ptolemais with the coast road to Phœnicia and the north. To the northeast, by way of the Sea of Galilee and Capernaum, a branch of the main central highway ran to Damascus. The quiet upland city, Nazareth, was therefore peculiarly open to each of the many varied influences that emanated from the cities and lands of the eastern

Mediterranean and from the great Græco-Roman world across the sea.

View from the Heights Above the City. Probably the ancient city extended farther to the west, possibly climbing the heights that overshadow the town and rise to the height of one thousand six hundred feet above the level of the sea. Here was spread out before the eye of the young boy of Nazareth one of the most beautiful and significant views in all Palestine. To the west was the Bay of Haifa and the long line of Mount Carmel running out to the blue Mediterranean. On the southeastern end of this massive plateau was the Place of Burning, where Elijah appealed to the dull conscience of his nation. Below, on the farther side of the Plain of Esdraelon, was the huge ruin of Megiddo, beside which had been fought so many decisive battles in Canaan's history. Directly south lay the hills of Samaria, with the lofty height of Mount Ebal in the distance. Standing out boldly to the southeast was the battle-field of Gilboa. Behind it was the deep gorge of the Jordan and beyond the lofty hills of Gilead. In the immediate foreground lay Little Hermon, with the town of Nain on its northwestern side,[(9)] looking out upon the Plain of Esdraelon. Eastward, in the immediate foreground from Nazareth, was the rounded, tree-clad top of Mount Tabor. Over the hills to the northeast ran the road to Cana and Capernaum. On the north rose the lofty plateau of upper Galilee, and on its summit Safed, "the city set on a hill that could not be hid." Beyond rose the cold, snowy top of Mount Hermon. To the northwest, only five miles away, was Sepphoris, Herod's earlier capital, the chief stronghold of his kingdom.

The Spring at Nazareth. Nazareth has but one spring, situated on the side hill, in the eastern part of the town, probably outside the ancient city. It leaps from the native rock a little north of the Church of the Ascension. Thence it is conducted to the famous Mary's Well,[(117)] where the water spouts from the wall under a covered stone arch and thence is conducted into a great square stone trough. Here the women and children gather to draw water to-day as they gathered in the days of Jesus. About this ancient spring, as well as in his home, the keen, thoughtful boy of Nazareth was able to study human life, so that it was unnecessary that he be told what was in the heart of man. Nazareth was so small that the character and deeds of each of its inhabitants were like an open book, and yet it was large and central enough to feel the pulsations of all the great world movements.

Roads to Jerusalem. From Nazareth three or four pilgrim roads led to Jerusalem. One, apparently little used, led westward along the eastern side of the Plain of Sharon, and thence over the famous passes of Beth-horon to Jerusalem. The direct but more arduous and dangerous road led due south across the Plain of Esdraelon past Jezreel and Ginea, the ancient En-Gannim, which stood at the point where the great plain penetrates the Samaritan hills. Thence the main road turned a little westward, running through Samaria and Shechem. A more direct branch ran due south, past Sychar, joining the other branch just east of Mount Gerizim. It was while journeying northward along this road that Jesus paused at Jacob's Well,[(17, 18)] on the eastern side of the fertile plain that opens to the northeast of Mount Gerizim, and conversed with the woman of Sychar, who perhaps had been working in the fields near by. The third pilgrim road from Nazareth ran from Jezreel eastward along the plain to the Jordan valley. From there it was possible either to take the more direct route on the west side of the valley or to cross the river at the famous fords opposite Scythopolis and thence to follow the highway along the eastern side of the Jordan. This eastern route was on the whole more attractive and lay in the territory of Antipas, beyond the reach of the hostile Samaritans. From Jericho a road led through the barren, waterless, robber-infested wilderness of Judea, that suggested to the Great Teacher his parable of the Good Samaritan.

Jesus' Educational Opportunities. Along the central or the east-Jordan route travelled the young boy of twelve to participate for the first time in the worship of the temple and to ask of the great teachers of his race the eager questions which aroused their wonderment. Luke has told in clear and graphic words the history of these earlier years: "The child grew, and became strong, filled with wisdom; and the grace of God was upon him." The light that comes from the study of Jesus' geographical environment richly supplements the meagre biblical narrative. Every year his parents made the journey to Jerusalem and Jesus doubtless went with them. The same highways frequently brought to Nazareth itinerant scribes and teachers of the law. Ample opportunities were also offered to secure copies of the scriptures of his race and thus to acquire that intimate knowledge of their contents which Jesus showed throughout all his ministry. Above all, Nazareth was in close touch with the outside world and revealed to Jesus the crying needs of the "lost sheep of the House of Israel," which ultimately drew him from the seclusion of his home to undertake his great life work.

Scene of John the Baptist's Early Life. John the Baptist is one of the most meteoric characters in biblical history. Only one scene in his life can be identified with certainty, and that is the grim castle beside the Dead Sea, where he fell a victim to Herod's passion and fear. Apparently a large part of his early life was spent at or near Jerusalem, where his father ministered as priest and where he was able to observe the crimes of the people, against which he later so vehemently and effectively protested. The wild, treeless wilderness that runs up from the Dead Sea almost to the gates of Jerusalem furnished a fitting setting for this stern prophet of righteousness, this herald of a new order. Here, undisturbed by the distracting life of the city, he could effectively deliver his message to the thoughtful ones who sought him in his solitude.[24] Here also dwelt that peculiar Jewish sect, the Essenes, whose ascetic life and strict ceremonial régime were an extreme protest against the corrupt Hellenizing tendencies of the day.

Field of His Activity. Like the early Hebrew prophets, whom John so closely resembled, he also sought out the places where men could be found in great numbers. The later Maccabean rulers and Herod transformed the hitherto comparatively deserted valley of the lower Jordan into fruitful fields, irrigated by the brooks from the hillside, studded with prosperous villages and guarded with mighty strongholds. The Jordan valley, which touched all the Jewish parts of Palestine — Judea itself, Perea, Samaria, and Galilee — was the chief field of John's work. Bethabara (House of the Ford) has been generally identified with the famous ford called Abarah, opposite Scythopolis. The best Greek manuscripts, however, read "Bethany beyond the Jordan." It is doubtful whether John's work extended so far north as the Decapolis. It is exceedingly probable that the variant readings are due to a confusion of the original, which read Beth Nimrah, which is represented by Tell Nimrin beyond the Jordan northeast of Jericho, at the point where the Wady Nimrin breaks through the Gileadite hills. It was evidently an important town, commanding the road which leads inland from this point and was within the field of John's activity.

The Baptism of Jesus. If so, the ford where Jesus met and was baptized by John was probably a little northeast of Jericho, just below the point where the Wady Nimrin joins the Jordan, rather than farther south at the traditional scene of the baptism.[118] In any case, it is easy to picture the coffee-colored stream pausing in its tempestuous course just before it enters the Dead Sea. A thicket of bushes and overhanging trees shut in the view on either side, making a strange but fitting sanctuary for the meeting of the fearless prophet and the disciple from distant Nazareth, who had doubtless come, attracted by the rumors regarding his work and words. Whether John knew it or not, that moment marked the culmination of his own life task. To Jesus it meant the consecration of himself not only to that for which John stood, but also to that vastly larger, broader task that had been revealed to him in the quiet years at Nazareth. His act, simple yet profoundly significant, brought to Jesus a full divine assurance of God's approval. He was yet to find the place, men, and means with which to work, but henceforth he was completely committed to his task. The biblical narrative implies that after this wonderful meeting with John there came to Jesus, as at frequent times in his ministry, a great reaction. He was led to seek the solitude of the wilderness west of the Jordan, there to battle with the temptations that assailed him, there to win the surpassing peace and poise that characterized his acts and words in all the great crises of his ministry.

Machærus Where John Was Beheaded. The Synoptic Gospels, as well as the Fourth, imply that for a brief period Jesus took up the message and adopted the methods of John, preaching with great success among the country villages of Judah. His work appears to have been brought to a sudden end by the arrest of John, whose fearless denunciation of Herod's crime in putting away his own wife, the daughter of Aretas, had aroused the resentful hatred of Herod and of Herodias, the partner in his guilt. In keeping with the methods of the age, John was seized and imprisoned at Herod's most distant fortress, Machærus,[38] which lay three thousand and seventy feet above the sea, on the top of a long flat ridge running for more than a mile from east to west. According to Pliny, it was, next to Jerusalem, the strongest fortress in the land. It had been reared by Herod the Great in the place of the old Maccabean stronghold. In the centre of it was an impregnable citadel. The encircling wall, one hundred yards in diameter, can still be traced. The interior is singularly bare, but a very deep well and two dark dungeons remain. Apparently Herod the Great also built a strong Roman city at the head of this valley. It rested like a swallow's nest on the lofty edge of the Moabite plateau. Acres of hewn stone with crumbling walls testify to its size and strength. In the centre are the ruins of a huge palace or castle about two hundred feet long and a hundred and fifty feet wide, with traces of rounded towers. Several passages lead to underground cisterns and dungeons, suggesting that this may have been the castle of Herod Antipas, beneath which John the Baptist was confined. Either here or in the citadel farther down the valley the intrepid prophet spent his last days. In this sinister spot, associated as it was with Alexander Janneus, Herod the Great, and his son Antipas, John the Baptist was beheaded.

Effect of John's Imprisonment Upon Jesus. The news of John's imprisonment evidently made a deep impression upon Jesus. It led him to change the scene and method of his work. He left Judea, with its harsh scenery and narrow life, and returned to the simpler and more joyous scenes in Galilee. He still continued in part to preach, but more and more he devoted himself to the task of the teacher and sought to draw from the multitudes that gathered about him certain disciples who would stand in closest personal touch with him and embody in their lives and teachings the message which he wished to impart to his race.

Jesus' Appearance. The gospels record the inner spiritual growth of the divine Son of God; but the environment amidst which he lived suggests the nature of his physical development. Nazareth is still famous for its attractive, wholesome type of men and women. Its wholesome surroundings, soil, and air all make for perfect health. The artists of the Middle Ages had no basis other than their morbid religious fancies in painting their grotesque pictures of the Christ. Constant exposure to the hot oriental suns meant that his complexion was deeply browned. The out-door life among the Galilean hills meant that he was probably tall in stature; his labors and long journeys reveal great strength of muscle. He probably had the thin nostrils and lustrous eyes that still characterize the pure Semitic type. The impression which he made at first glance upon all whom he met indicates that his was a perfect physical development. Had he permitted the enthusiastic multitudes that followed him to proclaim him king he would indeed have graced a throne. Through his mien and bearing was revealed the serene heart, in perfect harmony with the Divine Father and throbbing in sympathy with the needs and aspirations of all mankind. Thus there is every reason to believe that Jesus was in body, as well as in mind and in soul, the supreme and culminating product of God's creative work.

XXIV

THE SCENES OF JESUS' MINISTRY

Why Jesus Made Capernaum His Home.—Site of Capernaum.—
Archælogical Evidence.—Ruins at Tell Hum.—Testimony of the
Gospels and Josephus.—Statements of Early Pilgrims.—Site of
Chorazin.—Bethsaida.—Probable Scene of the Feeding of the
Multitudes.—The Night Voyage of the Disciples.—Places Where
Jesus Taught His Disciples.—Northern End of the Sea of Gali-
lee.—Contrast Between Its Northern and Southern Ends.—Jesus'
Visit to the Gadarene Territory.—The Chief Field of Jesus' Minis-
try.—Journey to Phœnicia.—At Cæsarea Philippi.—The Journey
Southward from Galilee.—At Jericho.—Situation of Bethany.—
The Triumphal Entrance Into Jerusalem.—Jesus' Activity in the
Temple.—The Last Supper and Agony.—Scenes of the Trials.—
Traditional Place of the Crucifixion.—The More Probable Site.—
The Place of Burial.

Why Jesus Made Capernaum His Home. At the beginning of his Galilean ministry Jesus transferred his home, as well as the scene of his work, from Nazareth to
Capernaum. The choice of this city reveals the breadth of his purpose. Capernaum
was the commercial metropolis of northern Palestine. Here converged the great
highways from Egypt, central Palestine, Gilead, and Arabia on the south, which in
turn led to Phœnicia, northern Syria, Damascus, and Babylonia. Although it was a
strongly Jewish town, its population was necessarily cosmopolitan. Many different occupations were here represented. The fish that were caught, especially in the
northern part of the lake, were famous throughout Galilee. The basaltic, well-watered plains about the northern end of the Sea of Galilee bore rich crops of grain;
while on the rocky but fertile hills shepherds pastured their flocks. The position of
the town also made it an important commercial centre. Roman tax collectors and
centurions made it their head-quarters. Thus Capernaum was an epitome of the
varied life of Galilee. Teachings implanted at this strategic point would also quickly spread in all directions along the eastern Mediterranean seaboard.

Site of Capernaum: Archæological Evidence. The exact situation of Capernaum has been the subject of long dispute. The two rival sites are (1) Tell Hum, at
the northern end of the Sea of Galilee, and (2) Khan Minyeh, or the neighboring
hill known as Tell Oreimeh on the northwestern side of the lake.[33] Although extensive excavations have not yet been conducted at these points, the archæological

evidence thus far discovered points clearly to Tell Hum as the site of Capernaum. On the top of Tell Oreimeh, which rises about two hundred and forty feet above the level of the lake, are the ruins of an old Amorite town. At this point, however, as well as at Khan Minyeh and in the neighboring plain, not a single trace of Roman ruins can be discovered. At Khurbet Minyeh, farther north, near the shore of the lake, are the extensive ruins of a large Arab town which flourished during the Middle Ages. In the absence of any trace of Roman ruins it is incredible that the great metropolis of Capernaum could ever have occupied this site.

Ruins at Tell Hum. Tell Hum, on the contrary, is the centre of a vast area of ruins which come from the Roman and Arabic period, and clearly was once the site of a huge city.[119] Great, black, basaltic blocks are strewn in every direction, with occasional fragments of capitals and columns of white limestone. In the neighboring valley is an extensive Roman necropolis, which is itself clear evidence that near by was once a great and flourishing city. In the centre of these ruins are the remains of the largest synagogue thus far discovered in Galilee. It was built of white limestone and lavishly decorated. Of the many artistic figures which were thus employed the seven-branched candlestick, palms, and vines are distinctively Jewish. The foundations and many of the fallen pillars of this noble structure still remain, and are jealously guarded by the Franciscan monks, who have surrounded the whole by a high, enclosing wall. The synagogue evidently faced the lake. In front was a raised pavement, to which steps led up from the east and west. Like most of the synagogues of Galilee, it was entered by three doors, of which the central was six feet in width and those on the sides four and a half feet. The synagogue itself was seventy-eight feet long and fifty-nine feet wide. The inner court was surrounded on three sides by rows of columns on which rested an upper gallery. The synagogue of which the ruins survive probably dates from the second Christian century, but there are distinct indications that it stood on the site of an older building. This older synagogue was in all probability the one so frequently mentioned in the Gospel narratives (cf. Mk. 1:21-27, Lk. 7:1-10, 8:41, Mt. 12:10-13).

Testimony of the Gospels and Josephus. The parallel passages in John 6:17 and Matthew 14:34 clearly imply that Capernaum was on the northern border of the Plain of Gennesaret. By many scholars this has been recorded as decisive evidence that the city, which was the scene of the greater part of Jesus' ministry, was at Khan Minyeh or Tell Oreimeh, which lie in the northern part of the Plain of Gennesaret. A reference in Josephus, however, leaves little doubt that during the first Christian century the term Gennesaret included the low-lying territory to the northeast of Tell Oreimeh, which rises in the midst of the plain, and that its northeastern end was the famous spring Of Tabighah[120] which bursts from the hillside at the point where the northern hills descend close to the lake. After describing the marvellous fertility of the Plain of Gennesaret Josephus says: "For besides the good temperature of the air, it is also watered from a most fertile fountain. The people call it Capernaum. Some have thought it to be a vein of the Nile because it produces the coracin fish (the catfish) as well as that lake which is near Alexandria." During the Arab occupation this spring was enclosed in an octagonal basin which keeps out the catfish that abound in all the inlets on the northwestern side of the lake and originally were doubtless found in this copious fountain, as is stated by Josephus (*cf.* Masterman, *Studies in Galilee*, 80). His statement also implies that the Roman city of Capernaum extended westward to the fountain Tabighah on the border of the Plain of Gennesaret. In his *Life* (§ 72) Josephus also tells of his being wounded in a skirmish near Bethsaida Julias, east of the Jordan. From there he was "carried into a village named Capharnome." This reference points clearly to Tell Hum, only four miles from Bethsaida Julias, as the site of Capernaum, rather than to Khan Minyeh, two and a half miles further west on the same road.

Statements of Early Pilgrims. The first Christian pilgrim to give an account of Capernaum is Bishop Arculf who visited this region about 670 A.D. Proceeding from Tiberias, he crossed the Plain of Gennesaret, and from a hill near the spring Tabighah he viewed Capernaum, which he thus describes: "It had no wall, and being confined to a narrow space between the mountain and lake, it extended a long way upon the shore from west to east, having the mountain on the north and a lake on the south." The description, while general, accords perfectly with the peculiar topography of the northern end of the Sea of Galilee. Near the spring Tabighah the hills come close to the shore, and then eastward gradually recede, leaving a narrow but ever-widening strip of land which extends northeastward for two miles to Tell Hum. Inasmuch as the inhabitants of Capernaum drew their water supply from the lake and were chiefly engaged in commerce and fishing or else in cultivating the rich fields of black, basaltic earth which sloped northward from the town, it was natural that the town should extend for at least two miles along the shore. Later Christian pilgrims echo the same testimony regarding the site of Capernaum. The Dominican monk, Burkhard, at the close of the thirteenth century, in describing the fountain Tabighah says: "Josephus calls this fountain Capernaum because the whole land from the fountain to the Jordan—a distance of two hours—belonged to Capernaum." Not until the seventeenth century was it suggested that the ancient site was situated at Khan Minyeh instead of on the northern side of the lake. This identification by a certain Quaresmius was apparently due to the extensive ruins of the large Arab town that flourished there during the Middle Ages.

Site of Chorazin. Two miles north of Tell Hum, beside a wild, volcanic gorge, on a rocky bluff about eighty feet high, that projects far out into the valley, are the remains of another Roman town which bears to-day the name Kerazeh. This is the Arabic equivalent of the biblical Chorazin.[121] This site agrees with Jerome's statement that Chorazin was two miles from Capernaum. Although it was not directly on the Sea of Galilee, as his description implies, it commanded from certain points a view of the lake which lay below. The ruins of the ancient town are scattered over several acres, and indicate that Chorazin was probably once as large as Capernaum. Its chief public building was also a synagogue, seventy-four feet long and forty-nine feet wide, and entered by a triple gateway. Its Corinthian columns were elaborately decorated, in a style that suggests that it comes from a period not earlier than the second Christian century. Like that at Capernaum, it probably stands on the site of the older synagogue in which Jesus taught the Jewish inhabitants of this retired Roman city. The remains of olive presses indicate that the town was once encircled by olive groves. Near by are also fields, the rich, basaltic soil of which doubtless bore the superior quality of wheat for which, according to the Babylonian Talmud (*Menahoth* 85 A), Chorazin was famous.

Bethsaida. Bethsaida, which also witnessed many of Jesus' mighty works, was, according to Pliny and Jerome, on the east of the Jordan. Here Jesus retired from the territory of Herod Antipas when the news came of the death of John the Baptist. The town was situated immediately east of the point where the Jordan enters the delta through which it discharges its waters into the Sea of Galilee.[122] Philip, the son of Herod the Great, rebuilt and transformed it into a Greek city, giving it the name Julias in honor of the daughter of his patron Augustus. It is represented to-day by the ruins known as Et-Tell. The site was well chosen. To the south is the rich, alluvial plain made by the delta of the Jordan. It rested on a rounded hill which rose fifty or sixty feet above the plain. Extensive Roman ruins reveal the importance of this southern metropolis of Philip's territory.

Probable Scene of the Feeding of the Multitudes. At this secluded point, which commanded a marvellous view of the Sea of Galilee to the south, lived three of Jesus' disciples, Andrew, Peter, and Philip. The waters of the lake immediately below the delta are still the best fishing grounds[123] in all the Sea of Galilee. Eastward and northward of the Jordan delta is a wealth of grass which covers the rich plain and runs up the slopes of the eastern hills. This point, which was a lonely place beyond the limits of the city, fully accords with the statement of the Fourth Gospel, "Now there was much grass in this place." Although early Christian tradition fixes the scene of the feeding of the multitudes on the northern borders of the Plain of Gennesaret, it is probable that here on the northeastern side of the sea Jesus, undisturbed, was able to teach the multitudes and to satisfy their great spiritual as well as physical needs.

The Night Voyage of the Disciples. The evidence that there was a Bethsaida west of the Jordan breaks down on close examination. The crucial passage, Mark 6:45, which states that after feeding the multitude Jesus told his disciples to cross over in advance to Bethsaida, would perhaps mean that they were simply to go in the direction of Bethsaida. The continuation of the narrative in Mark, as well as the parallel passage in Matthew 14:34, states that they crossed over and landed on the Plain of Gennesaret, while John 6:17 adds that their destination was Capernaum. The physical characteristics of the northern end of the Sea of Galilee throw much light upon the night voyage of the disciples. The actual distance from the lonely spot southeast of Bethsaida to Capernaum was only about six miles. Their course was almost due westward toward the point where the Plain of Gennesaret and the wadies behind lead to the heights of upper Galilee. Through this open gateway sudden wind storms rushed down across the lake with terrific violence. While we were riding by this spot one beautiful day in March a storm of this kind suddenly swept down across the valley near Khan Minyeh, transforming the placid lake into a mass of windswept waves and compelling some men in a sail-boat to lower their sails and drive before the storm. Even the members of our own party had difficulty for a time in keeping in the saddles, so fierce was the wind, although at the same time the southern part of the lake was almost undisturbed. Against such a western gale the weary disciples struggled all night until morning. At last, as the Fourth Gospel states, Jesus, ever solicitous for the welfare of his friends, came out to meet them as they were near to the land.

Places Where Jesus Taught His Disciples. On the southern side of the Plain of Gennesaret, where one of the streams that waters the plain flows into the sea, was the little town of Magdala, under the shadow of the bluffs that come close to the shore on the south.[33] It was a walk of only four or five miles from Jesus' home at Capernaum. A little east of the road which ran from Capernaum to Nazareth were the rounded, treeless heights known as the Horns of Hattin, where, according to tradition, Jesus sat down and taught his disciples the great truths contained in the Sermon on the Mount. To the north and west of Capernaum are many quiet heights commanding exquisitely beautiful views across the sea below. To these Jesus doubtless often retired, sometimes accompanied by his disciples. The earliest Christian tradition (that of Arculf, about 670 A.D.) fixed the scene of the giving of the Beatitudes and of the Sermon on the Mount on the top of the hill at the end of the wady that leads up to the north of the famous fountain of Tabighah.[129] Euge-sippus writing in the twelfth century says that "the descent of the mountain where our Lord preached to the multitude was two miles from Capernaum," thus confirming the older identification with the central, commanding, and yet secluded site near the city that witnessed most of Jesus' teaching and work. It would appear that (as Dr. Masterman urges in his *Studies in Galilee*, 87) the difficulties which later prevented pilgrims from reaching the northern shores of the Sea of Galilee led them to transfer the traditional site of the "Mount of Beatitudes" to the Horns of Hattin nearer Tiberias. Along the northern shore of the sea are also two or three picturesque bays with the land sloping gradually upward like an amphitheatre. Here it requires little imagination to see Jesus sitting in the boat with his disciples, surrounded by attentive crowds. These quiet spots, apart from the city, were of profound significance in Jesus' ministry, for his great work was that of a teacher, and they afforded the needed opportunity for quiet conversation, for question and answer, and for that intimate personal touch which was the secret of the Master's power.

Northern End of the Sea of Galilee. Jesus' active ministry was performed almost entirely about the northern end of the Sea of Galilee and was limited to a radius of four or five miles with its centre at Capernaum. This fact shows convincingly that Jesus' method of work was intensive rather than extensive. To-day the sadness of the lament which he uttered over Capernaum, Chorazin, and Bethsaida still overshadows this most beautiful but loneliest spot in all Palestine. Save a few monks who live at Tell Hum, each of these sites is almost absolutely deserted. A hush seems to rest upon the whole land. The traveller often goes for miles without meeting a human being. Only occasionally are sails seen upon the northern end of the lake. It is like an ancient ruined temple, whose sacred memories and associations are undisturbed by the footfall or voice of man.

Contrast Between the Northern and Southern End. On the other hand, the southern end of the lake has already felt the touch of the modern commercial world. Tiberias, on the southwestern side, has a population of over five thousand, of which two-thirds are Jews. At Semakh, on the southern point of the lake, the railroad from Haifa to Damascus has a station and is rapidly bringing in not only the tourists, but the products and life of the outside world. In the time of Jesus also the Græco-Roman world had largely taken possession of the southern end of the Sea of Galilee. Tiberias, the city of Herod Antipas, was either completed or else in the process of building. The site of Tarichea, whose name suggests its Greek characteristics, was at Kerak, on the southwestern end of the lake. Across, on the heights opposite Tiberias, was the thoroughly Greek city of Hippos, already reckoned as one of the Decapolis. To the southwest, on the bold bluff two thousand feet above the Sea of Galilee, lay the splendid city of Gadara. Its great theatre and acropolis commanded a magnificent view of the sea. Along the height to the west of the city ran the paved Roman highway with its row of columns, flanked on either side by magnificent villas. Still farther west, looking down toward the sea, were the tombs of the rich citizens.

Jesus' Visit to the Gadarene Territory. Only once is it recorded that Jesus left the Jewish atmosphere that characterized the northern end of the sea to enter the Greek world so near at hand. The exact scene of his healing of the demoniac was apparently uncertain even in the minds of the Gospel writers. It is sometimes described as the land of the Gadarenes and it is exceedingly probable that at this time the authority of the powerful city of Gadara extended along the eastern border of the lake which lay only six miles away. Josephus, in his *Life* (9:10), refers to certain Gadarene villages close to the shore. On the eastern side of the Sea of Galilee the hills recede at every point from a quarter to a half mile from shore, except at one point across the lake from Tiberias. There the hills approach within forty or fifty feet of the shore, and slope abruptly to the water, making it easy for a frightened herd of swine to plunge headlong over the steep place referred to in the Gospel narrative. Gerasa, from which is derived the other designation of the region (Land of the Gerasenes), is without much doubt represented by the ruins of Kursi or Kersa, on the left bank of the Wady Semakh, about a mile from the sea.[32] The ruins indicate that it was a small village, surrounded by a wall three feet in thickness. The ruins also extend outside the walls toward the lake. On the hillsides which rise immediately above the town are ancient tombs. Here Jesus probably met the maniac whose belief that he was possessed of a legion of demons reflected the strong Roman environment in which he lived.

The Great Crisis in Jesus' Ministry. The Gospel narratives are so fragmentary and the topographical evidence is so meagre that it is impossible to trace with any degree of assurance Jesus' various journeys. Once, and possibly often, he visited his kinsmen at his native town of Nazareth, following the well-beaten highway along the lake to Magdala and thence past the village of Hattin to Nazareth. From the cities on the northern end of the Sea of Galilee, which were the scenes of his public ministry, the rumor of his work spread in all directions and multitudes came streaming to him from Galilee, Judea, the cities of the Decapolis and even distant Phœnicia. It soon became evident, however, that the majority came merely to be healed, or attracted by the hope that he was the Messiah of the popular expectation. To such his strong ethical message was a disappointment. They represented the stony or shallow ground of the familiar parable, and, therefore, in their lives the seed which he sowed bore no fruit. Scribes sent by the Jewish hierarchy at Jerusalem also came to entrap him with questions and to stir up distrust and opposition even in the ranks of his disciples. Thus he suddenly found himself surrounded not by enthusiastic multitudes but by suspicious, relentless foes.

Journey to Phœnicia. This great crisis marks an important turning-point in Jesus' ministry. Influenced by the evidences of the loss of public favor and of the open opposition of the Pharisees, he withdrew from public activity in Galilee and devoted himself more and more to the instruction and training of his disciples. Through them he realized that he was to accomplish his divine mission. On one occasion he departed with his disciples to the borders of Tyre and Sidon. It was a circuitous journey through the lofty, picturesque valleys of upper Galilee, down toward the fertile, warm plains of Phœnicia. The biblical narrative indicates that he did not enter the ancient city of Tyre, but proceeded northward, probably along the great coast road that ran through Sarepta and Sidon. At this time both of these cities were important commercial centres. Sidon lay on a promontory jutting out into the Mediterranean, with shallow, sandy harbors both on the north and on the south. The fertile fields and groves that encircled this northern metropolis, and its warm, sunny climate doubtless reminded Jesus and his disciples of their home at Capernaum. The Gospel narrative also implies that Jesus returned to Bethsaida through the Greek towns east of the Jordan, thus completely avoiding the territory of Antipas.

At Cæsarea Philippi. Soon after, or possibly in connection with the same journey, Jesus visited Philip's capital at Cæsarea.[30] It lay at the head of the Jordan valley, on the highway from northern Palestine to Damascus. About were picturesque hills, covered with poplars, oaks, and evergreens, and fertile gardens watered by the many streams that sprang from the base of Mount Hermon. The Roman town was situated on a triangular terrace, with the present Wady Hashabeh on the north and the Wady Zaareh on the south. On the east there was also a protecting moat, while the inner city was surrounded by thick walls and guarded by towers. It was not within this heathen city, but on the quiet hilltops and the spurs of Mount Hermon that rise to the north of the town, that Jesus found the refuge and quiet which he sought. Here, away from the Judean multitudes and the popular hopes of a temporal Messiah, Jesus told his disciples that he must accomplish his mission not by the sword or with the outward signs of triumph, but through suffering, ignominy, and death. Here, therefore, is to be sought the scene of that transfiguration which was so closely connected with his announcement to his disciples of the supreme sacrifice which he was about to make and which revealed to them his true character.

The Journey Southward from Galilee. From Luke 13:31 it is clear that at this period Herod Antipas was endeavoring to put Jesus to death, even as he had John the Baptist. This fact doubtless explains why Jesus avoided the territory of Antipas, preferring, as he himself implies, to end his work in Jerusalem rather than in some gloomy fortress like that of Machærus (Luke 13:33, 34). Hence, as he returned southward from Cæsarea Philippi, passing through Galilee, probably along the western side of the lake or by boat to the southern end, he was careful "that no man should know it" (Mark 9:30). The most direct route from Capernaum to Jerusalem was down the western side of the Jordan valley. Luke 17:11 states that on his way he passed along the borders of Samaria and Galilee. It was probably in one of the little villages not far from Scythopolis that the ten lepers sought his help. From Luke 9:51-56 it appears that he first planned to pass thence through Samaria, probably by the road that ran through Teiasir and Tubas and joined the main central highway near Sychar (*cf.* p. 54); but the inhospitable reception accorded him by the Samaritans evidently led him to avoid this road and keep instead to the Jordan valley. Mark 10:1 indicates that he followed the east-Jordan highway. This road took him into the territory of Perea, which was under the control of Herod Antipas, but at a distance from his capital. Here, in the field of John the Baptist's activity and near the scene of Jesus' early work, the people again rallied about him in great numbers.

At Jericho. The multitudes still followed Jesus after he had crossed the Jordan on his way to Jerusalem. The Gospel narratives have given two vivid pictures, one of the blind men who sat by the way as he passed along, and the other of Zaccheus, the prominent tax-collector. The Herodian Jericho evidently lay on both sides of the Wady Kelt, whose waters irrigated the city and its fertile gardens that extended far across the level plain.[35] The ancient ruins indicate that the larger portion of the Roman city lay on the southern side of the Kelt; but its suburbs extended northward to a point east of the older Jericho, which lay near the western hills. The plains about the Roman Jericho were probably cultivated for miles in each direction. Here the date-palms grew in great profusion and their fruit was one of the chief exports of the place. Strabo states that balsam was produced here in large quantities. In summer the climate was exceedingly hot and oppressive, but in winter it was balmy and equable. Josephus describes with unwonted enthusiasm its marvellous fertility and healthful climate (*Jew. Wars*, IV, 8:2, 3). Through it ran the great caravan road to Gilead and the desert. It was the eastern outpost of Judea. The collection of customs at this point was, therefore, of great importance. The city was as different from the other cities of Judah as was its physical environment. Plenty, luxury, and corruption were its chief characteristics. It was the heir of the traditions of the ancient Canaanite cities of the plain. Its immediate associations were with Herod the Great, Cleopatra, and Archelaus, three of the most sinister characters of this corrupt age.

Situation of Bethany. From Jericho the road led up through the barren wilderness of Judea[25] to Jerusalem. It was an almost steady climb of three thousand feet. Probably Herod the Great had already joined these two important cities of his empire by a Roman road, following the general course along which runs the modern carriage road. In striking contrast to the barrenness of the brown, rocky wilderness is the lofty plateau which stands at the top of the final ascent. On this southeastern spur of the Mount of Olives lay the little town of Bethany.[124] It was surrounded by small, rock-strewn grain fields and stood in a bower of fig, almond, and olive trees. To the northwest rose the higher ridges of the Mount of Olives, shutting off the view of Jerusalem. Above was probably situated the little village of Bethphage, less than a mile away and closely associated with Bethany in the minds of the Gospel writers. The view to the east was through the broad hollow down which went the road to Jericho. To the southeast the eye looked beyond the barren hills of the Judean wilderness to the Dead Sea and the lofty line of the plateau of Moab.[24] It is significant that Jesus chose this village as his home while in Judea, for it was retired, yet near to Jerusalem and one of the few places that commanded a wide outlook. This fact suggests the impression which Jerusalem made upon the mind of the great Prophet of Nazareth. Shut in by its surrounding hills and by its narrow fanaticism and ceremonialism its atmosphere must have seemed to him stifling.

The Triumphal Entrance Into Jerusalem. Near Bethany, his southern home, where Jesus apparently spent many days, he secured the ass on which he made his memorable journey to Jerusalem. The occasion was the Passover Feast, and pilgrims from Perea, Galilee, and eastern Judea, the fields in which his ministry had been performed, accompanied him on the journey. As they saw him riding on an ass, the royal beast in the days of David, the earlier hopes of the people were suddenly revived. Quickly the news of his presence spread through the long line of pilgrims. Those ahead tore branches from the trees by the wayside or else spread their garments in the way along which he was to pass, while they all joined in a triumphant song suggested by Psalm 118:25, 26:

> Hosanna to the son of David!
> Blessed is he who cometh in the name of the Lord!
> Hosanna in the highest!

Slowly the procession wound around the southern spur of the Mount of Olives, with the deep gorge of the Kidron on the south, until Jerusalem suddenly burst into view. Thence descending into the valley, Jesus entered the city and found his way to the temple just as the sun was setting behind the western hills. He sought not a waiting throne, but a place for quiet worship. Then in the hush of the evening, refusing to give the slightest encouragement to the selfish, material hopes of the people, he returned to his humble home at Bethany.

Jesus' Activity in the Temple. Jesus' activity during the last week of his ministry gathers about the temple.[125] The remark of his disciples regarding its huge foundation stones was used by him as a means of calling their attention to the temple not built with hands. It was probably near the entrances in the southern part of the great court of the Gentiles, under the huge portico with its four rows of Corinthian columns, that the extortionate money-changers and those who sold doves plied their trade. To secure a place within the sacred precincts, they must have bribed the temple officials. Jesus' act in expelling them was, therefore, not merely a reassertion of the sanctity of the temple, but also a rebuke of the corrupt practices of the Sadducean nobles. Solomon's Porch, where Jesus walked and taught, was the long colonnade with its double row of pillars on the eastern side of the Court of the Gentiles. From this eastern side one magnificent gate, with doors adorned with Corinthian brass, led directly into the Court of the Women. Within this small eastern court were probably placed the thirteen offertory chests into which the people cast their free-will offerings. Here only men and women of Jewish faith and parentage were allowed to enter. It was probably within this court that Jesus stood with his disciples and watched the people as they cast in their offerings, the rich of their plenty and the poor widow her mite.

The Last Supper and Agony. The place of the upper chamber, where Jesus ate the last supper with his disciples, is not definitely known. Tradition fixes it at a certain place on the western hill. Equally uncertain is the exact site of the Garden of Gethsemane. Its name indicates that it was probably an olive grove containing an oil press. It was doubtless enclosed with a fence like similar gardens about Jerusalem to-day. It was situated somewhere to the east of the Kidron, on the side of the Mount of Olives. A tradition which is probably not older than the sixteenth century identifies Gethsemane[126] with a garden low down in the Valley of the Kidron, opposite the temple. This garden, with its eight old olive trees, aids the imagination in picturing the spot, probably farther away and more secluded, where Jesus met and overcame his last great temptation, and gave himself wholly and voluntarily to the completion of the divine task entrusted to him.

Scenes of the Trials. The Gospel narrative implies that Jesus was not tried before a formal meeting of the Sanhedrin, which would have convened in one of the chambers immediately adjoining the temple, but in the house of Caiaphas, the high priest. This midnight session was, therefore, not a regular trial, but a preliminary examination by his Sadducean enemies, with a view to formulating definite charges against him. The house of the high priest was undoubtedly near the temple, probably somewhere to the west. According to the Fourth Gospel, the trial before Pilate, the Roman governor, was held in the Prætorium. The judgment seat of Pilate may have been connected with the palace reared by Herod on the western hill, which was then the home of the Roman rulers of Jerusalem, but more probably it was in the tower of Antonia, immediately to the north of the temple, opening into the Court of the Gentiles where the mob which was in league with the high priestly party was assembled.

Traditional Place of the Crucifixion. The exact scene of the crucifixion is also uncertain. The biblical records indicate that it was outside the city wall and yet in a conspicuous position near the city and also near an important highway. In the vicinity was a tomb, and the name, Golgotha, suggests that it was either at a place of burial or else on a hill, the form of which suggested the shape of a skull. In Luke the place is called The Skull, supporting the conclusion that it was the peculiar form of the rock that gave the place its name. Jerome speaks of it as the little mountain, or hill, of Golgotha. It was the practice both of the Jews and Romans to put to death public offenders outside the city. In the case of those, like Jesus, charged with rebellion, a conspicuous public place was chosen in order to make the object-lesson more impressive. The traditional site of the crucifixion is due west of the temple, across the upper end of the Tyropœon Valley. It is possible to infer from recent excavations that it was just outside the northern wall of the Roman city. Tombs discovered at this point show that it was also a place of burial. While this identification is not impossible, it cannot be traced farther back than the fourth Christian century.

The More Probable Site. A more probable site is somewhere near the rounded skull-like hill five hundred feet north of the Damascus gate, above the so-called

Grotto of Jeremiah.[127] It is near the great northern road and, because of its height, can readily be seen from the northern side of the city. It is the continuation of the northern ridge on which Jerusalem is built and its bold form and abrupt face are due to the rock cuttings at this point. Vast quantities of stone used in the repeated restorations of the walls have been taken from these quarries. Probably Herod quarried at this point much of the stone used in extending the temple area southward. The bold, rocky bluff on the northern side of this quarry was well adapted to public executions. If this was the scene of the crucifixion the place where the cross rested has probably been cut away by later excavations.

The Place of Burial. In a little garden to the left is shown to-day a well-preserved, rock-cut tomb.[128] It is an excellent example of the family tomb of the Roman period and may have been that of Joseph of Arimathea, although there is no conclusive evidence. It possesses great interest, however, because it is a type of the tomb in which the body of the Master was laid.[129] Most significant is the fact that not one of the places which witnessed the closing scenes of his life can be identified with absolute assurance. Occidental as well as oriental Christianity has shown itself too eager to worship sacred sites and in so doing to forget the deeper meaning of the events which have made the places memorable. Though most of the scenes will remain forever unknown, the work and teachings of the Master will abide and occupy an increasingly larger place in the life and thought of mankind.

XXV

THE SPREAD OF CHRISTIANITY THROUGHOUT THE ROMAN EMPIRE

Original Centre at Jerusalem. The spread of Christianity throughout the civilized world bears conclusive testimony not only to the life-giving truth of Jesus' message, but also to the supreme wisdom of his method. His heroic death at first daunted, but the vision of his living presence, which, according to the oldest records, came to his disciples amidst the familiar scenes on the northern shores of the Sea of Galilee, quickly inspired them to take up the mission which he had left them and to proclaim abroad the good tidings of God's love for men. Strangely enough, Galilee, which had been the scene of the call, the training, and the sending forth of Jesus' disciples, again sinks into oblivion. Capernaum, Chorazin, and Bethsaida had failed to respond to their great opportunity. In accordance with the implied, if not the expressed, commands of Jesus, his disciples soon transferred their homes and work to Jerusalem, the religious home of the Jewish race, to which they, as well as their Master, at first alone appealed. Here it was possible at the great annual festivals, when the pilgrims streamed to the temple from all parts of the Roman empire, to touch the entire Jewish world. Following the example of the Great Teacher, his disciples took up the task of teaching and preaching within the precincts of the temple and especially at Solomon's Porch on the eastern side, where he had often walked and talked.

Spread of Christianity Outside Judea. The stoning of Stephen, which was outside the city and probably in the deserted quarries immediately to the north of the temple, marked a new epoch in the life of the early Christian community, for it was the beginning of a bitter persecution at the hands of the Jewish authorities, which soon drove the disciples in all directions from secluded Judah and transformed them into a world-conquering missionary force. In this early dispersion the apostles naturally followed the great highways, which led northward, southward, and westward from Jerusalem. Philip the Evangelist preached with great success at Samaria. Here he was building on an older Hebrew basis, for the Bible of the Samaritans contained the first five books of the Old Testament with portions of the book of Joshua. The mixed Samaritan population, however, ever open by virtue of their geographical position to the diverse influences that surged up and down the eastern Mediterranean, never proved a stable element in the early Christian church.

Philip's Work in the South and West. Leaving the Samaritans, Philip set out for the coast city of Gaza. He probably took the central highway from Jerusalem southward by way of Hebron. A late tradition places the spring where he baptized the Ethiopian official on the tortuous road, practically impassable for chariots, which leads southwestward from Jerusalem, but the older and more probable tradition identifies it with that beside the main road southward, a little north of Bethzur. Thence Philip turned westward, preaching and teaching with success at the old Philistine town of Ashdod, which lay three miles from the Mediterranean, on the border line between the fertile plain and the drifting sands, at the point where the main coast highway divided into its eastern and western branches.

Extension and Expansion of Christianity During the First Decade. Peter, likewise, turned westward, and at the flourishing city of Lydda, which stood where the main highway from Jerusalem to Joppa crossed the great northern coast road, found a well-established Christian community. Joppa[130] stood on a bold hill looking out over the western sea. It was fitting that here Peter, the natural leader of the rapidly growing Christian church, should have a clear vision of the great and needy Gentile world that lay beyond the narrow bounds of Judea. Joppa was indeed the gateway between Jerusalem, which represented Judaism, and Rome, which stood as the embodiment of regnant heathenism. From Joppa, with its small, rocky harbor, the apostle followed the messengers of Cornelius, the Roman centurion, along the road which closely skirted the shore to Cæsarea, the new door which Herod the Great had opened between Palestine and the Gentile world along the shores of the Mediterranean. Here Peter was far beyond Jewish atmosphere and civilization. The population, the public buildings, and the language of this busy seaport were either Greek or Roman. Thus, before Herod Agrippa in 41 A.D. entered upon his brief but brilliant reign of three years, Christianity had swept over the borders of Judea into the great strategic cities of the western coast plains and even to Damascus, far in the north. It was also breaking the narrow Jewish bonds and following the great western highways that were guiding it on to the conquest of the empire.

Situation and History of Tarsus. The man who led this forward movement and formulated the world-wide policy of the Christian church was born in a city of southern Cilicia, which stood midway between the east and the west. There the influences of the ancient Orient and of the more active Occident met and mingled. The city of Tarsus lay on a rich, moist, alluvial plain, ten miles north of the Mediterranean and only eighty feet above the level of the ocean. Two miles farther north rose the foot-hills that led up to the lofty, massive peaks of the Taurus Mountains. These northern heights shut off the cooling winds, making the climate of Tarsus hot and enervating. In ancient times the sluggish river Cydnus flowed through the centre of the town on its way to the sea. The strength of Tarsus consisted in its position at the southern end of the great Cilician Plain. At this point the main highway from Antioch to Ephesus and Smyrna touched the Cydnus and thence turned northward, crossing the Taurus range by the famous Cilician Gates. Its commercial prestige, however, was not so much the result of its natural position as of the energy of the early population. They had drained the marshes about the Cydnus and transformed the lake immediately south of the town into a large inland harbor. They also cut the road beside the narrow stream that penetrated the Taurus range, making Tarsus the seaport of the wide plains to the north. Tarsus in the days of Paul was a magnificent city of fully half a million population. Its citizens were supremely proud of their city—a pride which the great apostle to the Gentiles clearly shared. The energy which characterized the inhabitants, as a result of their successful struggle with adverse natural conditions, was also reflected in the character and work of its most distinguished citizen.

Influence of His Early Home Upon Paul. Probably from the days of Antiochus Epiphanes, Tarsus had been the home of a large and influential Jewish colony. They were doubtless permitted, as an independent social and religious group, to share in the citizenship of the proud Roman city. This Roman citizenship not only delivered Paul at many crises in his stormy career, but also brought him into intelligent and sympathetic touch with the great empire to which he bore the message of the cross. The atmosphere, therefore, of Paul's early life was distinctly Roman and cosmopolitan. The influence of this broad environment is traceable in all his work and teachings. From the port of Tarsus ships ran frequently to Cæsarea and Joppa, the ports of Jerusalem. Thus the journey was easy and natural for the young Jew of Tarsus as he went back to the sacred city of his race to study at the feet of Gamaliel, the greatest Jewish scholar of the age. His life in Palestine brought him into closest touch with the growing Christian church. The energy which he had inherited from his native city found expression at first in active persecution of the members of the new sect. The open-mindedness which he had acquired from his youthful environment, and which later led him to appreciate that which was good in the heathen religions, prepared the way for the supreme experience which came to him as he was crossing the desert on his way northward to Damascus.[42]

Work at Antioch. The history of the spread of Christianity for the next decade is chiefly a record of the work of the great apostle to the Gentiles. The graphic passages in the second half of the book of Acts present a remarkably vivid picture of his journeys and experiences. It was natural that Paul, a native of Asia Minor, should not remain in the narrower atmosphere of Palestine, but should find instead a congenial environment and field of work in Antioch, the great and opulent capital of Syria, the third metropolis of the Roman empire. Here he was able to observe the impression which Christianity made upon the heathen, and especially upon the Jews of the dispersion. Antioch was also the natural geographical centre from which to set out upon his missionary journeys.

Importance of the Pioneer Work of Paul. In all his missionary activity, Paul evidently followed a definite plan. He selected as the scenes of his work the great cities, situated on the main highways of communication and commerce. This choice was in part due to the fact that in the larger cities of this character were found Jewish communities, with synagogues which opened doors of opportunity to the pupil of the famous Rabbi Gamaliel. During the two preceding centuries the Jews of the dispersion had become an exceedingly active proselyting force. The influential and honorable position which they had won in many of the Græco-Roman cities, as well as the character of their faith, commended them to the most worthy of their heathen neighbors. The result was that many of the Gentiles had accepted the essentials of the Jewish religion and worshipped with the Jews in their synagogues. This class is ordinarily described in the narrative of Acts by the designation "devout Greeks." Thus Judaism had prepared the way for the spread of Christianity. From the ranks of the devout Greeks was drawn a large proportion of the converts, who responded to the early preaching of Paul and of the other Christian apostles.

Paul and Barnabas in Cyprus. With these conditions in mind, Paul and Barnabas planned their first missionary journey. Cilicia belonged within Antioch's sphere of influence and was indeed a part of the province of Syria. Paul and Barnabas turned to the immediately adjacent island of Cyprus and the Roman province of Galatia, lying respectively to the southwest and northwest. Cyprus possibly attracted them because Barnabas was a native of that island. Throughout all its history it had stood in close commercial relations with Syria. Salamis, its chief eastern city, was first visited. It lay at the mouth of the River Pediæus on the eastern edge of a fertile plain which extended far to the west. The Ptolemies, as early as 295 B.C., had transported many Jews to Cyprus, and Herod the Great doubtless sent many more to work the copper mines there which he controlled.

At Paphos. From Salamis two Roman highways ran across the island to Paphos, the chief city on its western shores. The Roman city which Paul and Barnabas visited was the new Paphos. It was situated on the sea-coast, being in fact the seaport of the older inland city ten miles to the southwest. The older city had been famous throughout the ancient world as the seat of the corrupt worship of the Paphian goddess, whom the Greeks identified with Aphrodite. At the new city Paul came into contact both with the Roman ruler and a representative of the local superstitions.

Journey to Antioch in Galatia. From Paphos it was easy to secure a passage northward to the coast of Pamphylia, for along this course passed many of the merchant ships from Alexandria to Rome. The apostles probably landed at Attalia and thence went to Perga, the chief city of central Pamphylia. It lay five miles from the river, on a plain at the foot of a bold, extended acropolis. The climate of these low-lying coast plains was sultry and malarial. The city was dominated by the worship of a local goddess and there is no evidence that there was a Jewish synagogue at this point. Because of these unfavorable conditions, Paul and Barnabas simply passed through this southern city on their way to the great strategic centres farther north. The journey thither through the deep valleys and over the rough heights was exceedingly arduous. Here Paul doubtless experienced many of those perils of rivers and perils of robbers which he mentions in II Corinthians 11:26.

Conditions at Antioch. It was at the Roman colony of Antioch,[131] that the apostles found their first great field of activity in Asia Minor. The town lay about three thousand six hundred feet above the level of the sea, on an isolated plateau two miles in circumference, which rose from one to two hundred feet above the western plain. On the east it was protected by a rocky gorge through which flowed the River Anthios. The city was, therefore, a natural fortress, able to resist the frequent attacks of the warlike Pisidian mountaineers. It had been made a Roman colony by Augustus a little before the beginning of the Christian era and hence was an outpost of Rome itself and dominated the southern part of the great Roman province of Galatia. The worship of the local deity had recently been abolished, so that the city offered an unusual field for missionary work. The Jewish colony was apparently large and influential, for many Gentiles joined with the Jews in worship at their synagogue. From the first Paul and Barnabas appear to have made a profound impression upon the people of this important city. It was their success that aroused certain of the Jews and the Roman magistrates of the city so that the apostles were forcibly expelled.

At Iconium. From Antioch they turned eastward, following the Roman highway that led to Lystra. Instead, however, of going at once to Lystra, they turned to Iconium,[132] eighty miles east of Antioch. This town lay on a level plain three thousand three hundred and seventy feet above the sea. It was protected on the west by a lofty mountain range, from which emerged the river, which first irrigated and then lost itself in the wide, thirsty plain on which Iconium lay. Unlike Antioch, Iconium had no natural barriers. Great energy and skill were required to utilize successfully the waters of its main stream and to protect it from the annual floods. Here grew up a flourishing commercial city with an active, resourceful population. A Jewish colony and a synagogue offered an excellent field for the apostles' work. Here they remained for a long time, preaching, teaching, and laying the foundations for the strong Christian church which made Iconium long after an important religious centre. In time, however, the opposition of the Jews crystallized and the apostles were driven forth by a mob.

At Lystra and Derbe. From Iconium they turned southward to Lystra,[133] twenty miles distant. It was a quiet town, situated in a pleasant valley in the midst of which rose a bold, elongated hill about one hundred and fifty feet high, which was the acropolis. The valley was watered by two streams which flowed from the western hills. While it was a Roman colony and connected with Galatian Antioch, it was aside from the great highways of commerce. The apostles evidently turned to it as a refuge. Antioch and Iconium were strong Græco-Roman towns, but at Lystra Paul and Barnabas came into contact with the native Lycaonian population. The readiness with which the natives identified the energetic spokesman, Paul, with Hermes, and the more reserved and dignified Barnabas with Zeus, reveals the naïveté of the small provincial town. Again the attack of a mob, incited by Jews who came from Antioch and Iconium, compelled the apostles to seek refuge in Derbe, on the southeastern end of the Lycaonian plain. The town was probably situated on a low hill that stands in the midst of the great plain about forty-five miles south of Iconium.[134] On the south the lofty range of the Taurus shuts it off from the sea. Here the apostles were among the native people, with little Roman, Greek, or Jewish influence to interfere with their work, which appears to have been successful and undisturbed by persecution. From this point they retraced their steps through all the cities where they had recently labored. Thence going southward they stopped for a short time at Perga and then sailed from Attalia back to Antioch.

Decision of the Great Council at Jerusalem. The successful work of the apostles, extending probably through two years, raised a great controversy in the church as to whether the Jewish institution of circumcision was necessary for salvation. Paul and Barnabas journeyed southward through Phœnicia and Samaria, telling the Christians on the way of the results of their work among the heathen. Fortunately the church met this great crisis wisely and in the spirit of Jesus. The narrow Jewish bonds were broken and Christianity went forth comparatively untrammelled on its world conquest.

Work of Paul and Silas in Asia Minor. Paul and Barnabas, accompanied by Judas and Silas, two representatives of the church at Jerusalem, devoted themselves for a time to the work at Antioch, the Syrian capital. They soon, however, felt the call to the larger field beyond. Barnabas, accompanied by Mark, returned to Cyprus, and Paul, taking Silas, set out on his second great missionary journey. His object was twofold; first to visit and encourage the churches already established, and second, to carry the message of the Gospel to Ephesus, the great commercial, political, and religious centre of western Asia Minor. They first visited the churches of Syria and of the sub-province of Cilicia. Thence they followed the great military road westward, stopping at Derbe, Lystra, Iconium, and probably Antioch.

Paul's Vision at Troas. Being prevented from entering the northern province of Bithynia, Paul and Silas went on through Mysia to Troas, on the extreme western boundary of Asia Minor. While at this seaport town, which stood at the end of the great overland route from Asia,[135] facing the Ægean and the continent of Europe beyond, a vision came to Paul which marked a new stage in the expansion of Christianity. The experience was remarkably similar to that which came to Peter at the port of Joppa. In response to this vision, Paul left behind his work in Asia Minor and took ship for Neapolis, the port of Philippi in Macedonia. In so doing he was following the most direct highways between Asia Minor and Rome (*cf.* p. 55).

Paul and Silas at Philippi. The city of Philippi lay about nine miles northwest of its seaport, Neapolis. It was on the southern side of a great plain that extended to the north and northwest. Its chief river flowed along its eastern side into a huge marsh that flanked the city on the south. Like many of the cities chosen by Paul as the scenes of his labors, it was a Roman colony. It was probably chosen because of its strategic value as one of the outposts of the great empire whose conquest for

Christ was already the goal of Paul's endeavor. Also, as the event proved, Rome's protection was of great value to the apostle, who could claim citizenship in the imperial city. Apparently there was only a small Jewish colony at this point and no synagogue, so that Paul established connection with his countrymen at the open place of prayer beside the river and beyond the city walls. The success of their work aroused the inevitable opposition and led to their imprisonment; but on this occasion they were sent forth from the city at the request of the magistrates rather than by force.

At Thessalonica. From Philippi they proceeded westward along the well-travelled Egnatian Way to Thessalonica, the capital and chief commercial city of Macedonia. It lay at the northeastern end of the Thermaic Gulf, the present Gulf of Salonica, in a great ampitheatre formed by the surrounding hills, which were crowned by a strong citadel. Vast plains lay behind the city and it commanded the trade of the northern Ægean. Because of its loyalty to the cause of Octavius and Antony it had been made a free city, ruled by its own assembly and magistrates, called Politarchs. Here, as at Philippi, Paul succeeded in laying the foundations of a strong Christian church, composed largely of the Greek converts to Judaism. The hostile Jews soon charged Paul and Silas with stirring up sedition and rebellion, a charge to which the rulers of a free city like Thessalonica were especially ready to listen. Much to his regret, Paul was therefore obliged suddenly to leave the city.

Paul at Berœa. As in his flight from Iconium, he now found refuge at a quiet, retired town. Berœa lay fifty miles southwest of Thessalonica, in the midst of groves of trees and flowing streams. It was flanked by a bold mountain range on the west and faced toward the Ægean, with a broad expanse of plain lying in the foreground. Here Paul found a nobler type of Jews, probably untouched by the mercenary spirit of those who had been attracted to the great commercial centres like Thessalonica and Philippi. His work among both the Jews and Greeks was very successful until emissaries came from Thessalonica. Paul's heart was evidently set upon returning to take up his work at the Macedonian metropolis, but events had proved that this was impossible.

At Athens. Accompanied by the Christians of Berœa, Paul next went southward along the Ægean to the home of that civilization which had surrounded him in his boyhood days at Tarsus and profoundly influenced the fields in which he had done his work. Landing at the port of Piræus, he proceeded along the new road to Athens, beside which stood the altars to the unknown gods. On entering the city he naturally went to the Agora, on the south of which Mars Hill[136] rose abruptly. East of this was the Acropolis, crowned by that most peerless product of Greek art, the Parthenon. Athens was still at the height of its artistic splendor, but it had already ceased to be the political and intellectual capital of the Greek world. Superficial philosophy and sophistry had taken the place of real intellectual leadership. Athens, being aside from the world's commerce, had little attraction for the Jewish colonists. The city, therefore, lacked the religious background which Paul had found helpful in all his previous work. The critical, speculative atmosphere of the city was uncongenial. Paul was accustomed to addressing himself to the vital, crying needs of humanity. He made a strong effort to adapt himself to the new conditions, not without some success, but there is no record of a church at Athens, and he soon left to find a more promising field.

Importance of Corinth. Corinth, to which Paul next went, marks an important epoch in his ministry. The city was called by the ancients the "Bridge of the Sea."[137] It lay on the narrow neck of land which connected the Corinthian with the Saronic Gulf. It was on one of the three great highways from the east to the west, and here all cargoes had to be trans-shipped. It was also the bridge that connected the Peloponnesus with northern Greece. By nature, therefore, it was destined to become a great and influential city. It was built on a broad terrace at the end of a gently sloping plain, with an almost impregnable acropolis rising one thousand eight hundred feet above the sea-level. When Paul visited the city it was the metropolis and Roman capital of the province of Achaia. From the days of Julius Cæsar it had been a Roman colony. Because of its commercial importance its population was cosmopolitan, including many Jews. Like most cities thus situated, it was exceedingly prosperous and profligate.

Paul's Work at Corinth. To this needy and important field Paul addressed himself with superlative devotion. Anxious regarding the results of his work in Thessalonica, harassed by poverty and weakened by sickness, he nevertheless devoted himself to teaching both Jews and Gentiles, at the same time plying his trade as a tent-maker. Finding the Jews hostile, he devoted his time almost entirely to the Gentiles, making his home with Titus Justus, whose name suggests Roman origin. Unable to visit the church at Thessalonica, Paul wrote to the Christian community there the two letters known as I and II Thessalonians. At about the same time he appears to have written his famous epistle to the Galatian churches. These letters mark the beginning of that remarkable correspondence which is recorded in the epistles of the New Testament. During this period or at a later visit Paul wrote from Corinth the letter known as the Epistle to the Romans, which contains the fullest and noblest résumé of his doctrines. Corinth was one of the few places which Paul was not compelled to leave under pressure of persecution. After a sojourn of about two years he departed for Syria, stopping for a short time at Ephesus, and finally landing at Cæsarea.

His Third Journey. After visiting the churches at Jerusalem and Antioch, Paul set out, probably early in the spring, on this third great missionary tour. As in his second journey, his aim was to visit the churches which he had established and to proclaim the Gospel in the city of Ephesus. He first revisited the region of Galatia and Phrygia, and thence, following westward the great caravan route, he apparently went on directly to Ephesus by the higher and more northern road. Ephesus, for the next year or two, became the head-quarters from which he made journeys to the churches in Macedonia and Achaia. Apparently at certain points, as for example at Illyria on the Adriatic, he extended still farther the sphere of his influence.

Situation and Importance of Ephesus. Ephesus was at this time the chief commercial city of eastern Asia Minor. Here converged the great highways from the east and north. The town lay opposite the island of Samos, on the bank of the Cayster River. Like most Greek cities, it was built on and about an imposing hill and was enclosed by a great wall. It was a characteristic Roman city, with a huge theatre,[138] a beautiful agora, a stadium seating over six thousand, a forum, and streets lined with colonnades; but its dominant life and ideas were Greek. This western culture was deeply influenced by that of the Orient, for Ephesus, by virtue of its position, was pre-eminently the place where the East and West met and blended. The population of the city was as cosmopolitan as its civilization. Here also Roman, Greek, Alexandrian, and oriental thought met and mingled. Next to Delphi, its temple was the most important religious force in the Greek world, but its influence, on the whole, was immoral and debasing. Here, in the face of active persecution, Paul and the Christian workers whom he gathered about him established what later proved to be the most influential church in Asia Minor. Paul did not leave the Ægean until he had established a Christian community at Troas, which he had visited on his second journey, and at the important cities of Colossæ and Laodicea, east of Ephesus, on the great caravan road from Syria and the Tigris-Euphrates Valley. The latter churches appear to have been established by his co-workers, for in his letter to the Colossians Paul implies that he had never personally visited their city.

Return to Palestine. Having planted the Christian faith in all the great strategic centres along the main thoroughfares which led to Rome, Paul set out by boat from Miletus[139] to return to Jerusalem. Following the usual course along the southern shore of Asia Minor, he landed at Tyre. Thence he went by land to Jerusalem, stopping at Ptolemais and Cæsarea. The bitter persecution which he experienced at the Jewish capital and his long, wearisome confinement at Cæsarea are familiar chapters in the life of the apostle.[115] They only intensified his oft-expressed desire to visit the capital of the great empire, whose strength and weakness he fully appreciated. Again his Roman citizenship enabled him to escape his persistent persecutors and to reach Rome, although as a prisoner.

Journey to Rome. In this last long journey his courage and faith, as well as his wide experience as a traveller, were dramatically illustrated. Sailing from Cæsarea, he, with his Roman guard, trans-shipped at Myra, a city of southern Lycia, on an Alexandrian merchant ship. Thence the usual sea route was followed along the southern shore of Crete until the storm drove them south of their course, past Sicily, to the island of Melita, the modern Malta. There the ship was wrecked and they were obliged to remain through the winter. Then by another Alexandrian merchantman they sailed northward, landing at Puteoli, and thence proceeded by land to Rome along the Appian Way.[140] At last at this goal of all his missionary journeying, Paul was able to extend widely the bounds of the church, already established in the capital, and through the medium of letters and messengers keep in close touch with the churches which he had founded.

The World-wide Conquests of Christianity. Whether or not Paul was able later to visit distant Spain, as certain early church traditions assert, cannot be definitely determined. At least it is certain that the goal which he had set before himself had been, in one sense, fully attained. Within less than thirty years after the death of Jesus, active, growing Christian communities were to be found in all of the important cities of the eastern and northern Mediterranean. Two or three centuries later heathenism was vanquished and Christianity was master of the empire. This marvellous achievement would have been impossible if Rome, in the course of its natural development, had not broken down all national and racial barriers and bound together the peoples of that ancient world into one great empire. It had opened and developed the natural highways, making communication comparatively quick and easy. The natural trend of civilization was also from the east to the west, and Christianity moved on the crest of a great wave which was sweeping over the western world. Thus the faith of the Hebrew prophets and of Jesus, first proclaimed among the hilltops of Judea and Galilee, was able to enter upon that world-wide conquest which is the most significant fact in human history.

APPENDIX

APPENDIX I
SELECTED BIBLIOGRAPHY

THE PHYSICAL CONTOUR AND CHARACTERISTICS OF PALESTINE

Baedeker, *Palestine and Syria*, 1911.

Buhl, *Geographie des alten Palästina*, 1896.

Conder, *Heth and Moab*, 1883.
—— *Tent Work in Palestine*, 1895.

Dawson, *Egypt and Syria. Their Physical Features in Relation to Bible History*, 1885.

Dunning, *To-day in Palestine*, 1907.

Forbush, *The Travel Lessons on the Old Testament*, 1900.

Fullylove, *The Holy Land Painted by John Fullylove. Described by John Kelman*, 1902.

Guérin, *Description de la Palestine*, 1868-89.

Guthe, *Palästina*, 1908.

Hull, *The Survey of Western Palestine*, 1888.

Huntington, *Palestine and Its Transformation*, 1911.

Libbey and Hoskins, *The Jordan Valley and Petra*, I, II, 1905.

Lynch, *Narrative of U. S. Exploration in 1848*.

MacMillan, *Guide to Palestine and Syria*, 1903.

Masterman, *Studies in Galilee*, 1909.

Meistermann, *New Guide to Palestine*, 1909.

Merrill, *East of the Jordan*, 1870.

Murray, *Handbook for Travellers in Syria and Palestine*, 1892.

Oliphant, *Land of Gilead*, 1880.

Petrie, *Tell el-Hesy*, 1891.

Palestine Exploration Fund, *Quarterly Statement*, 1869-1911.
——, *Survey of Eastern Palestine*, 1889.
——, *Survey of Western Palestine*, 1888.

Robinson, *Biblical Researches in Palestine, Mount Sinai and Arabia Petræa*, I, III, 1841.

— —, *Later Biblical Researches in Palestine*, 1856.

Schumacher, *Northern Ajlun*, 1890.
— —, *Pella*, 1889.
— —, *The Jaulan. Survey of the German Society for the Exploration of the Holy Land*, 1888.

Stanley, *Sinai and Palestine*, 1883.

Stewart, *The Land of Israel*, 1907.

Tristram, *Bible Places, or the Topography of the Holy Land*, 1897.
— —, *Landscapes of the Bible*, 1901.
— —, *The Land of Israel*, 1876.
— —, *The Land of Moab*, 1874.

Warren, *Underground Jerusalem*, 1876.
— —, *Plans, Elevations, etc., Showing Results of P. E. F. Excavations at Jerusalem*, 1884.

Wilson, *Picturesque Palestine*, I-IV, 1881-84.
— —, *The Recovery of Jerusalem*, 1871.

HISTORICAL GEOGRAPHY OF PALESTINE

Besant and Palmer, *Jerusalem, the City of Herod and Saladin*, 1888.

Calkin, *Historical Geography of Bible Lands*, 1904.

Conder, *A Primer of Bible Geography: Founded on the Latest Explorations*, 1884.

Geikie, *The Holy Land and the Bible*, 1897.

Le Strange, *Palestine under the Moslems*, 1890.

Macphail, *Historical Geography of the Holy Land*, 1900.

Miller, *Least of All Lands*, 1901.

Neubauer, *La Géographie du Talmud*, 1868.

Sanday, *Sacred Sites of the Gospels*, 1903.

Smith, *Historical Geography of the Holy Land*, 1894.
— —, Article *Jerusalem* in Hastings' *Dictionary of the Bible*.
— —, Jerusalem, I, II, 1909.

Stapfer, *Palestine in the Time of Christ*, 1886.

HISTORICAL BACKGROUND OF THE APOSTOLIC AGE

Hausrath, *Time of the Apostles*, 1895.

Ramsay, *The Cities of Saint Paul: Their Influence on His Life and Thought*, 1907.
— —, *The Cities of Eastern Asia Minor*, 1907.
— —, *The Galatia of Saint Paul and the Galatic Territory of Acts*, 1896.
— —, *Saint Paul the Traveller*, 1896.

Wright, *Cities of Paul, Beacons of the Past Rekindled for the Present*, 1906.

BOOKS OF TRAVEL

Archbold, *Under the Syrian Sun, The Lebanon, Baalbek, Galilee, and Judea*, 1906.

Buckhardt, *Travels in Syria and the Holy Land*, 1822.

Curtis, *To-day in Syria and Palestine*, 1903.

Doolittle, *Forbidden Paths in the Land of Og*, 1900.

Goodrich, *In a Syrian Saddle*, 1905.

Lees, *Life and Adventures Beyond the Jordan*, 1906.

Neil, *Rambles in the Bible Lands*, 1905.

Oliphant, *Notes of a Pilgrimage to Jerusalem and the Holy Land*, 1891.

Rix, *Tent and Testament*, 1907.

Scott, *Christ's Own Country: a Pilgrimage through Palestine.*

Smith, *Patrollers of Palestine*, 1906.

Sweetapple, *The Earthly Footsteps of Jesus*, 1909.

Thomson, *The Land and the Book*, I-III, 1881-86.

Van Dyke, *Out-of-Doors in the Holy Land*, 1908.

Wright, *Early Travels in Palestine*, 1848.

MAPS

Armstrong, *A Map of Palestine from the Surveys Conducted for the Committee of the Palestine Exploration Fund; Reduced from the One-Inch Map, six sheets*, 1881.

Photo-relief Map, from a Specially Prepared Copy of the Raised Map of Palestine, 1902.

Beazley, *Medaba Map*, 1905.

Bible Atlas, Issued by the Society for Promoting Christian Knowledge, 1903.

Conder, *Map of Western Palestine from Surveys Conducted for the Committee of the Palestine Exploration Fund*, 1890.

Gage, *Relief Map of Palestine*, 1903.

Kent and Madsen, *Topographical and Historical Maps and Chronological Chart for Biblical Students*, 1905.
— —, *Historical Maps for Bible Classes*, 1911.

Johnston, *Map of Palestine*, 1884.

Palestine Exploration Fund, *Map of Western Palestine in 26 Sheets from Surveys, Conducted for the Committee of the Palestine Exploration Fund*, 1880.

Philip, *Scripture Atlas*, 1906.
— —, *Imperial Atlas of the World*, Vol. II.

Sanders, *Special Edition of the P. E. F. Maps. Part 1, Illustrating the Divisions of the Natural Drainage and the Mountain Ranges* (6 Sheets).

— —, Part 2, *Illustrating the Old Testament, the Apocrypha and Josephus* (6 Sheets).

— —, Part 3, *Illustrating the New Testament, also the Talmud and Josephus*, 1882.

Smith, G. A., *A New Topographical, Physical, and Biblical Map of Palestine. Prepared under the Direction of J. G. Bartholomew*, 1901.

Standard Biblical Atlas, 1908.

Stanforth, *Atlas of Universal Geography*, 1895.

APPENDIX II
STEREOGRAPHS AND STEREOPTICON SLIDES ILLUSTRATING "BIBLICAL HISTORY AND GEOGRAPHY"

The following stereographs (or stereopticon slides) have been prepared to illustrate the physical characteristics of the biblical world and the most important events of biblical history. Inquiries in regard to prices, methods of ordering, and other details should be sent directly to Underwood and Underwood, 3 West 19th Street, New York City or to Underwood and Underwood, 104 High Holborn, London, W. C., England. Through them a supplemental booklet (with three locating maps) may also be secured, that gives detailed descriptions of each of the views. Sixty of the most important, that may be used repeatedly to illustrate different subjects and events, have been starred.

PHYSICAL GEOGRAPHY

* * 1. **Relief Map of Palestine** (*cf.* p. 9, pp. 27, 38 in text)
* 2. **Ruins of Ancient Tyre** (p. 14)
* 3. **Haifa and the Plain of Acre from Mount Carmel** (p. 14)
* 4. **Eastward across the Plain of Sharon** (p. 15)
* * 5. **General View of Gaza from the Southeast** (p. 16)
* 6. **Shephelah and the Philistine Plain from Tell Sandahannah** (p. 16)
* 7. **Highlands of Upper Galilee about Safed** (p. 18)
* 8. **Lower Galilee Northeast from Mount Tabor** (p. 19)
* * 9. **South from Mount Tabor toward Gilboa** (pp. 19, 106, 170)
* * 10. **North from Gilboa over the Plain of Jezreel** (pp. 20, 106)
* * 11. **Plain of Esdraelon and Mount Carmel West from Gilboa** (pp. 20, 106, 121)
* 12. **Northwest from Bethshean up the Valley of Jezreel** (pp. 21, 106)
* 13. **South from Gilboa over the Hills of Northern Samaria** (p. 23)
* 14. **The Rocky Gorge of the Wady Farah** (p. 23)
* 15. **The Plain of Dothan West from Tell Dothan** (p. 23)
* 16. **The Barley Vale Leading to Shechem** (pp. 23, 24)

INDEX OF NAMES AND PLACES

Lector House believes that a society develops through a two-fold approach of continuous learning and adaptation, which is derived from the study of classic literary works spread across the historic timeline of literature records. Therefore, we aim at reviving, repairing and redeveloping all those inaccessible or damaged but historically as well as culturally important literature across subjects so that the future generations may have an opportunity to study and learn from past works to embark upon a journey of creating a better future.

This book is a result of an effort made by Lector House towards making a contribution to the preservation and repair of original ancient works which might hold historical significance to the approach of continuous learning across subjects.

HAPPY READING & LEARNING!

LECTOR HOUSE LLP
E-MAIL: lectorpublishing@gmail.com

www.ingramcontent.com/pod-product-compliance
Lightning Source LLC
Chambersburg PA
CBHW020910160726
47993CB00005B/1898